Why Women Are Oppressed

Why Women Are Oppressed

Anna G. Jónasdóttir

Foreword by Kathleen B. Jones

Temple University Press

Philadelphia

Temple University Press, Philadelphia 19122
Copyright © 1994 by Temple University. *All rights reserved*
Published 1994
Printed in the United States of America

The paper used in this publication meets the minimum requirements
of American National Standard for Information Sciences—Permanence
of Paper for Printed Library Materials,
ANSI Z39.48-1984 ∞

Library of Congress Cataloging-in-Publication Data
Anna G. Jónasdóttir.
   Why women are oppressed / Anna G. Jónasdóttir.
     p. cm.
   Originally published: Love power and political interests. Örebro,
Sweden : University of Örebro, 1991.
   Includes bibliographical references and index.
   ISBN 1-56639-110-5. — ISBN 1-56639-111-3 (pbk.)
    1. Feminist theory. 2. Political science. 3. Patriarchy.
  I. Anna G. Jónasdóttir. Love power and political interests.
  II. Title.
  HQ1190.A56   1994
  305.42—dc20   93-24039

An earlier version of this book was published in 1991 in the Örebro Studies series under the
title Love Power and Political Interests: Towards a Theory of Patriarchy in Contemporary Western Societies

For Bjarni, Systa, and Sif

Contents

Foreword

The influence of poststructuralism in contemporary feminist theory has been profound. Perhaps its most significant effect has been to render suspicious, even pernicious, any efforts at "grand theory" building. Poststructuralism has taught us to be wary of all attempts to generalize about gender, or to speak categorically about women and men and what sexual differences have represented. In the Anglo-American context, this poststructuralist wariness has been compounded by the arguments of postcolonialist theorists and the research of feminists of color. These critics have rightly noted that Western feminists have produced theories that tend to depend on ethnocentric and hegemonic readings of "women's experiences" and have deployed definitions of "women's interests" that privilege the social location of some women over others. The combined effect of these criticisms is to render anachronistic any theory attempting to identify the general mechanisms reproducing contemporary social relations of sexuality, or aiming at "a general understanding of women's and men's social and historical conditions."

Yet, I am convinced that feminism need not, and should not, eschew all efforts at grand theory. We remain confronted globally with persistent social and political inequalities between women and men, even if they are not always present in the same form or to the same degree for all women and men. Without some specificity attached to the concept of sexual difference, and without some concrete effort to analyze the political effects of sexual difference, feminist theory and politics would be deprived of their object: analyzing and transcending women's exploitation as women. Even theories apparently the least dependent on stable notions of sex and gender—theories that take both sex and gender to be fabrications discursively manufactured—still paint pictures of patriarchally persistent patterns of sex/gender systems that are, at once, produced and subverted.

Recognizing that sexual differences are not the only differences constitutive of power and that, on an individual level, difference is illimitable and irreducible does not lead inevitably to the conclusion that sexual difference is unspecifiable in more or less precise analytic terms. Instead, we take the concept of sexual difference as the theoretical starting point and, on the basis of empirical studies, revise and refine the basic categories of analysis. The theoretical challenge, then, has been to develop analyses that acknowledge the diversity and cultural variance of the categories of sex and gender. Anna Jónasdóttir's *Why Women Are Oppressed* takes on this challenge, fully cognizant of the risks involved. And it is precisely what makes this work exciting and provocative.

Why Women Are Oppressed provides us with a way to move beyond the political impasse generated within feminism by the contemporary confusion of any generalization about sexual difference with essentialist reasoning. Jónasdóttir makes the important distinction between the theoretical concepts used to develop abstract theory and the lived experiences among different groups of women to which such concepts only indirectly refer. She argues powerfully for the need for a theory that can elucidate the ways that social bonds between women and men *as* women and men are constituted and transformed in order "to understand as thoroughly as possible the conditions of our existence as sexual beings." Recognizing that "sexual life always exists in definite socioeconomic contexts," Jónasdóttir nonetheless offers the view that men's appropriation of women's caring and love constitutes the fundamental nexus of women's exploitation *as* women. We will want to argue with her formulations. Yet the test of Jónasdóttir's theory should not be its degree of generality but whether its account of the construction of women as loving caretakers "for" men, instead of as desiring, interested subjects in reciprocally erotic relations, is persuasive.

By developing a theory rooted in a materialist analysis of the "political conditions of sexual love," *Why Women Are Oppressed* provides a still much-needed radical feminist perspective with a socialist feminist twist on the resilience of patriarchally defined gender relations under the conditions of postmodern liberal democratic systems in the West. Yet the relevance of the analysis is not limited to the societies with which it is most immediately conversant. As debates about the meaning of concepts such as "women's needs" and "women's interests" and the relevance of feminism in Eastern and Central Europe demonstrate, questions about the appropriation of women's caring and love are critical, albeit less widely discussed, to debates about whether economic liberalization marks a transition to democracy and for whom.

Jónasdóttir's analysis of sociosexual relational activities produces a theory protean enough to avoid the pitfalls of mechanistic or reductionistic readings of sociosexual relational practices. What is distinctive about her voice is her insistence on avoiding one-sided, compartmentalized characterizations of sexuality as the practice of violence. Not dismissive of questions of abuse, rape, or other practices of sexualized violence against women, Jónasdóttir wants to emphasize the ways that mechanisms other than direct and open coercion or violence are vital to "the sexual authority structure prevailing in the formally free and equal, contemporary societies." In this respect, Jónasdóttir brings a Foucaultian perspective to radical feminist theories of sexuality and a radical feminist perspective to Foucaultian histories of sexuality.

In other words, her theory outlines the broad parameters within which to continue research from the ground up about the conditions of democracy in different cultural contexts that could generate what she calls a "women-worthy" society. The radical implication of Jónasdóttir's assuming a degree of fixity to a category of sexual difference, so that sexual difference can be theoretically analyzed, is the possibility of imagining the shape of the territory that Monique Wittig once called "beyond the category of sex."

Jónasdóttir's work would have been available to only a few without this U.S. edition of a work originally published in English in Sweden under the auspices of the Örebro Studies and Göteborg Studies in Politics. There is an extraordinarily rich and vital production of feminist works by Scandinavian scholars whose unique perspective on socialist and radical feminist debates, as well as the contemporary "poststructuralist turn," has been largely unknown to American scholars. *Why Women Are Oppressed* should contribute further to a process of exchange and counterinfluence in many more directions that will enliven debates about sexuality and the politics of love in this postmodern era.

Kathleen B. Jones
San Diego State University

Acknowledgments

Many people have been involved, professionally as well as personally, in helping me complete this work. I tried to express my deep gratitude to them all in the first version, which was published in Sweden in 1991. Here, in this slightly revised, new edition aimed for a much wider public, I want to thank the following persons and institutions: Bo Särlvik and Mats Dahlkvist, Department of Political Science, University of Göteborg, for their continuous genuine—and demanding—support; Sören Holmberg and Rutger Lindahl (same department) for reading the manuscript and giving thoughtful comments; Helga Maria Hernes (now at the Center for International Climate and Energy Research, University of Oslo), whose comments at an early stage helped give me the courage to continue working on my ideas; Maud Landby Eduards, Department of Political Science, University of Stockholm, and editor of the two publications in which Chapters 6 and 8 previously appeared, for her constructive comments, especially on these chapters—I have benefited very much from her unfailing competence and lucidity; Kathleen B. Jones, Department of Women's Studies, San Diego State University, for her generous help with the English language and with the content of Chapter 7; and Carole Pateman, Department of Political Science, UCLA, for her kindness and constructive comments at an early stage.

I want to thank all my feminist colleagues, besides those already mentioned, who initiated and participated in the various Swedish, Nordic, and other international scholarly and civic activities—seminars, workshops, courses, and lectures—where I was able to present papers and discuss problems. Two of these colleagues and friends, Gun Hedlund and Ingrid Pincus, have a "room of their own" in my life and work. In addition I would like to thank my students, especially those in my women's studies courses—most of them women and a handful of brave men—who have through the years given me invaluable critical and supportive feedback with an openmindedness that sometimes is lacking in more advanced academic milieus. I thank my colleagues and all the other staff, not least the library staff, at the University of Örebro, for their friendship and support. Among these people I wish to give special mention to Ingemar Elander and Thord Strömberg and to all those who either translated from Swedish to English or corrected the English of the various chapters: David Anstey, Malcolm Forbes, Jan Teeland, and especially Ingrid Pincus. I thank JÄMFO (the Commission for Research on Equality Between Men and Women) for a grant I lived on for two years, the University of Örebro through its Research Committee for granting me leave with pay for six months as well as for helping to fund translation/correction work, and to the Adolf Lindgren Foundation and the Fredrika Bremer Society for smaller but much appreciated grants. I also thank Jane Cullen, Senior Acquisitions Editor, and those others at Temple University Press who have assisted in the publication of this book.

Finally, I am grateful beyond words to Bo Jonsson, my first teacher in political theory, later my colleague as well as my husband. His love for me and for the children I brought with me into his house has been for me a vital source of empowerment.

To my children, Bjarni, Systa, and Sif, who have grown up with a mother and her writing on a seemingly never-ending story, who have helped me both directly and indirectly with this work, and to whom this book is dedicated—I will be in debt forever.

Why Women Are Oppressed

chapter 1

Introduction: Patriarchy as a Problem in Political Theory

It is the very essence of the theoretical enterprise that, if and when it seems appropriate, it should feel free to sever itself from the bonds of traditional ways of looking at political life.

David Easton, *A Framework for Political Analysis*

An understanding of the relation between man and woman has not yet really begun to be tapped for insights into conceptions of community, though it is probably the most fruitful source of insight for such conceptions, and for discovering whatever it is that lies deepest at the heart of society. If power is all it can ever be, here may be the place to find out.

Virginia Held, "Marx, Sex, and the Transformation of Society"

This book examines the broad question of how contemporary inequality between women and men is to be analyzed and explained.[1] Specifically: Why, or how, do men's social and political power positions with respect to women persist even in contemporary Western societies, where women and men are seen as formally/legally equal individuals, where almost all adult women are fully or partly employed, where there is a high proportion of well-educated women, and where welfare state arrangements, which obviously benefit women, are relatively well developed?

Even after decades of benevolent and active policies for gender equality, inequalities between women and men in today's Western societies persist and, very likely, have increased in some spheres. We are still confronted with a continuous flow of evidence, in art, research, literature, political actions, and so on, that women are being restrained, against—or by—their wills. Even though equality exists in the form of legal rights and formally equal opportunities, there must be some underlying mechanisms that curtail women's actual possibilities of realizing their opportunities.

Since the late 1960s the quest for theories to deal with issues like these has been a prominent feature in the social and political mobilization of women. A new kind of theoretical knowledge was and still is pursued: one that will reveal the causes of male dominance and women's subordination and devaluation.[2] The feminist quest for explanatory knowledge is especially interesting from a scholarly point of view. Since 1970, many attempts have been made to define the "problem [with] no name" (Friedan, 1963:11), or the "sense of oppression" that women were "organizing around" (Rowbotham, 1974:24). New approaches have been designed, with names like "patriarchy," "women's oppression," and "male dominance" as core concepts. From the beginning, titles of articles and books, like "The Political Economy of Women's Liberation" (Benston, 1969), "The Politics of Housework" (Mainardi, 1970), *Sexual Politics* (Millett, 1970) and *The Dialectic of Sex: The Case for Feminist Revolution* (Firestone, 1971) indicated that the problem in question could be identified and investigated in all spheres of society, in the home as well as outside it. "The problem" also seemed to be connected with a specific social, transformative—even revolutionary—dynamic. Furthermore, titles like those listed above and to an even greater extent the widely embraced feminist slogan "The personal is political" expressed a new way of understanding that the dimension of sex should be viewed as one of society's fundamental dimensions and must be taken seriously in social and political theory. Many overviews and analyses have been published in the past decade that account for the ongoing development of feminist theory (see, for instance, Connell, 1987; Donovan, 1985; Eisenstein, 1983; Göransson, 1987; Jaggar, 1983; Jónasdóttir, 1984; Walby, 1986, 1990).

In this book I identify those mechanisms that hold together, produce, and reproduce contemporary society when seen primarily as a web of relations between the sexes.[3] Methodologically, I deal with the problem of patriarchy by comparing two influential strands of feminist thought: socialist feminist theory and radical feminist theory. Initially, both used historical materialism, that is, Marxism's metatheoretical assumptions and principles, to approach social reality. The so-called Marxist method was expected, somehow, to do "service [to] feminist questions" (Hartmann, 1981a:11). Sometimes the Weberian understanding of politics as *Herrschaft* (a relationship of dominance and subordination) was also applied to feminist theorizing.[4] In my view, these two branches of feminist theory moved away from their initial objectives, with detrimental consequences for the development of feminist theory in general. In radical feminism, the dialogue with Marxist theory, begun by Shulamith Firestone (1971) and others, ended rather abruptly.[5] Moreover, the Weberian framework, introduced by Kate Millett (1970), among others, was also let go of as an object of closer feminist critique and rethinking.[6] In socialist feminism, the Marxist method was taken too much at face value. The conventional Marxist methodological assumptions were not challenged sufficiently, and one reason for this was, simply, that the feminist questions were not posed radically enough. A third branch of feminist theory, envisioned by Juliet Mitchell and others around 1970, was dropped or lost along the way.

I propose an alternative mode of theorizing contemporary patriarchy, characterized by the specific way in which I rearrange the following three discursive elements: What feminist questions should be raised? How should historical materialism, alias the "Marxist method," be used to frame these questions? How should this feminist historical-materialist problematic be related to political theory, including theories of the state?

Actually, I could not find a "room" suitable for the questions I struggled with in any of the different schools of historical materialism that so many feminists have tried to refurnish during the past twenty years.[7] Yet I think that the development of the kind of feminist theorizing necessary to explain patriarchy can benefit from the materialist conception of history and, indeed, the reverse applies as well.[8] The Marxist variant that seems best suited to serve basic feminist purposes is the *realist view*, or the realist approach.[9] Most important here is that the realist view, as a set of metatheoretical principles, seems to be able to contain and support a distinct feminist materialist field of knowledge, within which patriarchy as a social and historical system can be specified and theorized.

By pushing the "distinctive theoretical project" of socialist feminism (Jaggar, 1983:118) further in the very direction pointed out by its originators, I restate the basic problem of patriarchy. I restate it as a question of a specific sociosexual power struggle, a struggle over the political conditions of sexual love, rather than over the conditions of women's work. This move implies that the concept of love can be understood, primarily, as sociosexual relational practices, and not only as emotions that dwell inside individuals.

By focusing on sexuality and love rather than on economy and work, I take seriously the "tentative and imperfect" attempts by early radical feminists, like Kate Millett (1970) and Shulamith Firestone (1971), to problematize the present form of male-dominated heterosexuality and the articulations of sexist power in modern society at large. I say "early radical feminists" because those who have continued to work on and with radical feminist theory since the late 1970s have lost something crucial in their mode of dealing with sexuality. I agree with Hester Eisenstein's claim that "the women-centered analysis brought radical feminism to a theoretical and practical impasse" (Eisenstein, 1983:xii). But I show also that socialist feminism, with its women-and-work-centered perspective, has for an equally long time been going around in circles. The conclusion of my theoretical exploration, thus, is that sexuality, as a field of social and political power relations, should be identified as the basic theoretical domain of feminism. The ontological views and the methodological principles applied to this domain, however, should be those of a revised, or re-oriented, historical materialism. The kind of "unmodified" feminist "domination approach"—I would say, reified violence approach—that radical feminists (most prominently Catharine Mac-Kinnon, 1987) now pursue, leads, in my opinion, into a blind alley.[10]

Readers of this volume will readily note that I do not deal equally with socialist feminism and radical feminism. I am occupied with the former much more and differently than with the latter, because my thinking developed along the winding path of attempting to make specifically feminist use of historical materialism, rather than along a direct path of consciously attempting to construct a better radical feminism. This means that I arrived at the field of sexuality through a method of exclusion. Again and again, when reading socialist feminist texts, I came to the firm conviction that the various socialist feminist modes of using Marxism had to be transcended. In other words, I did not simply start where the early radical feminists had ended in their attempts to modify and apply theoretical notions and historical schemes borrowed from Marx, Engels, or Weber. This is also the reason why I have not yet, to any greater extent, related my own way of theorizing to MacKinnon's radical feminism. Her original mode of inquiry, or, in her words, the "point of departure" with which she later broke (see preface in her latest book, 1989), is in certain ways similar to mine. However, a critical examination of how and with what consequences MacKinnon has displaced Marxism (which she claims to have done) as well as a comparison of her methods with mine will have to wait.[11]

To assume that historical materialism could be made to serve feminist questions is not the same as to have a clear idea about how this should be done. Nor has there ever existed a common view— even among socialist feminists themselves—on what variant, or variants, of this multi-branched research tradition that would be most fruitful.[12] And, remarkably little has been written by feminists about Marxism as a particular method.[13] As a matter of fact, a specific chapter on metatheoretical assumptions is also lacking in this volume. In Chapter 2, however, I present a very preliminary overview of what feminist theorists commonly find attractive in Marxism and how they differ in making use of it. I go on to underline an important division in socialist feminist theorizing, between theories of gendered "consciousness" and theories of gender relations. I am concerned with the development of the second type, that is, a theory of "social being" or "social existence."

Within Marxism, this is the type of theory that hitherto has focused solely on society's socioeconomic processes and work, and—within Marxist-oriented feminism—on the position of women in these processes. The result of my investigation is instead that the work paradigm in historical materialism now can and should be transcended (not invalidated). Feminist theory must identify and focus on society's sociosexual processes. This type of theoretical enterprise, I argue, moves beyond the theories of gender socialization that dominate the theoretical repertoire of today's socialist feminism. I believe also that sociosexual relations and "political sexuality" as theoretically significant fields—significant in and of themselves—have become possible to identify because of certain historical changes.[14]

What needs to be done in social and political theory, then, is to construct conceptually a whole new domain more or less from scratch.[15] And this, as stated above, should be done by putting both a reorientated Marxist method and a feminist re-reading of the best of political theory to the service of feminist questions. This stance presupposes that two feminist approaches that usually are seen as opposites somehow can be integrated. On one hand there is socialist feminism, the appropriator of the Marxist method. On the other hand there is radical feminism, the only branch of feminist theory up to now that has theorized about patriarchy in political terms. Socialist feminists consistently reject the radical feminist approach in both its older and its more recent forms. They reject it as being sex- or biology-fixated, as being ahistorical and nonmaterialistic; and with it they reject serious attempts to theorize "sexual politics." Radical feminists today, on their side, go against many core assumptions in socialist feminist analysis, such as the one that nurturant consciousness and ethics of care are connected positively with women's specific experiences and should be seen as advantageous for feminism. But they are particularly opposed to the idea that the development of an independent feminist theory of sexual politics needs any methodological "qualification" by conventional (read male-designated) "modifiers" (see MacKinnon, 1987:16). As far as I can see, this demand for total theoretical independence, when put into (theoretical) practice, entices people to be either naive or dishonest about influences from or similarities with other frameworks and lines of thought. What is still worse is, and here I agree with Moira Gatens (1987:16), that any theoretical separatism, "if presented as a long-term program, is utopian and runs the serious risks of reproducing, elsewhere, the very relations which it seeks to leave behind." This is not the place to go into detail about what "integration" would mean in an envisioned integrated feminist approach. However, this is what the rest of the book is about.

A few remarks should be made about the empirical testability and applicability of my theories. Much of my theoretical examination belongs on a metatheoretical level, and metatheory (i.e., ontological assumptions and methodological principles) cannot be tested empirically. My specific theory of contemporary patriarchy, however, which, stated briefly, proposes that men are empowered by exploiting women, is empirically testable, although only in principle or indirectly. Its chief task is to inform empirical studies, and to function in "communicative interaction" with more concrete and directly testable theories of the middle-range.

Some parts of my theorizing are more normatively oriented than others. Although I am well aware of the nondiscreet boundaries between empirical and normative issues, I still view my contribution to interest theory, as well as to democratic theory, as being more closely related to normative issues than are other parts of my work. I am not, however, occupied directly with practical-political problems. Even my interest theory is intended to function as an analytical framework, empirically applicable to social and political reality. Its aim is to clarify conditions rather than to deliver political answers.

Before leaving these considerations, one more point should be made about the empirical relevance of my theorizing. In Chapters 2 and 8, I identify certain situations characteristic of the contemporary form of the struggle between the sexes that would be particularly profitable to investigate. I am referring to situations and processes in various spheres of society, where women and men compete for scarce values—it might be a desirable job or a position of power in politics—and where all things are equal except sex. In these situations the men and women involved are about equally free from barriers like burdensome responsibilities at home, they are equally competent, and they are equally decided about what they want. Yet men—and for no obvious reason other than their malehood—most often come out as "winners." Exactly what happens in these processes? Conversely, what happens when women actually "win" over men in a zero-sum game? With this I am not implying that all processes of value distribution between women and men are zero-sum games, but some obviously are.[16]

This study has been in process for several years. A slightly different version of this book was edited specifically for my Ph.d. dissertation and published in Sweden in 1991. Before that, all but one of the main chapters (Chapter 5) had been published as articles in journals or as essays in books, in Swedish or in English. These earlier versions differ somewhat from what appears here. Chapter 9, as well as this Introduction, were written especially for the dissertation. Because of the mode in which the whole work has been carried out, a certain amount of overlapping in the different chapters has been unavoidable.

In Chapter 2 I specify the problem of patriarchy and account, briefly, for the whole range of issues dealt with in this book. My theoretical enterprise, like all theories that aim at a general understanding of women's and men's social and historical conditions, is highly abstract. The importance of differentiating abstract theories from more concrete ones, and the rationale for why and how abstractions are useful in the first place, is discussed in Chapter 3. Such considerations also inform the critical analysis of socialist feminist economic reductionism I undertake in Chapter 4.

The bulk of my constructive development toward an alternative theory of contemporary patriarchy is contained in Chapters 2, 3, 4, and 5. This includes a general methodological framework as well as the central concepts for a more specified theory. The question of whether and how the concept of "exploitation" is applicable to the relations between the sexes is covered in Chapter 5. There, and in Chapter 9, I present a theoretical explanation for the persistence of men's power today. I want to underline, however, that I am still working out the final form of this theory.

When dealing, critically, with social relationships in their contemporary institutionalized form, it is necessary to distance oneself, analytically, from the apparently self-evident nature of the present. For this, it is highly rewarding to look back, selectively, into history to observe how the web of institutionalized social relations, including sex, is patterned and understood differently in different periods. The analysis in Chapter 6 tells us how some of the most influential writers ever in modern political theory, Thomas Hobbes and John Locke, conceptualized and justified the historical reshaping of gender relations that occurred in the youth of capitalism and the nation-state. In reading these old texts, one is amazed to find how significant sex was in the early development of modern political theory.

Chapter 7 deals with the questions whether, how, and with what limits classical interest theory is applicable to women's concerns and of relevance to feminism. The chapter results in a decisive step toward a feminist political, or normatively oriented, theory of interest that claims to transcend many apparent contradictions and dilemmas in prevailing feminist debates. The question raised in Chapter 8, then, concerns the connection between citizenship, individuality, and sexuality in Western democracies. In short, the aim is to extend my main theoretical standpoints and arguments into the field of democratic theory. Finally, in Chapter 9, I present my critical assessments and my constructive proposals restructured into several theses.

chapter 2

Sex/Gender, Power, and Politics: Patriarchy in the Formally Equal Society

over the slow heavy movements
we have no control
for we usually do not know
ahead of time
their exact direction
and force
We are ourselves part
of the movement
The fixed point
for measuring the movement
does not exist

Marx nailed it to economy, in
the relations of production
and that is
a sensible point of departure
But not a fixed point

Göran Sonnevi, *Det omöjliga* (The impossible)

In studying, theoretically, contemporary power relations between the sexes, I use the term "patriarchy" (and "male domination" as a synonym) to designate a social and political power system.[1] A meta-theoretical assumption of mine is that sex/gender—women and men

The first version of this chapter was given as a lecture (in Icelandic) at the first Icelandic Women's Studies Conference, University of Iceland, Reykjavik, August 29–September 1, 1985. A revised Swedish version was published in the anthology *Feminism och marxism:*

as sociosexual beings—comprises a particular material base for generating and shaping history and society.[2]

Certain aspects of the total process of life and society have to do with the fact that we are sexual beings, driven by desire for and need of one another. These needs and desires enable us to empower each other as human beings, and to create others, as individuals and species. These sociosexual features must be comprehended in and for themselves; they comprise particular parts of the weaving together of society as a processual whole. Together with other human needs, such as food, shelter, and beauty, sexuality creates or constitutes social life.

How have the relations between women and men become a multidimensional power structure? Certain feminist researchers claim that inequality between the sexes has always existed, which is not to say that it must remain indefinitely. Others believe that a systematic and institutionalized inequality and oppression of women has emerged historically in connection with the development of other inequalities, mainly those of class.[3]

In addition to the question of the origins of patriarchy, we also have the extremely important issue of the historical changes in the power relations between the sexes. Can we distinguish any previous decisive changes in the sex/gender structure of society? If so, in what ways are they connected to other social changes? Can we locate any historical roots for the specific form of the sex/gender system that we live in today in the West? Some see these roots in the rise and development of industrialism; others say that they must be sought on a different level and farther back in time. In certain countries a fundamental social transformation occurred long before industrialism. This transformation encompassed the law, the state, the economy, sexual life, marriage, and religion.[4]

En förälskelse med förhinder (Stockholm: Arbetarkultur, 1986). An English version, translated by Jan Teeland, was published in *Acta Sociologica* 2 (31) (1988): 157–74. This third, revised version is published by permission of Norwegian University Press. The poem by Göran Sonnevi was also translated by Jan Teeland and is reprinted here by permission of the author.

To be able to ask the right questions about historical changes, however, we must have a theory of society as it looks today. How are we to explain the power relationships between the sexes that can be observed currently in society? Can we describe any basic mechanisms in this system that might provide a certain perspective on the many different practices through which women and men are related to each other, such as art, work, love, school, politics, and parenthood?[5]

There are in progress several attempts to capture, theoretically, the basic mechanisms of patriarchy. It is vital to this process of knowledge always to pose new questions, which means that reality is constantly being questioned. An interplay between empirical and theoretical studies is necessary and new questions require also, among other things, a critical study of older theories and concepts. I have been working with the following main theses.

- Sexual life encompasses its own production: the creation and recreation, the formation and empowerment of human beings—children and adults.

- The specific structural features and processual currents of society, referred to above as sexual life, not only are targets of change but also do comprise, in and of themselves, specific formative powers of social change.

- When we attempt to explain the unequal positions of women and men in today's society, we should envisage the set of relations between the sexes as a particular sociosexual and political power system.

- The fact that, considered from a gender perspective, our society is male-dominated in all areas does not mean that women have no influence at all; what they lack is authority—as women.

- It is necessary to keep the sex/gender perspective analytically distinct from a class perspective (or other social oppositions) if the aim is to explain the bases for male authority.

- The crucial issue in today's gender-political struggle is not that of women's position as producers of children, nor is it the position of women as a labor force (or reserve labor force). It is the issue of women as "empowerers" of social existence—for men.

- Now as never before women question being used as a source of pleasure and energy on conditions that they do not control, to be drained of their strength, which men convert to instrumental power—without empowering women in return.

- The extent to which the different social forces condition women's and men's possibilities in life differ historically. Today, sociosexual relations themselves are becoming more and more significant as a conditioning force.

The problem of describing and explaining patriarchy has at least three sides. I have previously called these the anthropological, the historical, and the theoretical sides.[6] These terms refer to the question of the earliest origins of patriarchy; its historical changes, including the historical roots of the form of male society that prevails today; and the question of how patriarchy is structured today and how it reproduces itself in contemporary society, which perhaps only now can be particularly manifest.[7] I have worked primarily with the third side, that is, I attempt to capture the essential characteristics of present-day male dominance in theoretical concepts. I would like to underline once again that my analysis applies only to societies comparable with our own, in which the most important criterion is that formal equality prevails between the sexes.

Feminist Questions

Since about 1970 the main lines in Western feminist theory concerning the basis of the oppression of women have been fairly clear. Simultaneously in several countries, perhaps first in the United States, England, and France, a break between conflicting points of view occurred, with very fruitful results. So-called radical feminism, which, as Juliet Mitchell wrote in *Women's Estate* (1986), had arisen like "a phoenix" out of the left-wing, male-dominated protest movements of the 1960s, stood against a rigid Marxism (p. 86). In the radical circles of the 1960s, where politics and scholarship inspired each other, the Marxists—mostly men—took upon themselves the right to define women's newly awakened insights concerning the unequal social positions of the sexes to be of absolutely less importance than the issue of class. In these circles feminists' tentative attempts to develop their new ideas were opposed. Both small and large self-appointed Marx and Lenin potentates claimed to have clear evidence that independent feminist analyses were scientifically meaningless, politically dangerous, and, at best, trivial. In other and more established research milieus where "class" was not the main weapon against the feminist perspective, the terms "individual," "humanity," and, particularly, "high scientific standards" and "intersubjectivity" were used in the same way—to deny women's demands for recognition of the fact that "humanity" consists of both men and women, and that something—not a small something either—was wrong in their relations with each other. Women also claimed that in order for the situation of the sexes to be studied properly, established concepts, theories, and methods had to be profoundly reconsidered.[8]

But Marxist environments meant not only opposition and the paralyzation of ideas but also powerful inspiration. The rapid development of Marxist ideas during the 1960s and 1970s meant a great deal to the new feminist perspective. Of the then prevailing lines of approach in the social and behavioral sciences, it was only within Marxism that concepts such as power, oppression, and liberation were used systematically. These concepts seemed opportune for many women who were far outside the traditional Marxist lines, women who were searching for words to apply to existing but almost invisible and unmentionable problems. Betty Friedan had, for example, begun to formulate them in the early 1960s, and Simone de Beauvoir had written about them as early as 1949—but then they went largely without any notice.[9]

In addition, Marxism comprised one of the very few approaches to the social sciences that made a point of proposing a theory that covered the totality of social mechanisms and their historical changes. There was only one serious competitor, structural functionalism, whose chief mentor was the American sociologist Talcott Parsons. Parsons had developed the fundamental ideas of family sociology and sex roles theory that were predominant during the 1950s and 1960s. It was against these polarized and, according to many, conservative theories about the separate roles of men and women that much of feminist scholarship was aimed.[10] A characteristic feature of structural functionalism—not only in its theory of sex roles—is that concepts like "power" and "oppositions" are made prominent by their absence. Another tendency in the ideas of structural functionalism is to equate what is with what is good and desirable, the idea being that manners and customs in a society would not have arisen had they not been functional for that society, and consequently good and desirable from the point of view of that society's aims. But since power, oppositions, and conflicting aims have no place in this line of thought, neither is there any place for the question of whether certain customs are more functional and desirable for certain groups than for others. Conflicts or relationships of dominance within marriage and the family are, for example, not easy to capture in the Parsonian theoretical net.

Socialist Feminist Theory

From the break between the self-sufficient radical feminists and the "abstract socialists" (Mitchell's term) emerged a third mode, which was initially formulated by Juliet Mitchell. Central to this approach is the use of feminist insights into problems; women's own issues must be the focal point. Marxist methods, reworked for our own purposes, can, however, be of assistance. According to Mitchell,

> It is not 'our relationship' to socialism that should ever be the question—it is the use of scientific socialism as a method of analyzing the specific nature of our oppression and hence our revolutionary role. Such a method, I believe, needs the understanding of radical feminism quite as much as of the previously developed socialist theories. (1986:81)

The American feminist and philosopher Alison Jaggar, in her book *Feminist Politics and Human Nature* (1983), reformulates Mitchell's manifesto, and in doing so reveals its most characteristic feature: "It attempts to interpret the historical materialist method of traditional Marxism so that it applies to the issues made visible by radical feminists" (p. 124). This analytic approach, which I call the third mode, is usually referred to as "socialist feminism," or "feminist historical materialism." The first expression is particularly difficult and, as used, vague and unclear. The second expression is much better as a name for a scientific analytic approach, its main disadvantage being that it is long and clumsy. Be that as it may, it is this line of thought that I tend to endorse. At the same time existing socialist feminist theory is the main object of my criticism; criticism I pursue from a standpoint best described as a certain kind of radical feminist stance.[11]

What then do these feminist theoreticians make of the so-called Marxist method? What follows is a four-point summary of what they extract and use most.

1   The materialist concept of history views unequal power relations, the oppression of certain groups of population and whole nationalities, as products of history, thus socially conditioned and therefore constantly subject to change and possible to eradicate. Prevailing inequalities and the exploitation of certain groups by others are seen, in other words, neither as God-given nor determined by nature, and consequently, not eternally necessary for the happiness of individuals.

2   Hence, the historical perspective is extremely important. It shows us, for example, vicissitudes in our conditions of life—what is has not always been—and thus it is not given that present social conditions and relationships will always exist. The historical view also entails that people both create their own history and are created by it; there is then no Development without there being people responsible for it. On the other hand, people cannot in any particular historical moment create a world independent of previously existing conditions: there are always limitations to the structural possibilities within which we operate, and these possibilities lie both inside and outside of people. This leads directly to the third point.

3 Marxism has preserved and developed a particular view of how we receive our knowledge and perspective of the world. This view is much older than Marx himself; it received its "modern" breakthrough with the fathers of liberal social theory—for example, John Locke in the seventeenth century—and proposes that our ideas and knowledge are not born and nourished exclusively and in isolation inside our minds and then directed outward through our actions to shape our environment. Instead we are both shaped by and shape our surroundings. Above all, we and our consciousness are formed by what we do, by our practical sensuous activities.

One of the cornerstones of the materialist concept of history is the assumption that "it is not the consciousness of men that determines their existence, but their social existence which determines their consciousness" (Marx, [1859] 1977a:389). Thus a special sort of causal connection is presumed to reign between our attitudes—feelings and ideas—and our practical activities. One of the most important arguments of women's studies research is founded on this, namely, *the theory of the gendered division of work and its consequences.* The fact that women and men live and act to such a great extent in different contexts must explain much about their differing attitudes, attributes, and capacities that otherwise seem to be so natural.[12]

The idea that the practical experiences of bringing up children and caring for other people does influence our sensibilities is not an invention of our contemporary women's movement. In 1612, the father of Western empiricism, Francis Bacon, wrote on this subject in his essay "Of Marriage and Single Life," in which his main message aimed at dissuading men from marrying and having children since:

> He that hath wife and children hath given hostages to fortune; for they are impediments to great enterprises, either of virtue or mischief. Certainly the best works, and of greatest merit for the public, have proceeded from the unmarried or childless men, which, both in affection and means, have married and endowed the public.

He continues as if to counter an obvious objection:

> Yet it were great reason that those that have children should have greatest care of future times, unto which they know they must transmit their greatest pledges.

But there are other qualities than the special "art of human discipline"—a discipline emanating from a loving co-existence with a wife and children—that the philosopher and politician Bacon would convey to his male readers, provided that they have ambitions of doing something in the service of the public. Unmarried and childless men make considerably better soldiers, for instance, not to speak of inquisitors ("more cruel and hard-hearted"), "*because their tenderness is not so oft called upon*" (emphasis added).[13]

Thus a man of Bacon's stature has assumed that there is a certain connection between how often our "tenderness" is "called upon" and how we behave in many public instances. How we then evaluate the various patterns of behavior is another question. Should we prefer the "discipline" attained through intimate sympathy and acts of love? Or shall we, as Bacon advised, value decisiveness and ruthlessness based on isolation from intimate emotional ties with other people? This is actually a classic theme in political philosophy, taken up in works of modern critical feminist scholarship, such as Carol Gilligan's highly noted book *In a Different Voice* (1982).[14]

4 All feminist researchers who are concerned with historical materialism make some use of its hypothesis of what constitutes the foundations of history and society. A section from Engel's *The Origin of the Family, Private Property, and the State* is most often cited:

> According to the materialistic conception, the determining factor in history is, in the final instance, the production and reproduction of immediate life. This again is of a two-fold character: on the one hand, the production of the means of existence, of food, clothing, and shelter and the tools necessary for that production; on the other side, the production of human beings themselves, the propagation of the species. The social organization under which the people of a particular historical epoch and a particular country live is determined by both kinds of production: by the stage of development of labor on the one hand, and of family on the other. (Engels, [1884] 1972:71–72)

The object of point 3 is to explain human consciousness and ideas, and the object of point 4 is to explain different social forms and institutions.

Socialist feminist theory can be divided into two main types. The first type is related to point 3 and entails a theory of how gendered consciousness is constructed in women and men: that is, how human beings are formed into sexually defined social characters—how gender, and above all, how the "second sex," comes about. It is concerned, then, with the social formation of both mind and body (see note 12). The second type is related to point 4 and focuses on society's socioeconomic processes: production and reproduction, and the position of women in these processes. Before I elaborate on these two main types of socialist feminist theory, I would like to say that I think most feminist theory that is informed by historical materialism is still too Marxism-fixated and too little guided by the insights of feminism.

The Theory of Gender Construction and Its Limitations

Some variant of psychoanalytic theory is often used as a complement to Marxism, and new and interesting ideas have been produced.[15] Some theorists, however, reject psychoanalysis and prefer to adapt the recent critical theories of ideology to feminist ideas.[16] Regardless of whether psychoanalysis or a theory of ideology is used, these studies tell us a great deal about how women and men are formed into different sexual characters, how this begins already in infancy in relations with parents, and how society's ideological forces form us into the sexual beings we are for the duration of our lives. But these studies do not focus on what must compose the crux of any theory of male authority, which, as I see it, is the relations between man and woman and women and men. The issues pinpointed are how psychosocial man and woman as individuals are "born" during childhood, or how adult masculinity and femininity as different role-sets are constructed by ideological powers. These are important questions to ask and answer. But questions such as What happens in the relations between adult women and men as sexual beings? are not given a central position in the above-mentioned theory of gender construction.

Women and men are involved in many different relationships with each other in which constant transactions are carried on ("transactions" is here a better term than "interactions") between them. They are "bound" to each other through erotic attraction, work relations, and political relations, as students, parents, and confidants, in sports, in artistic creation—in everything and everywhere. The feminist theoretical analysis of all these activities involving women and men as partners in discord and in harmony is incomplete. What is lacking is the focus on social processes that are driven and maintained by human beings *considered as sexes/genders*. Particular weight must therefore be placed on that relation, that process where the "sexual" can be isolated analytically, distinguished from all other activities people are involved in as women and men, that is, the erotic. By erotic I mean much more than the activity essential for sustaining life—sexual intercourse. So far I have not managed to find a better word for the complicated and in fact little-known material life processes in our bodies and souls that originate from the fact that we are sexual human beings. I imagine that the specific realities of sexual life (eroticism) entail a particular strength/power development in human beings and a transference of power between people that has great significance for how we are with each other and how we organize our societies.

To round this off, gender construction theory, or whatever it should be called, has been designated to fill the gaps that many have pointed to and deplored in the Marxist tradition. Marxism has no psychological or psychosocial theory, and many have felt themselves called upon to work out such a theory, with the assistance of psychoanalysis or other psychological theories. This orientation within feminist theory has contributed to making this complement to Marxism gender-relevant, and at the same time the psychological theories brought in have been criticized for their sexism and have been reformed. But this supplemented Marxism is still incomplete as an explanation for our present patriarchy—it does not pinpoint the problem. How then does it compare with the orientation of the feminist theory that has concentrated on socioeconomic themes (mentioned in point 4)?

The Production of the Means of Existence or the Production of Existence

According to historical materialism, the "two-fold" production (and reproduction) of "immediate life" is the most decisive factor in the development of society. What feminists have taken hold of is that the "production of immediate life," even in Marx and Engel's definition, has two sides: the production of the means of existence and the production of people, of life itself. There are significant differences, however, between feminist theorists in how they adapt these basic assumptions and what they make of them. Much is still vague, and there are even quite obvious misinterpretations of Engel's words (quoted above).[17] What is "production" and what is "reproduction"? What is "work" and what is "material"? Probably, however, the most crucial question is which production is the most decisive as regards *the explanation of the foundations of patriarchy?* Is it production of the means of existence or is it the production of life? Or both equally?

I have no doubt that it is the production of life we must focus on and examine if we are to understand as thoroughly as possible the conditions of our existence as sexual beings, and not principally as anything else, for example, as members of different classes or races. It is the socially formed and historically specific oppositions around *this* production process that must be explained. The unequal power relations between the sexes must now, in our type of society, explain themselves. This may sound strange, but what I mean is that the legal and political/ideological possibilities for equality exist in our society: neither the law nor officially authorized norms prescribe the subordination of women and the dominance of men any longer. ("Male domination is now upheld on a voluntary basis" goes one of the Frederika Bremer Society slogans, and in a way it is true.) Also economically and socially men's and women's possibilities of managing without forced dependence on each other have basically changed. What remains is the dependent relations we have with each other as sexes: the many-sided "bond" that relates us to each other as erotic beings, as parents to our children, as workmates, friends and playmates, in general, as women and men who wish to affirm the felt need to cultivate a good life and a good society—as, simply, women and men.

What, then, do I mean by the "production of life"? Much more than bearing, nourishing, and raising children, even though these activities are extremely important in this context. Women and men, in their total intercourse in pairs and groups, also create each other. And the needs and capacities that generate this creative process have our bodies-and-minds as their intertwined living sources. These needs and capacities must be satisfied and developed for the human species to survive, and for us as individuals to lead a good and digni-fied life. Our bodies and souls are both means of production and producers in this life process, and herein lies the core of the power struggle between the sexes.

Theories of Work and Their Limitations

With the above assertion I come into conflict with those writers who believe patriarchy to be a socially and materially based power rela-tionship (as opposed to those writers previously mentioned who work mainly with psychological and ideological definitions). In this connection I want to mention two writers, Heidi Hartmann and Iris Young, each of whom has her own interpretation.[18] What they have in common is that both see society's economic system—housework included—as the organizational framework for patriarchy. Hence they both also conceive of work as the activity that forms the base of patriarchy: sexual differentiation in work and the man's control over the woman's work comprise the key issues. Both then equate the "material" with the "economic."

What essentially differentiates these two writers is that Hartmann works with a "dual system" theory, while Young propounds the ne-cessity of a new total theory. Hartmann claims that patriarchy and capitalism form two separate systems, which, however, must be studied and analyzed as interwoven systems. Her defense of this idea is that in reality they do not exist separately in "pure forms"—in reality there is patriarchal capitalism. According to Hartmann, what is most important to describe and explain are the points of intersection between the two systems. In contrast, Young polemicizes against every form of dual-system theory, arguing that all oppositions and oppressions in society must be included and explained within some sort of total theory. The Norwegian feminist researchers Live Brekke and Runa Haukaa argue along similar lines (1980).[19]

The Sexual Struggle Today

In our society neither women's economic dependence on men nor the unequal division of work between the sexes constitutes the pivotal point in men's continuing ability to maintain and regenerate their dominance over women and in society at large. The crux of the problem lies on the level of existential sexual needs, which are materially and socially formed, and basically not economic. The activities that the sexual struggle revolves around are neither work nor the products of work but human love—caring and ecstasy—and the products of these activities: we ourselves, living women and men with all our needs and all our potential.

My assertion should not be taken to mean that I think the extremely unequal economic relations between women and men (e.g., most women having double jobs) is meaningless or scientifically and politically uninteresting. But I still maintain that the weight of the social forces that shape our possibilities in life as women and men are historically shifting, and that this weight has now shifted to the sexual relationship itself, which has become central in the way it was not when our chains were directly formalized and perfectly visible in laws, or fixed in almost insurmountable economic obstacles.

To test my propositions empirically may seem very difficult if not impossible; yet I do not think it is in principle more difficult than any other empirical testing. So far, however, there are not many systematic studies to turn to for support; at present, descriptions of reality in this area are more or less restricted to fiction.[20]

One way to test my ideas would be to study power positions in couple relationships in which both parties are fairly equal professionally and also share domestic tasks relatively equally. My argument would suggest that it is highly probable that the man nevertheless appropriates an disproportionally large amount of the woman's caring and love, both directly and through children; and also, in most cases, it is the man who decides the prerequisites or conditions for living together. All this does not necessarily mean that the man is the stronger half if the relationship breaks down, but the man normally finds himself a new partner much faster than the woman in a parallel situation—for this there is clear evidence.

When I argue that the core of male domination now lies in the sexual relationship itself, I am referring not only to intimate couple relationships in a marriage or cohabitation but also to a similar unequal exchange of care and pleasure that occurs between men and women in other contexts, such as in work or within politics, as individuals or in groups.

Toward a "Relative" Dual System Theory

On the question of a single or dual system, I would first say that Young's (1980, 1981) and others' demand for a total theory is unreasonable. I think that at least Young's motive for asserting a total perspective is more political than scientific. She often mixes political and scientific arguments; that is, she underpins theoretical standpoints with political arguments that I consider completely untenable. Generally, I do not think that society's various conflicts and oppositions all share the same cause.

In contrast to standard classic Marxist theoreticians, Hartmann claims that "capital and private property do not cause the oppression of women as *women*" (1981a:5). But men as wage earners, husbands, and fathers gain by women's less favorable position in the labor mar-

ket and take advantage of their work and service in the home. And
in an unholy alliance with men subordinated by class, capitalists
have an interest in exploiting women as a work force as cheaply
as possible.

Thus Hartmann makes no clear distinction between her two systems, even though sometimes it may sound as if she does. The result
is that it is not clear what actually "causes the oppression of women
as women." I think this vagueness is inbuilt, since she sees the purpose of the theory as explaining both systems simultaneously, which
leads to a dead end, not because knowledge is still incomplete, but
because it is in principle an impossible route to take. Despite this,
however, I advocate a kind of dual system idea, but one that is relative.

While we focus on the mechanisms of unequal sexual power, we
should also pay attention to how life is for women and men as members of different social classes, since sexual life always exists in definite socioeconomic contexts. But the crux of the *theoretical* concept,
the core of the explanation, has to do with gender—women and
men—regardless of class, though only certain extremely thin or diluted aspects can be encompassed by this core. Preliminarily, I offer
the following brief formulation: prevailing social norms, accompanying us from birth and constantly in effect around and in us, say that
men not only have the right to women's love, care, and devotion but
also that they have the right to give vent to their need for women
and the freedom to take for themselves. Women, on the other hand,
have the right to give freely of themselves but have a very limited
legitimate freedom to take for themselves. Thus men can continually
appropriate significantly more of women's life force and capacity
than they give back to women. Men can build themselves up as
powerful social beings and continue to dominate women through
their constant accumulation of the existential forces taken and received from women.[21] If capital is accumulated alienated labor, male
authority is accumulated alienated love. Exactly how this works can
vary greatly in both individuals and different social classes, but this
variation does not invalidate the theory. The problem is an empirical

one, that is, the theory must be anchored in studies of how these sexual processes vary. And such testing must be done with the help of more concrete models.

Equally, a theory of gender cannot be proffered as a logical consequence of a theory of class. Gender differences must be seen as empirical and historical generalizations to the degree that they can be proved to exist. Therefore when we work with a theory of sexual relations we must assume that they are influenced by class, and a theory of class relations must openly admit that these relations are sexually differentiated. *But the core of the theory must concern either the one or other, not both gender and class at the same time.* In a theory in which gender is the pivotal point, questions of class are of only relative significance; in a theory where class is the point of departure, questions of gender are only relative. In Chapter 3 I discuss more closely the grounds on which to distinguish between highly abstract theories and more concrete ones, and in Chapter 4 I criticize, more thoroughly, Hartmann's theory of patriarchy.

Today's Male Authority as Political Theory

Finally, what about "politics," "power," and "authority"? What do we gain by defining inequality in sexual relations as a matter of political power relationships? Why do I wish to define today's patriarchy as a political system and not in the more common, primarily ideological, psychosocial, or economic terms? And what do I mean when I say that women are not totally powerless but that they lack authority? These questions cannot be answered briefly, since politics and power are among the most complicated and contested concepts in the whole of political science. But, having said A, we can also say B— even though we cannot go through the whole alphabet.

My wish to use "political" as a basic determinant has to do with my conception of the sex/gender system as a comparatively independent feature of society. Thus we have a conception of society that says that every society rests on and grows out of a two-fold material base: the production of those things we need for our existence, and the production of us ourselves, for we also need each other as human beings to "live off" and with. Both of these relatively independent processes of production are sustained by unequal power relationships, and both can, supported by arguments that cannot be developed in more detail here, be called political.

There is a clear tendency among those feminist researchers who apply the other determinants mentioned above to see inequalities in sexual life as more or less a direct consequence of the economic system. Hence they ascribe very little causality to sexual relations themselves. In my opinion we should study what happens in the living relationship between women and men, what women and men do together in all the various social contexts. Examining the effects of the economy and upbringing on individual women and men is not sufficient, which is not to say that these aspects are unimportant—they set limits, provide a framework, structure possibilities. But in each instance, people themselves determine how they will handle the possibilities.

We need the designation "political" to denote a comprehensive characteristic of male domination. An example: in "Structures of Patriarchy and Capital in the Family" Annette Kuhn (1978:42) writes that patriarchy is a structure that unites property relationships and psychological relationships, and notes that patriarchy seems relatively autonomous within the family. This may be true, but my reaction is that such descriptions of patriarchy are incomplete. The battering of women and rape are examples of actions that are insufficiently described by the terms "psychological" or "economic." It is a question of a complex and tangible struggle over who is master of the situation, who has the power to decide *who is/does/gets what, when and how.* If politics has any particular core of significance it is about a field of power for wills and the consequences of will-power, where it is determined how we are with each other. Sex/gender relations constitute one such relatively independent field of power.

Disputes often arise over the question whether women have a lot of power, little power, or no power at all. I shall not attempt to sort this out in any conclusive way, but a certain degree of clarity can be achieved if we divide the concept of power into influence and authority.[22] The differences between the two terms are that authority means open acknowledgment, that is, legitimate power, while influence means effect, or power that can exist but is not always openly recognized as legitimate or "of right." We women have a fair amount of influence in various areas, and we do not always face opposition when we want to increase our influence, especially if we hide the fact that we are women as much as possible. It is mainly when we demand authority as female human beings that opposition arises— "women's voices are not appropriate for the pulpit" according to one argument against female clergy recorded in a Swedish investigation a few decades ago.

The sociosexual system, the whole set of interdependencies relating people as sexes, is to be seen as politically state-organized and— like the capitalist economy—simultaneously private and "free." But in contrast to the economic system, it is also personalized and "free," in particular male-dominated conditions. This means in turn that various forms of dynamic sexual power relations (or sexual politics) operate in every sphere of society and are not limited to the family, the economy, or the state (or whatever divisions of society we make). It follows from this, first, that women as women are free in the particular sense that is in accordance with this particular society's nature; second, that women do have some power, also as a sex; and, third, that men's oppression of women comes about as a matter of struggle, best conceptualized as a struggle of interest (see Chapter 7).

The Politics of Gender and Established Political Theory

Does the political theory of sex/gender being developed in this essay have any significance for and connection to established political theories—that is, those theoretical constructions that are meant to describe and explain political life in the sense we usually ascribe to the phrase? Very generally I would say that the investigation of society as a complex political system based on sexual conflicts, class conflicts, and other cleavage bases will successively come to challenge and transform more and more aspects of political theory and philosophy. For the past decade this process has been in full swing and developing along several different lines.[23]

To look at one area more concretely, I have argued in other contexts that traditional research on political behavior has landed in a cul-de-sac when it comes to explaining differences in the patterns of women's and men's political participation.[24] The large gender difference in participation in the political elite and in society's organs of power are particularly striking. But in those instances where the focus of study has been the absence of women in the organs of power, and their difficulties in asserting themselves, little energy has gone to explaining the problem. (In general, the explanatory variables, or rather, the social contexts of political behavior, regardless of whether they refer to choice of political party, views on political issues, or participation in decision-making bodies, are often a weak link in modern political science research.) The past twenty to twenty-five years of feminist research has prepared the ground for the disappearance of indifference to gender problems and the frequent frivolous attitudes to questions that are raised.

The above sketch of an explanation of our society's gender-political structuring constitutes an example of the type of basic theory formation that has up to now been very rare in modern political science. "Who is/does/gets what, when, and how" in the "authoritative allocation of valued things" is in fact decided on several different levels, and in gender-structured, class-structured, and other "fields of action."[25]

Aristotle, one of the mentors of Western political thought, explained and legitimized sexual hierarchy in society by using the image of light and beautiful male seminal fluid carrying society's higher formative sensibilities (with some men higher than with others). Women's dark menstrual blood, on the other hand, indicates that their defining element is pregnant with massive chaos.[26] However, he also claimed that the essence of politics is the relations between equals. No one today takes Aristotle's theories of the sexes seriously scientifically, yet there is the risk that similar ideas continue to exist on more obscure levels. We can nonetheless use his political notion as a point of departure and as a goal: that the good society requires that its members are equal, and that they "alternate being the leaders and the led."

Let us end with quotation from D. H. Lawrence. We hope that in the future we can smile in amusement at his words in much the same way we today smile at Aristotle's gender theory. At present, however, we are compelled to admit the truth of Lawrence's words.

> Man is willing to accept woman as an equal, as a man in skirts, as an angel, a devil, a baby-face, a machine, an instrument, a bosom, a womb, a pair of legs, a servant, an encyclopedia, an ideal or an obscenity; the only thing he won't accept her as is a human being, a real human being of the female sex.[27]

Common Oppression and Specific Experiences: Abstraction and Concretization in Feminist Theory

A recurrent assumption in the women's movement and in feminist theory and research is that all women live under a common oppression that is sex/gender specific. Thus, the assumption goes, women have certain interests in common and this commonality must be the foundation for all theoretical description and explanation of patriarchy. Many people, however, claim the opposite: that the oppression of women is specific in different groups of women, that it is dependent on different social, historical, and cultural borderlines. Such lines, the arguments go, divide women so that class, race, ethnicity, historical period, or culture are more basic determining factors than the sex/gender affiliation. Both sides of the argument lack precise definitions and quite often aspects that should be distinguished in thought (i.e., analytically) are confused with one another. The issue here is that we must create certain abstract distinctions in order to understand the complexities of reality. What follows are three propositions to help clarify these issues.

1 We must consciously and explicitly operate with theories on different levels. On a basic theoretical level,[1] women and men must

The first version of this chapter was prepared for the Theory Conference at the Second International Feminist Book Fair, Oslo, June 21–27, 1986. A Swedish version was published in *Häften för kritiska studier* 2 (1988):35–45. This revised version is reprinted by permission of *Häften för kritiska studier*.

be conceptualized as sex/gender–defined groups (and not as groups determined by class, race, or something else), if the purpose of the theory is to describe and explain sex/gender–specific oppression, that is, the oppression under which women suffer as women. In partial or middle-range theories, however, the assumptions about women's oppression and the analytical concepts must be such that the social and historical variations in the experiences and concrete circumstances of different groups can be captured in empirical studies.

2   Sex, class, and race are often mentioned together in feminist theory as the three main sources of contradictions and subordination in society. Here it is important to specify what is different and what is similar in the layers of reality these three categories refer to, and thus on what theoretical levels they should operate and how. I think that, while class and sex can and must be conceptualized on both the general and middle-range levels, race/ethnicity can only be developed on the more concrete middle-range level.[2]

3   My assertion in point 1 may sound as if I mean that patriarchy is to be seen as eternally the same, unchangeable in time and place. That is not the case. On the contrary, I claim that a basic theoretical conceptualization and explanation of patriarchy also needs distinctions. But these distinctions are different from those referring to various groups' specific experiences and circumstances. Here it is a question of theoretical distinctions or definitions of history and societal organization, which refer to the sex/gender relationship itself that must be isolated theoretically. Thus we have the question of structural determinants in regard to both contemporary societies (syncronic) and history (diacronic). We must ask, for example: How is the sex/gender relationship itself structured? In general? In specific forms of society? How does it change? And how is it related to other societal structures and processes, those of economic production, the state, and so on?

Basic Theory

To begin with I want to distinguish between what I here refer to as basic theory and what I have called total theory in another context.

The total theory assumes that all main forms of contradictions and oppression in a society should be covered by one and the same theory, and—as it seems—at the same level of abstraction. This is common among socialist feminists.[3]

At the bottom of this line of reasoning is the Marxist methodological principle that dialectical wholes should not be separated or divided into parts because then a genuine understanding of the whole is lost (see Eisenstein, 1979:36). To break out one part is thought to be especially injurious if we want to understand relations of power within the whole. However, the dialectical method also, and not least, demands a clear analysis of the different inherent parts and an understanding of the different character of each part. If we do not have that knowledge then the understanding of the whole will also be distorted.

Thus, when I speak about wholes (as distinguished from totality) I speak about relative wholes, about composite and complicated whole social processes. And the kind of basic theory of patriarchy I refer to must be a theory of one such relative processual whole, which at the same time is a part of the composite and complicated "total" social process. The content of this particular wholeness is the composite relationship between the sexes and the specific mode of production (and reproduction) that involves women and men socially as sexual beings. A basic theory of the sex/gender relationship and patriarchal societies assumes that we have chosen the perspective of sex/gender and the production of life as a structural basis of society; and that the purpose of this theory is to define and explain the changing structure of patriarchy and its reproductive mechanisms. A basic theory of class societies presupposes the choice of a different set of social relations and practices, another relative wholeness—that of class and the production (and reproduction) of the means of life—and aims at defining and explaining the structure and process of that basis.

A theory on this level is necessarily extremely abstract, that is, it must isolate certain elements from the concrete whole.[4] For its specific purpose it must disregard every concrete determination other than those that it means to explain. In our case, it is the specific agents and activities of the sex/gender system that must be theoretically isolated. Furthermore, the specific character of these elements in specific forms of societies must be identified and defined. The core question with which I am concerned is how to determine theoretically the specific form of sex/gender system operating today in the formally equal Western societies.

From my point of view, it is possible and fruitful to strive for a general theory of the production and reproduction of life/people, and the changing patriarchal forms this mode of production has taken (see also Chapter 4, "Conclusion"). This would be a theory centered on sexuality rather than work, in a manner parallel to Marx's theory of classes and the production of the means of life. Here I challenge many, actually I think all, feminists who have presented historical materialist theories of patriarchy or women's oppression. Chapter 4 is the outcome of a thorough critique of one such theory. Yet I find it fruitful to apply historical materialism as a method to feminist problems. What I do not find fruitful is to localize a theory of patriarchy within the framework of political economy or in any kind of symbiosis with that specific theoretical field. That is the line of thinking predominate among Marxist feminists as well as socialist feminists. At the bottom of this view lies the belief that if we leave the specific field of Marxist basic theory, that is, the field of political economy, we will find ourselves in a theoretical vacuum. In a way we do: we are confronted with a theoretical chaos, not a material/substantial emptiness. And we must orientate ourselves and create theoretical order of the chaos. It is the human sociosexual materia of our bodies-and-minds that is the substance here.

In his theory about the basic structure and dynamics of capitalism Marx abstracted, that is, sorted out, all concrete determinations except those necessary to make comprehensive the specific nature of this particular mode of production. As a construction of thought he "thinned" society until he grasped those very powers or capacities that had been historically forced to live their own (alienated) lives, namely, labor power, which had become a commodity of its own, and money, which had become a power of its own.

To comprehend the basic structure of the current formally equal patriarchy we must "thin" this society until the historically specific sex/generic nature of it can come into sight. (I discuss this further, below.)

The kind of basic theory I am speaking of does make claims about truth: it claims to be testable in principle. Thus what we have is neither a question of ahistorical, that is, empirically empty, analytical frameworks (in the manner of Talcott Parsons or David Easton) nor a set of normative propositions. What we have is a question of empirically founded conceptualizations, of so-called substantive theory about social reality, and it must therefore, as such, be testable. However, one of the specific traits of this theoretical level is that its theories are not testable directly or as a whole. They cannot be verified or falsified at one go, and their concepts are hardly applicable directly in empirical analysis. The basic theories must be tested in the form of derivated, or related, assumptions on a level of partial or middle-range theory. They must be operationalized in different parts and thus tested indirectly.

To exemplify: Heidi Hartmann, in her dual systems theory, argues that the basis of patriarchy is men's control of women's labor (or labor power) and that an alliance between men across the boundaries of class guarantees this control. This alliance, she assumes, is embodied in the institutionalized family-wage system. Further, women's lack of organizational resources outside the home keep them from changing their circumstances. To be tested these propositions must be broken down in several ways and the central concepts operationalized. And even if we find certain evidences against some of the propositions, this does not mean that the entire theory falls. The theory as a whole can only be "tested" theoretically, that is, criticized and rejected from the vantage point of another basic theory. This is what I attempt to do in Chapter 4.

Partial Theories and Middle-Range Models

The partial theories and middle-range models I refer to do not claim to have any explanatory value at the basic level, that is, they do not claim to explain patriarchy as a whole.[5] They are substantive propositions about the situation of women and the relations between women and men in the different areas of society—work, politics, family, education, and so on. They are also analytical models or conceptual frameworks that are directly applicable to reality and allow people's different experiences to assert themselves in empirical studies. At this level we can use many traditional instruments of analysis, on the premise that we examine their possible limitations or sexistic implications. Role theory is only one example of traditional middle-range thinking that continues to be of considerable use. An excellent example is Hanne Haavind's relationist role theory of femininity and masculinity, in which the idea is that women's relative subordination is continuously reproduced through symbolic interactions between women and men. Juliet Mitchell's four "structures" (in women's situation and life processes) and Berit Aas's five-dimensional model of culture can be looked upon as valuable contributions to this level.[6] These are examples of analytical frameworks for empirical research that are not univocally bound to any specific basic explanation of patriarchy or the oppression of women. These frameworks are, in addition, examples of models that marked a new phase in the empirical studies of women's situation.

I assert, above, that basic theories must be tested empirically at the middle-range level in derivated forms. Yet it is important not to see this as a strict or one-sided deductive procedure. The theoretical development on the middle-range level, and its close interplay with empirical facts, must partly lead its own life. The middle-range theories and models must have a kind of relative autonomy with respect to basic or general theories. Theorizing on each of the two levels should be done with an awareness of the existence of the other, and, as far as it is appropriate in any particular case, theories of different levels should be related to each other, in order to acquire the kind of confirmation that each of them seeks. This is dealt with in somewhat more detail in Chapter 9.

Sex, Class, and Race

Sex, class, and race are often mentioned together in theoretical discussions as the most fundamental bases of conflict in society. However, Ann Ferguson seems to be right when she writes that no one has presented an analysis that "makes clear how *race* fits in as a basic social division between people rather than as an effect of capitalism and/or patriarchy" (Ferguson, 1979:280). Still, in 1994, I am not aware of any such analysis. I will not attempt to solve this problem here, but I do think it is important to specify some of the similarities and differences between the concepts of sex/gender, class, and race.

What I have to say about this is something I have come to believe during my own work on a theory of patriarchy based on sexuality. The core of this theory is that I move beyond "oppression" as a core concept (see Chapter 5) to the more precise conception of sex/gender specific exploitation in the social and practical process of sexuality and love. This exploitation is codified in the principles of rights in the institution of marriage, although it is not limited to the family circle or to the sphere of the home. In several countries, for example, the Nordic countries, suppressive rights in marriage are rarely legally sanctioned. But they are still practiced, most often under appearances of freedom and equality. This specific exploitation must, in order to be historically and materially meaningful, have a social and material basis of its own. And I think it has.

Women and men, and people as sexual beings in general, are related to each other in the specific process of production (and reproduction) of life. In this process we (people as gendered sexual beings) are the productive agents as well as the products. And in this process our living human bodies-and-minds are both the raw materia (which in this case is social by nature) and the means of production. What men control and exploit in this mode of production is not primarily women's work and labor power but women's *love* and the *living power* love results in. The specific product, the result of this process of human practice, which men appropriate incomparably more and otherwise than women do, is thus not directly or primarily of an economic nature. The sex/gender specific product is not "surplus value" measurable in money or capital. It is *surplus gendered dignity,* that is, a legitimate socioexistential power of agency. This surplus power, then, is used (consumed) for achievements and accumulation of gendered control in economic, political, and other social activities. The collective, structured form of this male power should be defined in terms of *Herrschaft,* or authority in the Weberian sense.

What I am aiming at by this summing up of my theory of patriarchy is to assert that sex and class are the only societal relational concepts that point to such kinds of *productive processes* (of life and means of life) that *cannot be substituted by anything else* (that is, how or why they are "determining in the last instance"). Racism, or ethnic oppression, on the other hand, is not rooted in any specific production. The parties in racist relationships are not involved in any race-specific structural or necessary relations,[7] comparable to those consisting of sexuality/love and economy/labor. The racist oppression can probably be seen as more of a direct consequence of how patriarchal class societies operate than can sexual oppression. Theoretical assumptions about racist/ethnic oppression would then fit in exclusively at the more concrete partial level. I think it is meaningless to search for a theory of racism that would have to abstract its elements as far as I claim is meaningful—not only in the case of class structure but also in the case of the sex/gender structure.

Specifying "The Common"

The sex/gender problematique, which I claim must be isolated theoretically on a so-called basic level, refers by no means to any universal truth supposed to be valid in the same form in all periods and places. It must be specified along several dimensions. The point, however, about the "common" remains because women and men are not two formally different aggregates of individuals who happen to be women and men. The uneven power relations between the sexes should not be seen, as, for instance, Margrit Eichler (1980:12) does, as "social inequalities which *happen to coincide* with certain biological differences" (emphasis added). Women and men are the two substantial sections humanity is built of. Women and men as sexes (who are social by nature) are the generative source of the species. It is on the strength of the sex/gender capacities, the capacities for love and the creation of sexually "empowered" and generically dignified persons, that women do have a common basis for experience and thus a common basis for struggle.

To be sure, this commonality is very "thin" and very limited; there are many other elements in our lives, and the historical circumstances determine if, or in what form, this diluted common basis of women as "real human being[s] of the female sex" actualizes itself (see quotation at the end of Chapter 2). But sisterhood is powerful, even if it is not omnipotent, or felt or seen as the most important issue for the time being in all social contexts. In "Contextualizing Feminism: Gender, Ethnic and Class divisions," Floya Anthias and Nira Yuval-Davis write that their analysis "problematize[s] the notion of 'sisterhood' and the implicit feminist assumption that there exists a commonality of interests and/or goals amongst all women." They argue for what they see as an opposite assertion, namely, that "*every* feminist struggle has a specific *ethnic* (as well as class) context" (1983:62). I do not think that what they say contradicts what I propose. The practical sex struggle occurs always in several social contexts and varies from one situation to another. But to deny that the sex/gender position itself has some uniting actuality for women (and men) is like denying that the class position has any common importance for workers (and capitalists) of both sexes.

All over the world sex/gender capacities are practiced under oppression, and women suffer more and otherwise under this oppression than men do. So it is important to realize that we are united both in suffering and in strength. An oppressed group of people cannot define away that part of their relatedness that is rooted in suffering. Of course the suffering in itself cannot be exclusively a basis for change. But our common suffering and our strength are two sides of the same coin.

To reiterate: The terms in which we should specify the commonalities of sex/gender at the most abstract level are *structural* and *historical*, and the concepts of this level should not refer directly to the lived experiences among different groups of women. At this abstract basic level we must construct a specific mode of production concept based on sexuality and love (not on economy and work), that is, a mode of production and reproduction of people. At this "thin" level, this mode of production must be localized at the side of the economic mode of production, not integrated into it. Furthermore, following historical materialism as a method, we should in the mode of production of life, as in the mode of production of the means of life, distinguish between its historical changes and how its internal elements are structured and reproduced in historically specific forms of societies. We can formulate certain main questions, such as: (*a*) What are the inherent components of the mode of production of life/people? (*b*) What kind of inherent dynamic is there in the mode of production of people? This is a question that also asks in what way it is historical and, thus, raises the issue of theoretically founded periodization. (*c*) What is specific about the contemporary modes of production of people, in other words, of patriarchies of today?

At the general level we are striving to develop a feminist theory of history and society. But there is a third dimension, besides the historical and the societal/structural ones. If we follow the method of historical materialism, we should also define our main concepts metatheoretically, that is, ontologically or philosophically. We must define, for instance, sexuality, love, work, power, production, sex/gender, human nature, and so on, ontologically as distinct from the different historical forms in which these "things" are organized and looked upon in different societies. Gayle Rubin's well-known definition of the sex/gender system underlines the importance of this distinction (Rubin, 1975:168). For Rubin, the concept "sex/gender system" is the metatheoretical dominance-neutral (her term) referent to the concept of patriarchy, or rather to "male-dominated sex/gender systems."

The question of history and periodization is not only about chronology. It is also about theoretically founded assumptions of what kind of inherent dynamic exists in the mode of production of people, and how changes in this specific mode of production are connected to changes in, for instance, the economy and the state. This means that gender-relevant periodization must be constructed at different levels of abstraction. It means also that gender-relevant periodization should be developed both on its own, that is, based primarily on sociosexual relations themselves, and as concretized elements of, for instance, economically and politically based divisions of history.[8]

An example of a periodic framework that is somewhat concrete is Gunnar Qvist's division of the history of Swedish women into six periods. Qvist's division is founded on three types of variables: (1) so-called background variables—political, demographic, and economic (the labor market situation), (2) public policy and organizational programs concerning the position of women in society, and (3) what he calls the "women's struggle," that is, "women's own strivings to influence the public policy concerning women" (1980:45). According to Qvist this should be seen as a preliminary chronological framework. He also points out that "in a wider context one should of course speak about 'policies concerning the sexes'" (*könspolitik*) rather than policy concerning women. All measures taken regarding women have consequences for men, and all decisions that traditionally have been seen as internal solutions of problems that matter only within the "male society" actually do affect women. "In such a wider perspective," he continues, "there exist no sex-neutral policies" (p. 45). Here Qvist touches on still another distinction, the distinction between women's history and the history of the relations between the sexes. The former refers to research of women as a social category and the latter to sex/gender history, the development of which presupposes more abstract theoretical underpinnings, including a sex/gender–specific periodization.

One of the very few attempts to address specifically the theoretical aspect was presented by Joan Kelly-Gadol in "The Social Relation of the Sexes: Methodological Implications of Women's History" (1984). She proposes the "benefits" women gain—or, as in most cases, do not gain—in comparison to men, during periods of great transformation, as a criterion of periodical shifts in the "status of women." I do not think that this is a fruitful way of conceptualizing the most essential dynamic in the history of men-women relationships. Determining what are "benefits" and assessments of women's status in terms of better or worse (or "advances") could prove to be very difficult. Feminist anthropologists have also pointed out and demonstrated these difficulties (Rosaldo, 1980:401). But the most serious shortcoming of this way of theorizing about history is that it emphasizes quantitative changes too one-sidedly. Qualitative aspects of main alterations in the man-woman relationship itself should be focused on more directly.

For the sake of comparison, one might describe history by contending that the lower classes advanced less than the upper classes in periods of substantial historical change, that people of the lower classes were "excluded from the benefits of the economic, political, and cultural advances made in certain periods" (Kelly, 1984:4). But the directly measurable patterns of economic, political, and cultural value distribution remain unexplained as long as the internal mechanisms in the class relationship itself are not revealed. The limitations of Kelly's line of reasoning are similar to those of Hartmann's (see Chapter 4). She fails to conceptualize sexuality as a relatively independent structural relationship fit for historical definitions on its own. When she gets on to the qualitative determinants, the qualitatively different ways in which various forms of society are organized and transformed, she connects "the social relation of the sexes" much too close to the economic relations of property and to work.

The main concern of feminist theory should not be to look at how "women's status" or "women's situation" varies according to changes in the economic property relations or changes in the labor process (even if these concerns are also important). If the aim of feminist theory is to understand basic societal structures and historical transformations in terms of the "social relation[s] of the sexes," it must identify more directly the set of "bonds" or "interdependencies" between women and men. How do these dependencies, that is, the social practices that constitute them, change?

Kelly (1984) suggests that "we continue to look at *property relations* as the basic determinant of the sexual division of labor and of the sexual order" (p. 12). This must be modified, I think. What we should aim at primarily is to comprehend the possessive sex/gender relations themselves, that is, the relations of possessive rights and the appropriative practices that have associated women and men as sexes through history. It is here that the institution of marriage comes to the forefront. In a feminist theory of patriarchy the institution of marriage would have the same position that private property has in Marxist analyses of class-society. Then "marriage-society" would be a concept fit for further theoretical development and, perhaps, replace patriarchy as a sex/gender parallel to class-society. (Engels' book should have been named *The Origin of Marriage, Private Property, and the State!*)

If we look historically at the various kinds of interdependencies that connect women and men directly, that force them together in relations of social necessity—in practice or legally framed—we are able to see variations that to a certain extent are comparable to, but not identical with, the changes in the class relations. The formally equal welfare societies of today may, for instance, be conceived of as particularly "pure" or clearcut sex-societies. The economic, political, judicial, and other bonds/dependencies that have connected women and men personally through history have become fewer and weaker. What remains is a relatively isolated and clearcut bond of nature (socially formed, of course), that is, the dependency of love: of care and of erotic ecstasy.

Given that we do not overemphasize the comparison, we could say that this is a structural parallel to the economic compulsion inherent in capitalism. Even if wage-labor often is experienced as debasing and constraining, propertyless people continue to sell their labor power because realizable material alternatives do not exist. The laborer needs that which can be bought for his or her wage. No far-reaching external rules of legalized coercion is needed for the labor-capital relationship to continue. Women continue to give/attach themselves to men because they need that which they get and are allowed to do in the intimate couple relationship and in other relations with men. The reciprocity, however, is most often limited in these relations.

As I point out in Chapter 2, the system of male authority (or the marriage-society) should not be seen as localized only in the family, or in intimate relations and concrete marriages. The "marriage-society" should denote the whole set of relations in which women and men interact directly as persons. That may be at work, in political life, at school, and so on. But the normative and formative pattern of the sex/gender relationship at large (as a structural feature of society) is steadily produced and reproduced by its practices on the personal level.

A conclusion that can be drawn from these preliminary thoughts is that a theoretically founded periodization of the history of sex/gender relations must be based on how the qualitative elements that constitute the sex/gender relationship itself are contained or transformed. How do women and men relate to the control over and the appropriation of the sociosexual capacities of their bodies and souls. The point of this would be to distinguish between different historical forms of patriarchy. A typology of this kind would necessarily be very general in the same way that the Marxist typology portrays the history of class society. This means that to produce valuable empirical knowledge of concrete societies the concepts of the typology must be made concrete.

My main purpose in this very schematic chapter is to raise the question of different levels of abstraction in theorizing about patriarchy. Given the way in which I problematize the social relations of power between the sexes, that is, as being basically distinct from class and other relations of dominance, this question is of central importance. The issue of theorizing on different levels needs to be discussed much more if our goal is to produce feminist knowledge that is both empirically founded and theoretically informed.

chapter 4

Patriarchy, Marxism, and the Dual Systems Theory

After Juliet Mitchell and Gayle Rubin, Heidi Hartmann has probably been the most important writer to pursue the feminist assertion that feminist questions and Marxist method can be combined to the advantage of both.[1] While Mitchell and Rubin put sexuality firmly on the Marxist-oriented feminist map, Hartmann is the socialist feminist who, without abandoning Marxism, has most clearly pinpointed that men and not just the "system" are an active interested party in the organization and maintenance of the oppression of women.[2]

The Dual Systems Theory

Hartmann works within the framework of dual systems theory, a term that refers to patriarchy and class society as two relatively independent power systems that are integrated and mutually influence each other.[3] She rejects the economic reductionism of Marxist unitary thinking: it is not capital and private ownership that oppress women as women, it is men. At the same time she criticizes radical feminists for placing too much emphasis on biology and psychology, and for lacking a historical perspective. She also is concerned with

A slightly different version of this chapter was published in Swedish under the title "Patri-arkat, marxism och tvåsystemteori," *Häften för kritiska studier* 4 (1987):34–57. Jan Teeland translated that version into English.

correcting the ideological and psychologically fixated imbalance in current socialist feminist work and attempts to demonstrate that patriarchy is comprised not only of a psychological structure but of a social and economic structure as well. The term "the sexual division of labour" is not sufficient, however, as an explanation; it is what must be explained.

In short, Hartmann would "suggest a new direction for marxist feminist analysis." But she believes that Marxist categories do not provide any clues to understanding why women are subordinate to men both within and outside the family. Marx's theory of the development of capitalism is "sex-blind" because capital itself is sex-blind; "it is a theory of the development of 'empty places.'"[4] According to Hartmann, Marxism's contribution "enables us to understand many aspects of capitalist societies: the structure of production, the generation of a particular occupational structure, and the nature of the dominant ideology." And finally, Marxism offers "a method of social analysis, historical dialectical materialism" that can be put "to the service of feminist questions" (1981a:11). Hartmann then goes on to support her statements by quoting Mitchell's programmatic and oft-cited assertion:

> It is not 'our relationship' to socialism that should *ever* be the question—it is the use of scientific socialism [what we call Marxist method] as a method of analyzing the specific nature of our oppression and hence our revolutionary role. Such a method, I believe needs to understand radical feminism, quite as much as previously developed socialist theories.[5]

According to Hartmann, patriarchy thus comprises a particular social system that preceeded capitalism and that, in conjunction with capitalism, both changes and is changed by it. At the same time she claims that the two systems must always be studied together, and their points of intersection—how the two systems "interpenetrate" each other—constitute for her the core of the dual systems theory. Hartmann summarizes her definition of patriarchy as:

> a set of social relations between men, which have a material base, and which, though hierarchical, establish or create interdependence and solidar-

> ity among men that enable them to dominate women. [And:] The material
> base upon which patriarchy rests lies most fundamentally in men's control
> over women's labor power. (1981a:14–15)

Further, men maintain this control through their organizational
power, blocking women from access to essential productive resources such as self-supporting wages, and through sexual restric-
tions (1981a:15). Men's control is institutionalized in the family
wage system which, according to Hartmann, developed during nine-
teenth-century industrialization, and which, she claims, still exists,
constituting even today "the cornerstone of the present sexual division of labor."[6] Thus the subordination of women lies in men's interest as workers and capitalists, and in their interest as husbands and
fathers as well.

Hartmann believes that men's alliances over class boundaries
during certain critical phases in the development of capitalism become stronger than the logic of capital itself. The potential equality,
resulting from universal wage labor, between men and women that
capitalism offered was sabotaged by an unholy alliance of men. For
the working class this meant a lack of solidarity between the sexes,
greatly contributing to the absence of revolution in the West.

Hartmann's ambition is to specify the basic mechanisms of patriarchy more clearly than other theories have done. She wishes to
make the Marxist-oriented theory of patriarchy both "truly feminist"
and "truly materialist." She acknowledges the difficulties but refuses
to be daunted by them:

> What makes our task a difficult one is that the same features, such as the
> division of labor, often reinforce both patriarchy and capitalism, and in a
> thoroughly patriarchal capitalist society, it is hard to isolate the mechanisms
> of patriarchy. Nevertheless, this is what we must do. (1981a:29)

Hartmann's goals seem to be three-fold. She wishes to isolate the
basic mechanisms of patriarchy, especially with regard to how they
are formed and re-formed under capitalism. Her theory of patriarchy
is also meant to enrich our understanding of the historical origins of
capitalism. And in the end, she wishes to contribute to a more com-

plete analysis of our present form of society than traditional Marxism is capable of doing.

In the critical argument that follows I claim that to a very small degree Hartmann succeeds in what must be seen as her primary aim, that of exposing the specific power mechanisms of contemporary patriarchy. In my view, she suffers from the very limitation she criticizes in traditional Marxist analyses of feminist questions: Her Marxism clearly dominates her feminism (see 1981a:10).

Hartmann's contribution to feminist theory has been widely discussed internationally, and in Sweden researchers have applied her hypotheses empirically.[7] The clarity and relevance of her theory have been questioned as well.[8] Iris Young quite rightly points out that Hartmann has not succeeded in differentiating between the two systems' material foundations and structural characteristics. However, Young (1980, 1981) primarily criticizes the idea of dual systems as such.

Christina Carlsson and others have also criticized Hartmann for treating patriarchy in a functionalistic way: Carlsson attributes different needs and interests to patriarchy but no real internal conflicts, so that women seem not to have any active historical role (Carlsson et al., 1983:60). In a more recent work, Carlsson rejects the dual systems idea entirely, and, like Young, adopts a holistic or a "total theory" view. Capitalism is seen as *the* total societal structure, built around both social and biological sex differences. This duality must always be taken into account when studying the real actions of individuals and groups (Carlsson, 1986a:66).

In Hartmann's view, in contrast, capitalism should advance equality between women and men because of its structural gender neutrality; it is actually patriarchy that maintains inequality between the sexes, an inequality that existed prior to capitalism and that still exists. Young and Carlsson are among those who doubt the value of working with theoretical feminist questions on that high level of abstraction where capitalism can be conceived of as sociosexually neutral.

I believe that, in principle, Hartmann's idea of dual systems is fruitful: viewing society as a composite whole consisting of relatively independent parts that concur historically in their own processes at the same time as they are integrated in various ways and mutually influential. I also agree with Hartmann that men (and women!) as active sex/gender–interested parties must occupy an important place in the analysis. The problem must be formulated as being a combined structure/agency problem.

Hartmann is also correct to conduct her analysis in terms of appropriation and not only in general terms of oppression. Men appropriate certain advantages for themselves through controlling women—they gain something by it. However, Young is also correct: Hartmann does not succeed in isolating a material base in patriarchy. Her gender power system lacks specific structural characteristics that could qualify its relative independence. In her problem orientation— despite its revisory intentions—Hartmann never leaves Marxism's specific field of knowledge, that is, economy, class relationships, and work. Her thinking is riddled with economic reductionism. Her failure can also be attributed to the fact that she never really takes radical feminism seriously, despite her stated position. This leads to an extremely fuzzy concept of patriarchy and a neglect of the historical materialist potential present in the early pioneering, albeit limited, radical feminist writings.

Basically, I would conceptualize contemporary male authority (or patriarchy) in our type of society as a *political* sociosexual system. By this I mean that sexuality, gender relations, and love must compose those contemporary relational elements as well as those historical processes around which feminism bases its specific, and thus most abstract, fundamental theoretical problematique.

My decision to deal only with Hartmann's theory is partly due to her importance in the feminist analysis of patriarchy. In several respects Hartmann also represents a point of view that goes far beyond her own writings. Most important in this context is her focus on relations and practices of work as comprising the "basic problem" of the theory of patriarchy.

Consequently, much of my criticism could be addressed to most historical materialist-oriented feminist theorizing. My main critique of the socialist feminists, including Hartmann, is that they continue to be too dependent on Marxism, which, in turn, constricts the development of feminist theory (and, for that matter, the development of historical materialism as well).

My critique is organized into two main sections and a conclusion. In the first section I examine the way Hartmann utilizes the method of Marxism for posing feminist problems. I conclude that she makes very little use of the possibilities for new ways of thinking contained in the combination of historical materialism and feminist questions.

In the second section I look at Hartmann's conception of patriarchy: What are its fundamental relations and primary practices? I find that the lack of clarity in her concept of patriarchy prevents her from reaching her main objective — to analytically isolate the specific mechanisms of patriarchy.

In conclusion I attempt to specify my own points of view about relative dual systems theory. At the same time, these points of view are intended to be a contribution to the debate about whether the efforts to develop feminist conceptualizations of patriarchy on the level of the most abstract Marxist concepts are meaningful.

Marxist Method and Feminist Questions

Hartmann takes what at first glance seems to be an unequivocal stand on what parts of Marxism could serve feminist questions.[9] According to her, Marxist theoretical concepts are and can only be sex-blind. What can be used is the Marxist method. Upon closer examination, however, Hartmann's writing turns out to be inconsistent. In fact, she limits her theorizing about patriarchy to feminist questions of class and work processes. Indeed she makes common cause with the domestic labor theorists and other unitary Marxist theorists (whom she herself criticizes) in the sense that her theory is devoted to *complementing Marxism* rather than establishing a relatively independent theory of gendered power relations based on historical materialism. In addition, Hartmann is unclear about whether the materialist concept of history is also, like Marx's theory in *Das Kapital*, sex-blind. She herself seems to be blind to the possibilities to develop many radical feminist questions, should the opportunity arise for them to be asked and worked on from a historical materialist perspective.

Marxism's "Empty Places" and Feminist Theory

When Hartmann says that Marxist categories are sex-blind she exemplifies this by "class," "the reserve army of labor," and "wage laborers." In contrast to the domestic labor theorists, who would want to complement Marx's theory of value,[10] Hartmann concentrates on the social composition of classes under capitalism. She wishes to fill in the "empty places" in the demographical stratification of the class structure.

Under capitalism, the economically active sections of the population form a continually mobile class structure where the strongest forces of change are the necessity of capital to increase profits and the necessity of wage labor to earn its living. How the class structure of a given country is demographically constituted, that is, its constitution with reference to, for instance, sex, age, or ethnicity, is entirely an empirical question. It can vary considerably between different capitalist societies and between periods of time and even within different regions in one country. The *theory* of the capitalist class structure cannot explain, for example, why so many women and children were mine workers in England in the nineteenth century, while today nearly all miners are men; or why the leaders of Swedish industry, in the boom period in the beginning of the 1960s, consciously recruited Swedish housewives and not immigrants; or why women all over the world systematically occupy the worst paid and subordinate work positions as well as have inconvenient working hours to a greater extent than men. "The labor force" from a theoretical point of view refers only to value/costs and productivity.

Hartmann agrees with this way of understanding capitalism and Marxist theory—hence the "theory of empty places." But like the domestic labor theorists, she sees this "emptiness" as a gap in Marxism, which feminism theoretically should help to fill. Thus her theory of patriarchy should demographically, that is, regarding sex/gender, make concrete the otherwise abstract notion of class structure (strictly speaking, only the stratification within the working class).

This is of course an important field for feminist research, but we must be clear about its limitations. A theory whose specified problem concerns gender distribution within capitalism's variable occupational structure must deal with statistically describing and explaining just that. How and why women are subordinate to men in the occupational structure refers, however, to only one of the societal relationships that a fundamental theory of gender power should be able to illuminate. The purpose of feminist theory cannot be restricted to creating historical descriptions and empirical generalizations in the area of class theory.

Hartmann is right that studies of pre-capitalist societies' gender stratification provides a great deal of new knowledge about the origins of capitalism and the history of class society. And indeed it is also important to study present gender-related changes in the class structure and remedy the unnecessary gaps in knowledge found in many investigations in this area that are caused by lack of gender consciousness.[11]

For example, Hartmann stresses that labor unions are one of the most critical social institutions through which men control the labor market and women's work. There is sufficient empirical evidence to erase any doubt that labor unions both historically and at present provide one of the most central arenas of gender struggles outside the home.[12] However, women's repeated failures and inferior position with respect to men within unions must finally be seen as a consequence rather than cause of their fundamentally subordinated position as sociosexual beings.

The Materialist Conception of History and Sex/Gender

What does Hartmann make of those bases in Marxism that all social-ist feminists, including her, agree on as a common point of depar-ture: that is, the principles of a materialist concept of history as for-mulated by Marx and Engels? According to this concept, production and reproduction of immediate life has a two-fold character: on one hand, the production (and reproduction) of the means of existence; on the other, the production (and reproduction) of human beings themselves—the propagation of the human species (see p. 19).

Hartmann, however, explains away the theoretical feminist foot-hold in this historical materialism. When she confirms the impor-tance of apprehending Engels' formulation of "that second aspect of the *mode* of production [i.e., 'the production of human beings themselves, the propagation of the species']," she sees in this only "*how* we are created . . . as socially recognized genders"—that is, how we are shaped and differentiated socially into feminine and masculine individuals (1981a:16). In other words, she sees only an embryo of a socialization theory of gender, which is structurally re-lated only to the economy. She ignores the potential of historical materialism for creating a specific structural theory of the sex/gender relationship as a material base in itself. As we shall see later in more detail, Hartmann distinguishes no material relations or practices (or productive forces) that are necessary and specific for just this "sec-ond element" (or "second aspect") in the "two-fold character" of hu-man production. She also equates questions of race and the repro-duction mechanisms of racism with the question of sex and the social reproduction of gender. She views the "production and reproduction of human beings" as referring to any social character construction whatsoever. Sexuality loses the specificity it was actually ascribed in Marx and Engels' materialist concept of history, in which the sexual relationship occupies a particular position, that, however, was never developed further.[13]

The Materialistic

Hartmann criticizes current feminist theory for its ideological, biological, and psychological definitions of patriarchy, which, she sees as nonmaterialist. Hartmann believes that men's material interest in the continued oppression of women is primarily due to their having a "higher standard of living than women in terms of luxury consumption, leisure time and personalized services." Women's personal services "exonerate men from having to perform many unpleasant tasks (like cleaning toilets)," both within and outside the family (1981a:9, 15). Thus the materialistic is for Hartmann equal to the economic, that is, work. In her text there are, however, several possible turning points, or putative alternative (noneconomic) ideas. In certain respects she ascribes great value to the early radical feminist analyses, but she never reflects on the possibility of testing the materialist and historical development potential of these analyses on their own terms. For example, she strongly stresses the consciousness-raising importance of Shulamith Firestone's (1971) book on the power of men over women, especially the chapter on love. Hartmann writes:

> It is not just about 'masculinist ideology', which marxists can deal with (just a question of attitudes), but an exposition of the subjective consequences of men's power over women, of what it feels like to live in a patriarchy. 'The personal is political' is not, as Zaretsky would have it, a plea for subjectivity, for feeling better: it is a demand to recognize men's power and women's subordination as a social and political reality. (1981a:13)

Why does Hartmann not make more of these assertions? Why not test the possibility of remedying the gaps in the materialist historical view in radical feminist studies by retaining the focus on women and men as sexual beings? There is every reason to wonder what this "just" means in the question of ideology and attitudes. It is not self-evident that it concerns nonmaterial relations. A central element in the "new" Marxist way of thinking beginning in the 1960s is that the ideological forces are not wholly nonmaterial phenomena, but, on the contrary, seem exceedingly concrete and material in both our physical surroundings and our own bodies-and-minds.[14]

The concept of attitudes is problematic in this context. It is true that in the social sciences as well as in everyday language, "attitudes" often refer only to rather superficial opinions, and are, then, often specified as preferences or "rational choices." The classic social psychological definition of the concept of attitudes, however, contains three distinct components: emotions, cognitive reasoning, and the inclination to act.[15] With a materialist concept of attitudes referring to the social as well as the physical being, a mental and neural state of readiness in embodied human beings, organized through social experience, possibilities are opened for operating with more all-round conceptual tools with regard to relations in which we are continuously involved but which we are unaccustomed to "seeing" scientifically. For example, the fact that in all the different contexts in which women and men conduct relations with each other (work relationships, various family relations, friendship, etc.) we are at the same time sexual beings.[16] This is a further reminder that in human relations—love included—reason, feelings, and incipient actions run parallel, which tells us not only that the practice of sexuality and love is about emotional experience but also that it generates cognitive reason and readiness to act.[17] We are neither "involved" nor "detached" in political decision-making, work, and love; our psychosocial, material human life is continually gliding on a scale. Our various situations or states of experience are not discrete; they have neither a "definite beginning nor a definite end."[18]

Hartmann also perpetuates a view that fails to identify the specific nature of the power that comprises the sex/gender relationship, when she claims:

> The psychological phenomena Shulamith Firestone identifies are particular examples of what happens in relationships of dependence and domination. They follow from the realities of men's social power—which women are denied—but they are shaped by the fact that they happen in the context of a capitalist society. If we examine the characteristics of men as radical femi-

nists describe them—competitive, rationalistic, dominating—they are much like our description of the dominant values of capitalist society. (1981a:28)

The first sentence above indicates that there should be a universally valid relationship of dependency and dominance, in which sexual dependency and domination should constitute one particular form or appearance. This idea seems to me to lead nowhere; it seems to be idealistic in a "good old" Hegelian way.

We can, of course, *logically* construct a general category of dependence and dominance that can then take in various subcategories (like a variable in modern methodology), but *socio-logically*, so to speak—that is, empirically, as an object of study in the social sciences—such a general relationship does not exist. What we can expect to find in reality are various types of relations of dependency and dominance (which of course can demonstrate certain similarities)—various because they comprise qualitatively different substantial relationships in human life. For example: relationships of dominance based on economic dependence are one thing, sexual relations of dependence and dominance that develop around them are another. In women and men's concrete lives these different dependencies and relations of dominance can be interwoven, but the connections need not be of the kind usually assumed.

Hartmann is right that sexual power relations between men and women do not manifest themselves totally independently from the social and economic conditions in which they live. But the point is that sociosexual dominance is not and never has been only an effect of men's economic power position or reducible to the "dominating values" of society's current economic organization (capitalism or any other).

Why not then take seriously the radical feminists' "demand for the recognition of men's power and women's subordination as a *social and political reality*" (emphasis added)? That sex/gender relations comprise a specific political power structure is one of feminism's original and continuing assertions, and Hartmann herself has said it is an important insight. However, if this insight is to be worked into a historical, materialistically tenable hypothesis, we must establish the political as a historically specified theoretical determination, adapted to sociosexual relations and processes. This is a theoretical project that has still hardly been started.

The Historical

According to Hartmann the strength of radical feminism lies in its insights into contemporary relations between the sexes; its great weakness is that its consistent psychological focus renders it ahistorical. But precisely these "insights into the present" should qualify radical feminism's analyses for a historical materialist method at least in one important respect, since this method tells us that only when we have comprehended the current structure of society can we cogently investigate history.

Historical blindness suffuses not only radical feminist methods but also the "nature of patriarchy itself" in Hartmann's view. Radical feminists conceive of patriarchy as a remarkably resistant form of social organization, a social system that is characterized by men's dominance over women. Hartmann cites a definition from Kate Millett: "Our society . . . is a patriarchy. The fact is evident at once if one recalls that the military, industry, technology, universities, science, political offices, finances—in short, every avenue of power within the society, including the coercive force of the police, is entirely in male hands"; and she comments: "This radical feminist definition of patriarchy applies to most societies we know of and cannot distinguish among them. The use of history by radical feminists is typically limited to providing examples of the existence of patriarchy in all times and places" (1981a:14). Hartmann's last sentence may constitute a well-grounded criticism. But the assertion that Millett's idea of patriarchy should be in principle and irrevocably inappropriate in a historical-theoretical approach needs further attention. Even if it is true that radical feminists' definitions of patriarchy can contain "most of the societies we know of," they are not finally disqualified because they "cannot distinguish among them," that is, between different historical forms of patriarchal societies. "Patriarchy" (or male-dominated society) as a general or comprehensive historical social organization can be said to correspond to "class society" in the established Marxist sense of the term. Thus it is a question of a general historical concept that need not be seen as universal in an ahistorical sense. Class society is also assumed (by Marx) to refer to "most societies we know of," but class societies are presumed to have originated in history and are supposed to come to an end through political struggle, which many also think is true for male-dominated societies.

The criteria for differentiating between various forms of class societies lie in the Marxist class concept itself as a part of the concept of the mode of production. It has to do with what happens when the ruling class extracts surplus labor from the subordinate class. At the same time it deals with how social classes vary from a historical point of view: slaves and masters, serfs and feudal lords, wage laborers and capitalists, and this in turn is connected with what sorts of means of production the people in the different societies have developed. The patriarchy/male-dominated society should in a *comparable way* be able to be exposed to a theoretical analysis with the aim of developing criteria for distinguishing historical periods.

This point of view renders meaningless the common assumption that gender relations in our present type of society should be defined as "precapitalist," as "antiquated attitudes" or that their structure of authority should be typified as "traditional" (in Weber's term). Today's male dominance assuredly has its own form that must be specified historically, and for this, in my opinion, the early radical feminists' preliminary definitions offer valuable guidelines.

The Dialectic

Hartmann does not write much about the dialectic other than to state that by using Marxist methods she indicates "historical, dialectical materialism." She takes certain things for granted, however, that thus can be viewed in terms of the dialectical principles other Marxist-oriented feminists explicitly write about or refer to.[19] This applies, for example, to the demand for a comprehensive view of society so as not to fragment the whole into artificial parts, which then are represented and explained as if they were separate units, totally independent of each other. I interpret Hartmann's focus on the interaction between the two systems, capitalism and patriarchy, as an expression of how she thinks the dialectic should be applied. A central point in my criticism is, however, that, given the aim of a feminist-theoretical explanation of the bases of contemporary patriarchy, it is not constructive to try to focus on both systems simultaneously on all analytical levels.

Hartmann's emphasis on the interaction between the two systems is expressed, for example, in her criticism of feminists. In her opinion, Mitchell's failure to concentrate on how patriarchy and capitalism "interpenetrate" limits her analysis. And Firestone is criticized for discussing sexual dependence and dominance relationships without also observing that these "are shaped by the fact that they happen in the context of a capitalist society" (1981a:12, 28). In another place, Hartmann has written of Firestone:

> [Her] work offers a new and feminist use of marxist methodology. . . . Her work remains the most complete statement of the radical feminist position. Firestone's book has been all too happily dismissed by marxists. Zaretsky, for example, calls it a 'plea for subjectivity'. Yet what was so exciting to women about Firestone's book was her analysis of men's power over women, and her very healthy anger about this situation. Her chapter on love was central to our understanding of this, and still is. (1981a:12–13)

The question now is whether Firestone's acclaimed book on the power struggle between the sexes and on the conditions of love would have been better if she had tried to include "the fact that they exist within the framework of a capitalist society," and moreover, how should she have done this? For a start, it is not certain that it is capitalism, the mode of production in a narrow sense, that should be highlighted as central in the social and historical context. If that were the case, then power relations between the sexes would be qualitatively different in the "really existing socialist" societies whose basic economic structure is not capitalist. That such was indeed not the case comprised one of the women's movement's strongest initial insights: how much was similar between women's and men's situations as genders—despite the disimilarities in the relevant socioeconomic organizations? One refers here to things such as women's double work load and the lack of women in the various power positions in society—and it refers also to the conditions for sexual love.

This is a complicated matter that has been discussed very little in feminist theory. However, a historical specification of "our" type of male dominance clearly demands a more complicated definition than that of projecting capitalism as *The* independent variable. In Chapter 2, I present two preliminary criteria for qualifying contemporary Western society: the formal/legal equality between women and men, and women's actual—if often meager—possibilities for economic and social independence from individual men. Moreover, given the framework of capitalism, in what way could Firestone have acknowledged that framework in her chapter on love? First, one might ask, Is another theoretical explanation missing? For example, must the masculine and feminine characteristics that inspire human love relations be directly explained by the logic of capitalism or its ideology? Or, second, Is there a lack of reporting, suppositions, or awareness that the patterns of love relations and behavior as well as their institutional conditions can be empirically different in different social strata?

Considering Hartmann's other discussions on the connection between capitalist ideology and the social construction of masculinity, it is likely that it is the former she misses: she would want causal explanations of the social expressions of love to be found in economy. She would require an explanation that directly derives a capitalist ideology of love from capitalist economy. Such an explanation would tell us without more ado why women and men in our present society often have such uneven power positions, even in love (for example, why women are driven to making themselves vulnerable while men take for themselves). In my opinion, such demand for direct causal connections with economy are unrealistic.

I assume that people's patterns of emotions and behavior are historically changeable; the same is true of love relations. Socioeconomic relationships in every society assuredly play a major role in how people's feelings are manifested. However, I would argue from the assumption that the economic context is only one context and that people in their other capacities relatively independently form society. My assumption means, moreover, that women and men — needing, seeking, and practicing love — enter into specific productive relations with each other in which they not only quite literally produce new human beings but also produce (and reproduce) themselves and each other as active, emotional, and reasoning people. If we want to conceive of how all this happens and why it happens as it does, if we are seeking causal connections, it is both necessary, and sufficient, to seek these connections in the sociosexual life-process itself. However, to understand better the historically specific form of this social dimension today we must also have a clear conception of the historical specifics of society's other dimensions or processes. Presumably this applies particularly to the state and the economy. In the same way it would increase our understanding of the origins and development of capitalism and the nation-state if we observe how family relations, the institution of marriage, and sexual life have simultaneously changed forms.

This is not to say that we should seek the *causes* of the origin and development of capitalism or the nation-state in any of these other relationships. What I mean is that economic relationships, expressed in terms of "capitalist society" or "capitalist ideology" can only indicate the framework in which the actors move about when they practice their possibilities as sexual beings.

The question was also whether Hartmann, in criticizing Firestone's theory of love, was searching for class-related differences. There is no indication in Hartmann's text that this is what she is looking for. Class differences in women's and men's sociosexual conditions are otherwise heavily stressed by Marxist feminists, sometimes so heavily that hardly any common ground for theorizing over class boundaries seems to exist.

Regardless of what Hartmann means by searching for connections with capitalism as a societal context, we can only assume that Firestone's chapter on love would have been more informative if it had contained assumptions or facts about class variations. To the degree that Firestone has touched on the crux of gender-specific oppression, however, I question whether this could have been made more clear *theoretically* if she had demonstrated class variations. These, however, become extremely important in studies of concrete gender and love relations. The influence of class on gender relations and the gender differentiation of class relations can only be clarified empirically.

Hartmann's Concept of Patriarchy

Hartmann clearly states that Marxism's "woman question" must be reformulated as "the feminist question"; otherwise it is not meaningful to try to explain patriarchy by using Marxist method, for patriarchy is about "men's systemic dominance over women": "The feminist question is directed at the causes of sexual inequality between women and men, of male dominance over women, [and at] . . . how and why women are oppressed as women . . . the goal of feminist analysis [is] the relations between women and men" (1981a:3, 5, 7). How does she more precisely identify that "women are oppressed as women" in their relations with men? Or, in other words, what relationships, practices, and power relations constitute patriarchy? This question remains insufficiently analyzed and contradictory in Hartmann's work.

First, it is unclear whom Hartmann identifies as the main opposing parties in the patriarchal system: is it men and women (which she has repeatedly written); is it primarily men, in alliance with and against other men (which is what her summarized definition states); is it men *and women* of higher status who wield power over women *and men* of lower status (which she also states)? Or should patriarchy be seen as a multifunctional machine that grinds out all kinds of inequality and social hierarchies that are revealed when we study demographic variations in the class structure of capitalist societies—which her work also indicates.

Second, she claims that work is the basic material practice that relates men as men and women to each other as sexes. What the specific sociosexual power relations are about and from what generated is extremely unclear.

Patriarchy's Opposing Parties

The ambiguities begin in Hartmann's definition, in which patriarchy is said to be "a set of social relations between men" through which they can control women. Women themselves do not appear as real partners in this relationship but only as objects/resources used by men to be allocated in their exchange relations. The patriarchal interest conflicts in capitalist societies are said to be between men as private individuals (men "want their women at home to personally service them") and men as capitalists, and the conflict concerns the use of women's labor power" (1981a:19).

The model of patriarchy Hartmann sketches in her definition—men dealing with women as objects—is also present in Rubin (1975), who has clearly influenced Hartmann. Rubin has adopted the French linguistically informed structuralist view of gender relations, with which she would complement the historical materialist, gender-unconscious treatment of "the origin of the family, private property and the state." The primary source for this view is the anthropologist Claude Lévi-Strauss.

Lévi-Strauss conceives of women as words or signs and men as the users and signifiers of words. Both sexes exist in a timeless subject-object relationship where men are always and exclusively the subject (alone with the predicate in their power) and women always and exclusively the object (see Rubin, 1975:174–83). Rubin criticizes Lévi-Strauss for sexism (obviously rightly so); however her criticism is primarily ideological: he fails to point to the oppression of women, which he implicitly describes (Rubin, 1975:201). But the structuralist approach itself she adopts uncritically. This model of patriarchy, with only men acting and women only being acted upon, can be criticized in several different respects.[20] I especially question its historical validity, that is, its sensitivity to empirical data and its ability to register changes. This conception ignores, for instance, one historically new and important element in contemporary patriarchy (in our type of society), namely, the fact that women in a formal/legal sense have become "free" and "equal" with respect to men although in social life they are not. This means that women themselves in a new way have taken a position as a main party in the struggle over control of both their labor and their other "powers." I naturally do not claim that men, as the other party in the patriarchy, are not related to each other in an important (theoretically significant) way. That would be similar to saying in Marxism that there is no special bond within the capitalist class. The question concerns what relation is the most essential if we wish to understand the sex/gender power system's own dynamic and the changes in its historical forms.

Hartmann further confuses her analysis of the relationships that constitute patriarchy when she writes that even women (through their family connections) can exercise patriarchal power "over men lower in the patriarchal hierarchy than their [the womens'] own male kin" (1981a:18). In doing this she combines gender dominance and social status in general in one concept, which becomes analytically and historically unclear. In the end gender dominance and social status in general cancel each other out. This might have had a certain validity in, for example, feudal estate society, but it has little effect today other than to shuffle away the very cards feminist theory must look at. Hartmann's writing indicates that basically she imagines an unbroken historical continuity between the old patriarchal or paternal rule of husband and father and the present male authority in a formally equal society. She asks:

> Can we recognize patriarchal relations in capitalist societies? Within capitalist societies we must discover *those same bonds* between men which both bourgeois and marxist social scientists claim no longer exist or are, at the most, unimportant leftovers. Can we understand how these relations among men are *perpetuated* in capitalist societies? (1981a:19; emphasis added)

This is misleading. The patriarchal relations we strive to describe and explain, that is, the relation of dominance between women and men in our present, formally equal society—capitalist or not—are not the "same bonds" that existed in previous forms of society and that are perpetuated in the present. Hartmann in fact has not availed herself of the new use of the term "patriarchy," which the radical feminists first launched when they wanted to denote adult men's power over—and in comparison with—women: power that exists and that is steadily renewed without having clear support either in law or in juridical regulations. What is historically new in this male dominance or patriarchy is that men's power in relation to women is no longer so much practiced by virtue of fatherhood or the head-of-the-household institution as by virtue of "their collective adult maleness."[21] This means at the same time that women, formally and thus potentially, are actually responsible for themselves and take care of their own concerns.

Hartmann criticizes radical feminists for their lack of historical perspective, that is, their lack of perception that gender relations like other social relations undergo changes, and sometimes fundamental transformations. But she herself does not seem to be aware of what this means: that, especially if we wish to apply Marxist method, we must reckon with qualitatively different gender relations in different periods of history. Hartmann ascribes radical feminists' analyses of the present a certain value; their analysis "has its greatest strength in its insights into the present", but she seems not to understand that precisely this makes them so important, even, and not least, in helping us to comprehend history. If it is correct that radical feminisms' strength lies in comprehending the present, then the Marxist method (which Hartmann has chosen to follow) firmly tells us that the vicissitudes of history must be understood from a valid analysis of our present structure. In this context then it becomes of secondary importance whether radical feminists in fact provide faulty historical descriptions.

Hartmann's difficulties in isolating sex/gender relations as specific bonds between people are also apparent in her inability to see any fundamental differences between the bases for gender power and those for racial power relations. She includes both indiscriminately into "the second aspect" of the material base of society, that is, in the "production of human beings themselves." Both gender power and racial power seem to deal equally with the construction of people in different and ranked groups. Hartmann writes:

> Racial hierarchies can also be understood in this context. . . . Racial hierarchies, like gender hierarchies, are aspects of our social organization, of how people are produced and reproduced. They are not fundamentally ideological; they constitute that second aspect of our mode of production, the production and reproduction of people. (1981a:17–18)

As I mention in Chapter 3, I believe it is untenable to place race and gender in the same category of production, primarily because racial conflicts are wholly socially conditioned, while gender conflicts are *connected to fundamental needs*. This is not to say that male dominance and sex/gender inequality are fundamental needs. It means instead that sociosexual relations, seen in terms of meta-theory, can be conceived of as "essential" in a way that racial relations are not. In sexual relations a historical, human-materialist production process goes on that is necessary in the sense that it is *not substitutable*: it is necessary for the continuation of the human species.

Only the production of the means of life is comparable in this respect to the production of human beings. Both these social relations are also fundamental in another and related way: they encompass unique human *causal* powers[22] or creative capacities—work and love. It should perhaps be said that "essential" or fundamental in this argument is not about any gradation of how strongly people experience different types of oppression.

The fact that Hartmann equates race and gender hierarchies is in turn connected with two other flaws in her analysis. First, when she discusses human production and reproduction, she thinks only in terms of socialization theory. Second, she is too one-sidedly preoccupied with how people are slotted into the "empty places" of capitalism's class structure. The whole meaning of the theory of patriarchy would seem to hang on the ability to explain who populates which places in the hierarchy of the working class. But there is something unclarified here, something that should tell us how patriarchy and the theory of patriarchy relate to all the other social stratifications that can be distinguished in the work class:

> Capitalist development creates the places for a hierarchy of workers, but traditional marxist categories cannot tell us who will fill which places. Gender and racial hierarchies determine who fills the empty places. *Patriarchy is not simply hierarchical organization*, but hierarchy in which *particular* people fill *particular* places. It is in studying patriarchy that we learn why it is women who are dominated and how. (1981a:18)

The way Hartmann formulates the problem is at once too wide and too narrow. It is too wide in that she seems to expect that a theory of patriarchy should be able to explain the conditions for other kinds of social stratification (hierarchies) than those of gender, or that some sort of general theory of hierarchy can embrace them all. It is too narrow because a basic theory of patriarchy must be able to explain inequality between women and men in the whole society and not just the gender division of work in its most limited sense, within wage labor. Even if she adds up several "central elements" in the patriarchy, it is, in her view, to "understand patriarchal *capitalism*" (my italics) that all these elements must be examined. Since she attaches central importance—also theoretically—to the question of intersections, of how the two systems influence each other (understanding of the union between patriarchy and capitalism is placed before the analytical clarification of patriarchy itself), she becomes locked into the theory that already existed—that of capitalism. Women's and men's different conditions in the core area of this theory, the work process and class structure, automatically become the only given field for the examination of feminist questions.

The Totalization of "Work"

To discuss social relations in a historical materialist perspective is to also discuss practices. Ties between people are not mute couplings but organic channels through which run the processes of which society consists.

If patriarchy is constructed around the relations between women and men—which Hartmann, despite all, presumes—it is not simply given that the material practices that are constitutive of *these relations* should be work. If we speak of "women as women" (and men as men), we have actually said that the question involves people as sexual beings and thus a fundamental problem orientation should also be undertaken in the specific field of relations and practices of sexuality. With Hartmann it is just the reverse. She talks about women and men as sexes but treats sexuality theoretically as only a residual, and at best as a means in work and economic relations. Hence neither can she identify any social, materially based power relations that are basically sex/gender-specific, that is, that belong to sexuality: for her, such relations only grow out of capitalist ideology.

Not even housework, or as Hartmann puts it "the work process within the family," can give the sex/gender system the specificity that enables it to be essentially differentiated from the class system, because it is not necessarily a relation between women and men or between people as sociosexual beings.[23] Both women and men can purchase or allot themselves the household services of people of the same sex without generating any sexual or gendered relations. Men can also carry out these activities themselves or purchase equivalents on the market outside the home. But (a pivotal point in an empirical testing of my theses) the dominance of men over women does not cease today when or to the extent that housework is equally shared.

Here Hartmann would certainly intervene, saying, in effect: "Right! Equal sharing of household work is not enough; segregation and the unequal distribution of power in work outside the home must also cease." According to my premise this interjection also rests on an incomplete analysis. The only specific relations and practices that can qualify the distinctiveness of the sociosexual power system are those dependency relations and activities generated by the necessities of gendered person-to-person interaction, and of sexuality and love. Only when male dominance within these relations ceases can the strict gender division of work and men's control of women's work also cease. This does not contradict the fact that both paid and unpaid work are very important arenas for struggles between women and men, and scarcely any satisfactory situation has been reached in either sphere. What I want to point out is that not even with an equal division of household work, and probably not also with equal responsibility for children, will we have exhausted male dominance and oppression of women.

Hartmann's work contains glimpses of a specific sexual dimension. In a summary of her definition of patriarchy she writes: "Men exercise their control in receiving personal service work from women, in not having to do housework or rear children, in having access to women's bodies for sex, and in feeling powerful and being powerful" (1981a:18). But these glimpses lead nowhere; the order of the quotation is not accidental. Sexuality and existential sexual power relations are understood as wholly conditioned and directed—and as such, created by factors of economic development. Hartmann, in a manner common to Marxist feminists, also reduces sexuality to propagation: "An understanding of the demand (by men and capitalists) for children is crucial to understanding changes in women's subordination" (p. 37). This is certainly true, but what about the demand on women as love objects? This aspect of sexuality is seen only as a result of an economic/historical development that occurs when nativity becomes unimportant: "When children are seen as superfluous, women's sexuality for other than reproductive purposes is encouraged, but men will attempt to direct it towards satisfying male needs" (p. 37).

Hartmann makes the same mistake she criticizes the Marxists for: the economic system with its need for the reproduction of the labor force and inheritors of private property becomes womens' actual counterpart. Economy conditions and directs womens' sexuality, and only to the degree allowed by functional economic latitudes do "male needs" arise as a socially channeled force. Of women's needs, whether they be children or men, there is no mention.

I do not criticize Hartmann on the grounds that she is wrong in any simple sense of the word. I use her writings to illustrate the inadequacy of treating sexuality only from a socioeconomic perspective. Sexuality must be regarded as a distinct problem, a particular field of relations and practices in which women and men as sociosexual beings are the main agents. And as such, sexuality should be considered possible to study both materialistically (noneconomically) and historically—that is, approached in a feminist, historical materialist way.[24]

Like most other socialist feminists, Hartmann allows the concept of work to embrace too much. All possible mental activities, all material practices that could have any social and historical importance are conceived of as work. This is evidenced in Hartmann's treatment of, for example, Mitchell and Firestone. According to Hartmann, Mitchell's analysis would have been more substantial if she had identified women's activities in all the structured contexts of life (paid work as well as propagation, the sexuality and socialization of children) as work. She claims that Mitchell overlooks the material base of patriarchy in that she has overlooked the "relation between women's and men's labor power." According to Hartmann, Firestone has succeeded better (although she overemphasizes biology and reproduction) since she ascribes to patriarchy a material base, namely, "the *work* women do reproducing the species" (1981a:12, emphasis added).

Why this fixation with "work"? Is there anything to be gained by considering the various activities involved in sexuality, or *everything* that is involved with caring for one's children and others as work? The positive aspect of using a flexible concept of work is that it makes possible empirical historical analyses of what has actually been denoted as work in various forms of society and various epochs as well as indicating who has carried out what work.

Insights into the varying extent of societal work, its character and its division among social groups, are important in a Marxist methodological perspective. Not least in a society such as ours is "love on paid work time"[25] increasingly practiced, primarily by women. Severe crises seem to threaten, for it is becoming more and more difficult to recruit to the "sex-blind" places (seen in terms of class theory) in the "love professions." But Hartmann does not pursue this line of reasoning. Her fixation with work seems to be anchored in a very widespread and unreflected belief that if we abandon the concept of work, we will lose our historical materialist foothold. I do not think that need be true; on the contrary, "love" perceived as material practice must occupy that position in basic feminist theory that "work" occupies in Marxist theory. These two concepts refer to qualitatively different social practices and living processes; and we must be able to identify and clarify both. If everything is work, our perception of alternatives to the growing economization and instrumentalization of our social relations and practices is obscured.

"Work" should be limited to its position as an economic category, which can indeed be quite wide; and in practice, work is often simultaneously something else. Like love, it can contain both pleasure and pain. But the criteria for delimiting work, analytically, should involve *instrumentality*, or goal orientation: efforts by the practitioner to execute a given task, to create or shape a predesigned object. (According to Marx it was just this conscious purpose that differentiates the clumsiest architect from the most industrious bee.)

What should distinguish love as a typal concept is that its practitioner acts without aiming to shape the love object according to his or her own lights. On the contrary, it is essential that the object in receiving love win the capability of "shaping" himself or herself and his or her own goals. Work can be loving and love can be laborious. But we experience the contrasts and know that both are necessary for a good and worthwhile life.

The success of Hartmann's theory (compared with Marxist unitary theory) is diminished by her eagerness to remedy the radical feminists' and even Mitchell's alleged lack of history, overemphasis on biology and psychology, and the lack of a materialist basis in their concept of patriarchy. It would be wrong to claim that Hartmann concentrates only on class relations, but she limits herself to the economically material, to relations between women and men as creatures of labor. Her expanding the concept of work to include house-hold tasks and various services within the family does not compen-sate for this limitation. She neglects specific sex/gender relations and thus also the possibility of identifying a power base specific to the sociosexual system.

Conclusion

Hartmann's notion and treatment of the "empty places" in the class structure and of men's use and control of women's work in both patriarchy and capitalism is not wrong in any simple sense. But these issues do not comprise the "basic problem" of feminist theory. In my view the basic task for methodologically Marxist-oriented feminists lies in producing their own, relatively independent theories about sex/gender, gender power, human production, and so on that are equivalent to but not subsumed by Marxist theories.[26] This applies to the more general "theory" of society and history and the historically specific theory of capitalism. The dual-systems approach implies this view of equivalence or relative independence between Marxism and feminism. It involves acknowledging that feminist analysis of patriar-chy that is on the same high level of abstraction as Marx's theory of capital is as meaningful. The Marxist unitary view of the "woman question," however, denies this as do the feminist empiricists and the totality theorists. Hartmann seems to take a stand for the former, but she practices the latter.

Why are abstractions meaningful? To abstract is to analyze, that is, to isolate in thought certain elements in a complicated reality. The aim of abstraction is to identify conceptually and reveal those ele-ments that we believe to be the most essential in the context we wish to explain—and, possibly, consciously change. The weaker the analytical/abstract clarity, the greater the risk for concrete confusion.

How meaningful then are abstract theories about sex/gender rela-tions? Or in other words, how much do comprehensive or basic theo-ries explain? In my view they are both necessary and of limited significance. They do not free us from the task of carrying out empirical studies, and they cannot replace less abstract, more concrete levels of theory. Consequently, we cannot avoid the arduous task of seeking, testing, and developing concepts on a middle-range level. We must continue to work with more concrete, directly testable hypotheses when studying the situations of women and men in the various subdivisions of society, such as working life, school, the family, and politics. In my opinion Hartmann's idea about the importance of the institution of the family wage is more appropriate as a middle-range hypothesis than as a core concept on the basic level of theory.

To assert the value of an abstract sex/gender power theory does not contradict what many feminist scholars have argued and what experience, common sense, and scientific knowledge tell us: that sex/gender power relations can be different in different institutional contexts. Concrete case studies as well as comparative studies of the situation of women and the relative positions of the sexes in different institutions and organizations and in different (but comparable) countries are necessary to clarify such matters. How we shape all these more or less concrete intermediate-level concepts, analytical frameworks, and subtheories, what questions we ask in individual empirical studies, and what sorts of interpretations we make of the results depend, however, on what abstractions we presume—openly or implied—on the basic level of theory. Here we are concerned with the value of clarifying what ideas about the structuring fundamentals of society we use in our studies.

We can also ask how politically meaningful it is to attempt theoretically to distinguish an essential part in the complexities of sex/gender relations, a nucleus that is assumed to contain a dynamic, an explosive force of the greatest qualitative significance for a comprehensive transformation of these relations. If this succeeds, that is, if the theory is valid, can we then resolutely and effectively adopt measures and implement the desired changes? It is indeed not so simple, particularly if there is anything in what the venerable Marx once wrote when he was young that in the sexual relationship lies the greatest potential for humankind's development of itself, its social nature, and humanity.[27] A

theory, no matter how good, makes the struggle no easier or less pain-
ful, nor perhaps does it make the struggle shorter, but with such insights we should at least be able to *see* more clearly.

The idea of trying to encircle core assumptions also has another
side. Feminist scholars sometimes argue that one major difference between present-day oppression of women and capitalist class oppression
is that the former cannot be brought back to a single social relation
corresponding to Marxism's emphasis on the exploitation of surplus in
the relation between labor and capital. The oppression of women is
considered much more complex, an outcome of a whole system of
relations and structures. But I would argue the contrary. In the specific
theory of exploitation I have begun to develop, a certain structural similarity is assumed between the labor-capital relation and the love-male
authority relation. On the other hand, neither class nor sex/gender oppression is maintained (or eradicated) only through relations of exploitation themselves. *Both* are renewed and opposed in many different and
complex social structures.

Why do the previously mentioned groups of Marxist-oriented feminist theoreticians consider it meaningless to strive after special feminist
theoretical constructions on the same "diluted" level of abstraction as
that of Marxism? Assuredly for several reasons, among which, the argument that male Marxists have said as much.[28] Apart from that, however,
this standpoint implies that the Marxist perspective on society and history, actively or passively, is made absolute. Capitalism is erected as the
Fundamental Structure, a total force and the only one that influences
society on a deep level and in its entirety. Economic power is seen as
Power, changes and transformations of economic production are
equated with History.

If feminists wish to adopt Marxist methods for a comprehensive
theory of society and history, we should make Marxism's basis in economic production and class *one* fruitful perspective for the study of
history and capitalist society. To be successful this theory must be inspired by and continually reflect women's concrete experience (which
is both common and varied), and it must be based on careful empirical studies.

The isolated concepts in the most abstract sex/gender theory will then be "blind" to class, race, and other social-group criteria. If we choose sex/gender as a point of departure and a field of knowledge, then we have rejected the idea that a far-reaching *theoretical* specification or definition of other social elements should be pertinent.

A clear advantage to Hartmann's way of stating the problem, compared with dealing exclusively in terms of division of labor, is that she takes up the question on a level of agency where groups with diverse interests confront each other. Thus her model contains both structures and active bearers of structures. But Hartmann is fundamentally ambiguous in all characteristic attributes of the central concepts: the question of what *relations* are assumed to be included in the base of patriarchy and what *activities* or *practices* are performed in these relations is never answered satisfactorily.

Hartmann seems to be consciously ambiguous in that she sees the study of the *points of intersection* between the two systems and not the analysis of the patriarchal structure itself as the most important aim of Marxist-oriented feminist theory. This keeps her within Marxism's specific "sphere of interest," and the only important patriarchal conflicts she perceives are those occurring in the partnership between the patriarchy and capitalism. Her concept of patriarchy appears as a labyrinth of intertwining gender/class/status and race hierarchies. She does not take feminism's revised view of patriarchy seriously, that is, the view that the main partners in the patriarchal power system are adult men and adult women.

The core of Hartmann's theory is that women are economically dependent on men and that men control women's work. I argue, however, that the societal work process cannot comprise the basis for both a theory of capitalism (or other modes of economic production) and a corresponding or accompanying theory of patriarchy. This is not to say that women's weak economic and work position is uninteresting. A relative socioeconomic equality between women and men, or let us say a minimal economic independence and social security for women, are and remain crucial prerequisites for the eradication of sociosexual conflicts—even for their exposure.

chapter 5

Beyond "Oppression": The Exploitation of Women

I served his purpose
and believed it was love's

. . . .

through my eyes
which were man's within mine
he was given
a gift
to love himself

. . . .

his love for me
was to let me
love him
my love for him
was to let him
through me
love himself

Elisabet Hermodsson, *Gör dig synlig* (Make yourself seen)

Discrimination, oppression, and exploitation are the key concepts most often used to define women's estate and the relations between the sexes in a patriarchal society. Other commonly used concepts are stratification, hierarchy, suppression, and even enslavement. In this

The first English version of this chapter, translated by David Anstey, was presented in the workshop "Exploitation" at the ECPR Joint Sessions of Workshops in Barcelona, March 1985. The poem by Elisabet Hermodsson was translated by Myrtle Ternström and is reprinted here by permission of the author.

chapter I propose that of these concepts *exploitation* is the most fruit-ful one to work with, given the aim to explain, on a societal (or systemic) level, the dynamics of contemporary patriarchy. The argu-ments I advance apply in particular to the relationship between the sexes in the formally/legally equal Western societies of today. This proposal can be put into three distinct but related theses.

1   At issue is not primarily the exploitation of women's labor power by capitalists and by men. This I make clear in the preceding chapter. Neither are the benefits accrued through the exploitation of women as women only a question of men's freedom from something, to "be released from menial tasks and unpleasant burdens" (Farr Tormey, 1976:211). Instead we are here dealing with, analytically, the maintenance of men's power as *men* (in formally equal societies), the reproduction of which requires that men control the use and appropriate the effects of the specific kind of capacities or human powers women are endowed with as sociosexual beings. This appro-priation also usurps women's power to act on their own behalf in the wider context of the community, that is, as political persons.

This exploitative relationship is, thus, a three-party relation in which women (as women) and men (as men) constitute the two active parties, as individuals as well as collectives. The third party is that which is exploited: love power; understood as a creative and alienable, practical human capacity, used by people to act on one another's and one's own human materia (body-and-mind). The power situation in which this exploitation is acted out is primarily in person-to-person relations between women and men, that is, on the social existential level.

2   My first thesis, which proposes a distinct materialist (and thus causal) sociosexual power, is a precondition for my second one, namely, that the sociosexual system, alias the mode of production of people, must be explained in terms of itself rather than being re-duced to something else (such as the division of labor, the logic of capital, a universal pattern of dominance, etc.). This does not contra-dict the view that gender relations, as all human relations, are shaped in a historical context and, therefore, (self-)constructed under influence of other formative social forces, mainly those of the economy and the state.

3 That which associates the Marxist notion of exploitation with the feminist one postulated here is that ultimately both take as their point of reference such naturally social, physical, and mental powers or capacities of human beings as are uniquely essential for humankind's existence. These are the powers to produce the means of human life and to develop the very forces of this production; and the power to produce, or create, human life itself—and to develop the living source of this kind of creativity.

Furthermore, there is a third essential human capacity that I assume to be alienable and exploitable as well as fundamentally developmental. This is the capacity to organize socially and to act rationally to administer common concerns, one's own included.[1]

By "exploitation" I refer to the appropriation of certain human/natural powers or capacities that are indispensible to people. Appropriation refers to the situation where a person or a group of people extract these powers from others without exchanging them, or returning them, equivalently and where those who are exploited do not have control over the situation, that is, they have no real alternative to the exploitative relationship.

"Exploitation": Used and Dismissed in Feminist Theory

The term exploitation is used frequently by feminist writers. It occurs as one among many in the search for key concepts that would help to pinpoint with accuracy the central mechanisms that keep patriarchy going. But as feminists strove to explore the implications of the different concepts and to apply them more stringently in theory and research, "oppression" rose in conceptual status while "exploitation" was almost completely lost in the process. There are a few exceptions to this.[2] But in these cases exploitation is used exclusively to portray *economic* exchange and control over women's *labor* power. This is the case even when the body as a sexual means of production is dealt with.³

Without wanting to trivialize the significance of women's double workload or the effects of economic exploitation on laboring women's lives, I suggest that the concept of exploitation be used in circumstances other than these and more gender specifically. It should be used to designate the systematic extraction of power occurring in the sociosexual relationship in and through which women and men produce and reproduce themselves and thus society. This power is not labor power.

The intellectual heritage of Marxism has probably lent more inspiration to theoretical studies of the relationship between the sexes than any other tradition of thought (others being psychoanalytic theory, French structuralism, and poststructuralism). Marxism held assumptions and concepts that seemed to enable us to grasp much of that which could never really be problematized within role theory, which had dominated empirical studies of women since the 1940s. Marxist assumptions about a dominant ideology that shapes the minds of people lent substance and material support to the analysis of socialization. The hypothesis that certain groups must provide a reserve labor force if capitalism were to maintain its vigor also gave a much-needed perspective to women's free choice between home and wage labor. Terms such as power and oppression emerged as clearly appropriate for those students of sex/gender relations whose work had reached the limits of what the sex-role analysis of the complementary relationship and even the newer stratification alternative could embrace (cf. Jónasdóttir, 1984). However, without entering into a discussion about the "unhappy marriage between feminism and Marxism,"⁴ it is clear that Marxist circles in most countries had not only a stimulating but also a restrictive influence on the efforts of feminists to pose their own problems from their own points of view.⁵ Thus in the beginning the assertion that women as *women* were oppressed across class and race boundaries was met with resistance. This assertion implied that even upperclass women were in some sense oppressed and also that men as *men*, and not only as

capitalists, were oppressors. None of these assumptions correspond-
ed to the prevailing Marxist thought patterns.

What came to be the most important question in Marxist-oriented feminist theory was how the oppression of women and the
sex/gender system in general are connected with capitalism and its
class system. But the most burning question for feminist theory was
and still is, in my view: What does, specifically, the oppression of
women as *women* consist of, when understood as a distinct social
occurrence and a distinct historical process that is analytically isolated from class relations and the work process? And, assuming the
above-mentioned fruitfulness of Marxist method, how should this
method be used and developed to clarify and explain *this* dimension
of society? Here feminist theory meets something of a crosscurrent
within Marxism, namely, the question of to what areas of society,
other than the economically based mode of production, historical
materialism alias Marxist method can be extended. Expressed
slightly differently: What potential does Marxism have when applied
to new areas, new in the sense that these areas were not of interest
as fields of knowledge when Marxist thought was evolving?[6]

Jon Elster belongs to those Marxists who, partly in polemic
against feminist analysis, have written about the concept of exploitation. He consistently (1980, 1981, 1982) uses two counter-examples
to show what exploitation is not. One is the feudal extraction of
surplus labor, which, he says, should more accurately be termed
"extortion." The other counter-example is the exploitation of women
(as women), where Elster regards the concept of oppression as containing all that needs to be said on the matter. "Exploitation proper,"
according to Elster's view, exists only within capitalist economy. The
self-perpetuating economic necessity is the only real exploitative relationship.

Elster also puts forward the very reasonable point of view that
what is more important than a dispute over words is to arrive at a
description of the mechanisms that give rise to and perpetuate injustice in family and community life (Elster, 1981:410). This is, of
course, correct—but only to a certain extent. Realistic descriptions

and expositions that aim to get past a more superficial level require appropriate words. As I see it, feminist theorists have in their quest for knowledge consistently avoided too many disputes over words. Usage of the term oppression is a case in point. But we cannot, like Marianne Gullestad, in the long run accept it merely as a "moral and loosely defined umbrella term." Nor is her pragmatic view that "the concept is useful insofar as it leads our thinking forward towards strategies for liberation from oppression" (Gullestad, 1981:360) any more acceptable. If we fail to recognize the point at which we should deal specifically with the implications of our terms and ask ourselves if they cover what we are attempting to elucidate, we will soon be confronted at the very least by the fact that we have no clear idea of what "liberation from oppression" is all about. I suggest that oppression is no longer sufficient as an explanatory category.

Gullestad says, and as far as she goes, quite rightly: "By drawing a distinction between economic relationships (exploitation) and power relationships (oppression), we can also show how ideological and psychological oppression paves the way for economic exploitation" (1981:360). Here the concept of oppression is understood in a broader sense than that of exploitation and has, moreover, both ideological and psychological connotations. Oppression is seen as an ongoing manipulation of the senses that in turn forms people so as to accept being exploited. I do not argue with this. My objection is that the term exploitation should not be restricted to the economic field. For even if the term is allowed to assume certain wider implications—in this case the sexually based exploitation of women's capacity to love and care[7]—we will not lose sight of its distinctiveness from the more general term oppression. What we gain is the ability to include vital processes in society that the term oppression does not include. And these processes are different from those implicit in the class-based exploitation of the work process. There are, however, certain common characteristics. In both cases, a people's physical and living powers and capacities are being exploited; and we are dealing with the two human-natural prerequisites for the continuation of the species. Human sexual life and human working live cannot in this respect be replaced by anything else.

"Exploitation" and the Norm of Reciprocity

Usually, exploitation is understood as a moral term, meaning roughly, "taking unfair advantage of another person."[8] A fairly widespread assumption is, for example, that Marx, in his theory of surplus value, chose to use the word exploitation because he disliked capitalism. Yet, in a scientific study there is no reason to charge the very concept of exploitation with moral (i.e., normative) elements, and this applies to both our reading of Marx and our understanding of other areas. As Gouldner puts it: "It can be employed simply to refer to certain transactions involving an exchange of things of unequal value" (1960:166).

Still, the moral overtones or implications of the term exploitation are not entirely irrelevant because social relationships termed exploitative are *associated with the norm of reciprocity*, to "pay like with like," to use an old Nordic/Icelandic expression. This norm, which says that if you take or receive something from another person you ought to reciprocate in kind, or with something of equal value, is considered one of the oldest and most widespread norms known to history. Hypothetically or as an empiric generalization, we may treat the norm of reciprocity as universal. Gouldner compares its usage and cultural implications with the incest taboo (1960:171).[9] This alleged—and in innumerable studies confirmed—universality does not mean that its presence and application is unaffected by sociocultural or historical circumstances.

Gouldner draws an important distinction between the norm of reciprocity and a norm that has to do with the complementary rights and obligations between occupants of different social positions. In the latter case the expectations rest on obligations and rights implicit in the position itself, irrespective of what the individuals who occupy it actually do or do not do. (According to the traditional rules of the institution of marriage, for example, man and woman are obliged to love each other because they are lawfully married, and not because of what they are or what they do in respect to one another.) The norm of reciprocity, on the other hand, implies that a person has rights and obligations based on what another person has previously done for her or him and vice versa (Gouldner, 1960:170–71).

Older Usage of the Term

Because of its political-ideological connotations as well as its more general moral implications the term exploitation has long been seen within the social sciences as explosive. In fact the term became so explosive that it practically vanished from the discipline's vocabulary with the exception of Marxist theory. Indeed Marxists have hitherto claimed a kind of ownership of the term.[10] This is not reasonable, however, if the term is considered in the light of its own history. The term exploitation was used in both the English and the French sources[11] of Marx's thinking. In the classical vocabulary of political economy the word referred to "a relationship in which unearned income results from certain kinds of unequal exchange" (Gouldner, 1960:165). Gouldner also maintains that the notion of exploitation is present in Thorstein Veblen's term the "vested interests" to which he ascribes the meaning "the right to something for nothing," or as Gouldner (1960:165) understands it: "*institutionalised* exploitation."

The term exploitation acquired a wider usage among early sociologists (early 1900s). The American sociologists L. von Wiese and Howard Becker, for example, writing in 1932, described capitalism's economic exploitation as only "one of the forms which are found among the phenomena of exploitation." And furthermore: "The destruction of capitalism will not signalize the end of exploitation, but will merely prevent the appearance of some of its forms and will open up new opportunities for others" (quoted in Gouldner, 1960:165, note 18).

Apart from economics, these grand old men of sociology applied the term exploitation to the field of sex-gender relationship, where it continued to be used even after it otherwise nearly disappeared from sociology (Gouldner, 1960:166).[12] Why sexuality in particular came to occupy this special position is not explained by Gouldner, and I do not intend to explore the subject further here. My reason for highlighting these fragments from the history of the term is to show that it has a respectable heritage and that there is no historical basis for Marxists to claim ownership of its usage. The plausibility of their claim may instead lie in the fact that Marx's term has a specific scientific definition in a closely delineated theoretical construct. And this cannot be seen as an obstacle to its use in other theoretical contexts; especially if these other contexts have certain important links with the Marxist usage.

In a way I am inclined to agree with Waller's comment on his own use of the term in *The Family: A Dynamic Interpretation*, published in 1951: "The word exploitation is by no means a desirable one, but we have not been able to find another which will do as well" (quoted in Gouldner, 1960:166). Waller's misgivings were due to the fact that the word has such strong pejorative connotations in everyday language and is so controversial in the sciences; but he was unable to select another word that embodied as well the reality he wished to illustrate.

The Marxian Concept

Marx's use of the term exploitation is in itself not strictly normative or moral. It can, however, be said to have two different sorts of historical preconditions, one of which implies the reciprocity norm discussed above. In bourgeois society it acquired a very particular meaning. "Fair exchange" had from the very origins of the exchange principle meant "equal exchange." Whether it meant women exchanged for pigs, butter for woolcloth, or fish for iron ore and brandy, there was always the firm assumption that the exchange should be all square. Early liberal social theory had *equality* as an axiom. All human individuals were regarded as equal, or at least more alike than unalike (see Chapter 6) and the norm of equal value in exchange relations entered a new historical phase as money became more widely accepted as the equivalent of other objects. The idea that in economic exchange transactions one should receive, indeed have the right to receive, as much in return as was given was thus not something invented by Marx. Sale and purchase of different items, both work and other things, had equal value as its guiding principle.

The other principle underlying bourgeois-liberal theory and its system of norms was the principle of liberty. Equal individuals were by nature free and independent. As such they entered into necessary exchange contracts. But fears of envisioned conflicts and power struggles between individuals, physically and intellectually equal, gave rise to the need for an entity superior to the individual—the state. The political-economic principle underlying capitalist social theory is that of free individuals who—through equal exchange and with their liberty and private property guaranteed by the state—buy that which they do not produce themselves and sell that which they have excess of.

What Marx highlighted, among other things, was that the propertyless workers were neither free nor equal (compared with the aristocracy, priesthood, bourgeoisie, and the freeholders) other than in certain respects. They were free in the sense that they were not serfs, and they were equal (compared to property owners) in the sense that they had their labor power to sell. But they had no recourse if they did not obtain a fair deal on the market. Marx's premise was that the necessity for a worker to sell his labor power in order to eat was fundamentally different from even the necessity for a small farmer to sell his butter even if the price was low. The worker had no choice, no alternative. The farmer could for a time live off other products and postpone the purchase of that which he would have used the butter money for. When, therefore, Marx demonstrated that the capitalist economic exchange on the labor market was neither equal (i.e., labor power was rewarded according to its market price but not according to its productive value during the working day) nor free, one may say that this theory implied a norm—or, rather, a lack of norm—a violation of a social principle. But this was, as I have said, not discovered by Marx and was not in any simple way dependent on his moral standpoint.

Another and quite different premise for Marx's theory was his ontological or philosophical/anthropological view of the nature of man. Man was seen as a social, active, self-developing, and historically evolving being. Among the many things that this view of mankind implied was the idea that man would not voluntarily submit himself to bondage, literally or metaphorically. History also showed that the relatively independent small farmer did not leave his own land to sell his labor power until no other choice was open to him. But history showed, moreover, that man reconciled himself and adapted himself to conditions that, with the best will in the world, could not be called either free or equal. Presupposed by (but not contained in) Marx's empirically oriented theoretical concept of exploitation are, thus, certain social norms (reciprocity in exchanges, equality, and freedom), a certain ontological/anthropological view of man, and empirical observations from history of the actions of concrete people that were in harmony with his hypothetical view of man.

Still another underlying assumption must be brought forward more specifically. It has been implied in the above discussion but has not been stated explicitly. Evidence of historical changes in land control and the control over the means of maintaining one's livelihood in general formed in a certain sense the most fundamental part of Marx's studies. This is connected to an element in historical materialism which, for some reason, has always been and still is controversial, namely, that different areas in society are quite objectively ascribed different degrees of theoretical importance. Marx set out from the fact that people are physical, living creatures who die if they do not have access to food and protection of different kinds. He thereby also asserted that the material world and its historically changing circumstances assumed a different and causally more important position in society than, for instance, religious ideas or the political and judicial institutions that man has erected and continuously altered. What characterized the sociomaterial conditions under capitalism, and what was also new in comparison with the conditions during the Middle Ages, was that large numbers of people were, so to speak, suspended in limbo. They had no immediate access to any secure means of subsistence, no land, no livestock, nothing. In order to survive and provide for themselves they were compelled to work for others, who in a new sense *owned* the means of subsistence. Socioeconomic conditions had thus evolved, circumstances controlling man's livelihood, that more closely resembled the relationship between slave owner and slave than that of feudal bondage. An entire class of people had been rendered powerless in the face of the fundamental need for daily bread and a roof over their heads.

This complete dependence on other people who *owned* with the full consent of the law provided the necessary background for a new (capitalist) and more subtle form of economic exploitation to take place and become institutionalized. Dag Østerberg (1978) sums up this multi-level relationship in this way:

> The crux of the class conflict lies in the fact that one class does not have control over its own working situation and the products which are created. The other class decides what shall be produced and how it shall be produced, what shall be invested, etc. This lack of power is a form of what Marx (following Hegel) called alienation. Starting from contemporary social economic theories, Marx demonstrated that the alienation finds its expression as exploitation on the labour market, in the now famous theory of surplus value. This is often interpreted in the way that the worker is committed to an ostensibly fair contract with the owner of capital, which in actual fact means that the latter gains advantages through it. The workers get 'shortchanged' (they are exploited). From the sociological point of view the exploitation is not primarily of an economic, monetary kind, but more a question of self-determination, of power over one's own work and the proceeds from it. (p. 107)

The question is, should we talk about exploitation other than specifically economic rather than about alienation when referring to powerlessness and dependence with respect to the fundamental conditions of existence in a society? The economic form of exploitation implies the appropriation of labor power during a longer time than that for which the worker is paid. But the removal of control over the conditions of subsistence, over the opportunity to determine how labor power should be organized, how it should be expanded, and how its products should be used, can be said to constitute a sort of political exploitation, a crippling of people's organizational and administrative capacities or of people's *power of agency*.[13]

The notion of exploitation in Marx can thus be said to comprise two levels: one more fundamental, the appropriation and paralyzation of the human power of agency (i.e., a political exploitation), and one less fundamental (i.e., economic in a more restricted sense), the appropriation of labor power in excess of the price paid. My main objective here is to argue that the sex-gender specific exploitation of women has to do with the transference from women of a large proportion of their life power. By "life power" I mean those capacities and energies that are of crucial importance not only for the reproduction of the workforce but for how women and men perform or practice their social existence as sexual beings and, also, how the various power of agency fields are structured in society as a whole.

Farr Tormey's Conceptual Analysis

The philosopher Judith Farr Tormey seems hitherto to be the only one to have undertaken a thorough analysis of the term exploitation as applied to the situation of women. In her essay "Exploitation, Oppression, and Self-Sacrifice" (1976) she sees the demand for self-sacrifice, the social norm that requires of people to forgo their own rights and interests, as an important oppressive device. Since this norm is in particular directed toward women, says Farr Tormey, it contributes to maintaining a systematic exploitation of women. She sees her own notion of exploitation as being superior to the Marxist one: "My understanding of the concept has greater scope and explanatory power and examples of exploitation in the economic sphere can be subsumed under it" (Farr Tormey, 1976:214).

Farr Tormey draws certain helpful distinctions between the concepts of oppression and exploitation. However, in my view she has not been wholly successful in capturing the most vital point, the actual dynamics in the sociosexual exploitation process, and has not clearly explained who the main parties in the relationship are.

A fundamental difference between exploitation and oppression, says Farr Tormey (1976), is that the exploited party can equally well be people or nature, whereas only people can be oppressed. The exploiter, however, must be a person or group of people, while oppression can come from nonhuman sources, for example, nature. Among the more important differences between exploitation and oppression, she continues, is that one person can oppress another person without gaining anything, whereas exploitation necessarily always involves benefits or gains of some kind to someone. She ascribes to oppression the implication of a special form of slavery based on the assumption that the person believes that the conditions he or she lives under are those that he or she deserves or is supposed to live under (p. 207). Oppression thus differs from other forms of slavery inasmuch as the force or compulsion involved operates more at the mental than the physical level. Two necessary and, taken together, sufficient conditions must therefore be fulfilled before oppression can be said to exist: (1) Oppression is a relation whose object is necessarily a person or group of persons; and (2) Oppression requires influences on psychological states (p. 216).

By "psychological states" Farr Tormey means both so-called cognitive and noncognitive states, that is, both beliefs and moods. The expression to be "down" captures well the essence of what oppression is about, she continues, in the sense both of mental states and of actual social positions. In the socially significant sense of oppression one is down (put down and kept down) as a result of unjust or unfair treatment generated by irrelevant social distinctions (p. 216). Regarding noncognitive mental states or moods one can feel down, feel oppressed, and in that sense one *is* oppressed. Such moods can, according to this argument, be produced, for instance, by the weather or by certain physical processes in the body just as much as by something that other people do or are involved in. What is decisive here is that one *feels* oppressed. As far as the cognitive mental state is concerned, however, that is, the fundamental beliefs about oneself and one's environment, one does not need to feel oppressed in order to be oppressed. What is typical of "socially significant oppression" is that one is held "down" in a long-term process. The decisive factor in this process is that the person herself or himself by her or his thoughts, feelings, and actions takes part and thus maintains a low-grade social position, a serving role. Oppression, understood in this way, thus paves the way for exploitation. And the doctrine of self-sacrifice is, according to Farr Tormey, the moral principle and means of oppression that most effectively prepares women for exploitation.[14] She understands self-sacrifice as a special form of self-denial. It requires that someone else gains by it, and that one gives up certain rights.

Farr Tormey sets up three general criteria according to which a social relationship may be called exploitative, and a fourth that applies in cases where the exploited parties are people.

1 Exploitation is a three-term relation that requires a person or group of persons for at least one of its terms. More specifically, the exploiter must be a person or group of persons. (For simplicity she later uses "a person" instead of the longer "a person or group of people.")

2 Exploitation necessarily involves benefits or gains of some kind to someone (unlike oppression, as we have seen, which may exist without anyone's gaining from it).

3 Exploitation resembles a zero-sum game: what the exploiter gains, the exploitee loses; or, minimally, for the exploiter to gain, the exploitee must lose. (When the environment is the object of exploitation, the lose is commonly characterized by depletion.) That exploitation is like a zero-sum game does not imply, however, that the exploitee may not also gain something, so to speak, on the side. Farr Tormey uses an example from poker: "I may

thoroughly enjoy your company and the experience of playing poker with you even when I lose heavily" (p. 211).

4   When the exploitee is a person, exploitation requires a violation of principles of fairness consisting of either a disregard for the exploitee's interests or an infringement of the exploitee's rights: "This need *not* imply that the interests or rights of the exploitee are totally ignored; what is important is that they are given 'less than their due' " (p. 210).

The concrete exploitation situation around which Farr Tormey builds her analysis is the situation in most homes where the wife/ mother takes on a "major share of menial tasks and unpleasant burdens" (p. 211). The benefits on the part of the exploiter consists of freedom from these tasks. I will return to this.

She distinguishes between, on one hand, exploitation and, on the other, mutual compensation and fair exchange. This is a crucial distinction because the infringement of the qualitative mutuality, the absence of exchange that implies equal worth for the involved parties, is what exploitation is all about. She maintains that compensation is compatible with exploitation. It is therefore possible to assert that a wife/housewife is exploited with respect to item X ("menial tasks and unpleasant burdens") even if she is compensated by being relieved of economic burdens. It appears that Farr Tormey even accepts the assertion that, in the above example, the wife exploits the husband with respect to item Y (gainful employment), and that he in his turn is compensated by not taking on his fair share in item X. The point is that it is a question of mutual *compensation*. Mutual exploitation can thus exist, according to Farr Tormey, but this does not correspond directly to fair and equal exchange *because the mutual exploiters do not start from the same position* (she here refers to Rawls who, in his *Philosophy of Justice*, uses the term "original position," quoted on p. 212). An indication of the fact that compensation of the above-mentioned kind does not cancel out exploitation, continues Farr Tormey, is when a gainfully employed man claims that he is exploited by his wife, working in the home, but who at the same time would be most unlikely to change places with her.

To sum up those elements of Farr Tormey's analysis that I find relevant for my proposition here: Oppression is understood as a long-term (ideological) breaking down of people's fundamental beliefs about themselves and their place in life. The crucial point is that the individuals in question actively adopt this attitude and do not necessarily feel it as being something oppressive. The moral principle of self-sacrifice, living for others, operates as a tool of oppression that in a special way is directed toward women. Oppression with the doctrine to self-sacrifice as its most effective weapon thus prepares the way for exploitation.[15] The exploitative relationship itself implies that certain individuals, in this case housewives, take upon themselves an unreasonable share of menial and unpleasant tasks so that other family members are released from them and have more time to pursue other activities. Oppression for Farr Tormey can thus be understood as a limited concept or merely a precondition for exploitation, as opposed to being able to explain an exchange between two parties where one gains something that the other correspondingly loses. And this last point is, as I see it, of paramount importance. The discussion about sex discrimination and oppression of women often sounds as if no particular party wins anything by it.

I see shortcomings in Farr Tormey's analysis. First, she describes exploitation in the sociosexual exploitation relationship basically as only negative. The gains consist of *freedom from* something, and the exploiter avoids doing certain things: "Other members of the family . . . gain freedom from the tasks (menial tasks and unpleasant burdens)" and to the same extent the housewife loses this freedom (p. 211). The benefits and losses, I propose, also in a sense have a positive substance inasmuch as the exploiting party literally derives energy and the losing party is depleted of powers necessary, among other things, for independent action.

Second, sociosexual exploitation is not only a question of *work* or unevenly divided household chores.[16] These are certainly a very important factor, and far-reaching changes in this field must take place for the relationship between the sexes to change in any way at all. But the process of sociosexual exploitation goes beyond one party's carrying out more of certain chores than the other, and further than having more real free time than the other. The circumstances that allow this type of arrangement are imbedded in a more deep-seated power relationship; a relationship of appropriation and commitment. In this women are required (or require of themselves) to confer their vital powers, to make themselves totally available, with little or no power of control. If women desire access to the reproductive sources of sociosexual life, if they wish to be able to grow and assert themselves as independent social beings, as women individuals, they must do so more or less within the confines of submission.

Third, Farr Tormey's analysis must clarify who the exploiting party is, given that the exploitee is the "housewife." She speaks both of "other members of the family" and of the "husband." As I see it the main opposition exists between the woman/wife and the man/ husband. How the woman/housewife makes use of or is made use of by, for example, children in the family is subsidiary to the fundamental relationship between the adult man and woman. Of the family relationships this is the only one where the parties are potentially on equal terms.

Using the Marxist Method to Serve Feminist Theory

As the preceding pages indicate, I both accept and reject Marxism. More precisely: I am attempting to conceptualize the specific socio-sexual problematique, in particular, the persistence of patriarchy in an age of formally legal equality, by using a mode of comprehension similar to the one that enabled Marx to understand the nature of class society and of capitalism's power of constant renewal. But this ambition requires, simultaneously, a denial of Marxism as a universal mode of thought based solely on economy and labor. The idea is that in historical materialism it is by no means obvious that we can treat "material" and "economic" as one and the same. All that is material is not economic,[17] not even in the final analysis. I also contend that work neither is nor ever can be life's only and total "prime want."

Ultimately sex-gender issues arise from sociosexual material circumstances. This physical dimension forms a distinct element in human nature, is shaped historically and socially, and forms a fundamental part of human nature that is "interdependent with itself," that is, a part of nature as a whole.[18] Here it is more precisely the very materia of human bodies, including the sexual organs and the specifically human sexual power or capacity, that acts in a specific metamorphosis with itself. It is people's bodies-and-minds that supply both the raw material and the "productive forces" for this transformation. Thus, also, while the economic productive forces grow above all, through people's creating "the extension of body and mind," the sociosexual productive forces can be developed only by a more complete use of the body-and-mind themselves. But the unique human practice that mediates between the social and the natural in this transformative process does not consist primarily of *work*; it consists, I suggest, primarily of *love*.[19] Love, then, as a sensuous capacity and a specific creative force expressed in relational practice is, like work, organized in a specific societal or systemic process: sexuality.

In Chapter 4 I criticize the feminist fixation with "work" as a theoretical concept. In my view, the concept of work cannot grasp any specific sociosexual practice. Historical-materialist feminist theorizing has as yet lacked a notion of a distinct, organic process that comprises the relational base of patriarchy and, at the same time, is a source of resistance and a potential for change. This means, moreover, that the usual radical feminist way of substituting sexuality for work is misleading. Work and sexuality cannot be seen as conceptual parallels, Rather, work parallels love in that both denote (unique) *practices*, while economy parallels sexuality in that both refer to *systems*; the systems in which vital practical-relational processes are organized. The most serious critique I would direct against the radical feminist "dominance approach" of the type MacKinnon (1987) proposes (see Chapter 1, esp. note 6) is that in this approach there seems to be no organic source of societal change other than orga-nized violence and resistance to violence. This approach does not include, nor is it related to, any conception of societal, productive, or creative practice. Furthermore, in this dominance approach (or violence approach), all differences tend to disappear between, on one hand, the free-and-equal, contractarian[20] form of gender rela-tions that, I contend, is constitutive of and typical for today's patriar-chy, and, on the other hand, forms of gender relations that are shaped internally and maintained by overt coercion and violence. In the last section of this chapter I present a preliminary typology to distinguish sex/gender exploitation from economic exploitation and to differentiate between two forms of sex/gender exploitation, one characterized by overt dominance and the other—today's "exploita-tion proper"—by a pressure or force of a different kind.

Exploitation in the "Technical" Sense

To pursue my argument I shall clarify the distinction between exploi-tation as a "technical" concept and its normative preconditions. This distinction is important in defending the theoretical use of the term, but it also helps us to isolate other conceptual distinctions. It helps us, for example, to comprehend *historical differences* in what exploita-tion is about and what makes it possible. It is important to be able to clarify differences—even subtle ones (see, for example, Elster, 1980)—between exploitation built on direct and more or less open force, as in the slave-owner economy of antiquity and in feudalism, and the exploitation that takes place in voluntary transactions, as is the case under capitalism. In a similar way, as economic exploitation becomes less visible under capitalism, the appropriation of women's loving capacities becomes less visible in the formally equal society.

If a distinction between exploitation as a technical process and its normative preconditions helps us to grasp how exploitation itself (as a technique or a method) changes historically, it also helps us to see how its normative elements/preconditions are altered. It is thus reasonable to claim that the exploitation of surplus labor becomes genuinely unjust only under capitalism, since it is only then that people are declared free and equal. According to capitalist ideology, everyone is entitled to obtain maximum satisfaction of their needs and development of their capacities (Macpherson, 1973). This applies to sociosexual exploitation as well. Only when equality between women and men has become historically possible, that is, politically and ideologically recognized and enshrined in statute, is its absence genuinely unjust.

For the sake of comparison we return once again to economic production. By isolating exploitation's technical elements it is easier to understand the so-called internal economic coercion of capitalism, or what Elster calls the economic "causal chain" (1980:3). Although "no threats [take place between people] beyond the withholding of offers" (p. 3), one can discern the independent compelling force that the economy exerts. Self-acting economic power arises from private ownership of the means of production. Self-acting economic powerlessness is generated by the bitter physical necessity for people to support themselves—people who are both socially (politically and judicially) free and at the same time without control over the means of production. My assumption is that an equivalent relationship of power/powerlessness exists in our contemporary form of sociosexual life, and I will return to this.

The distinction between exploitation's technical and normative elements also helps us to see the actual substance or materiality in the exploitative relationship; it is a question of one group of people alienating or appropriating *something* from another group. This insight risks being completely lost when, for example, Giddens defines exploitation as "domination [over nature and/or human beings] which is harnessed to sectional interests" (1981:60). Here the term exploitation refers generally to hegemonic power; power is exerted for the interests of some and not for the good of all. A similar vagueness exists in most feminist writings where the term is used. When there are assumptions that something is being taken—that there is a transference of something involved and not only oppression in some vague sense—then only labor and time are considered, or other possible factors are reduced to labor.

This objection of mine in regard to other parts of feminist theory (especially radical feminism) may seem misdirected because the use and misuse of women's bodies and sexuality is the context where the term exploitation is most often found. It is true that the term is used, but as soon as the question of working out a theoretical understanding of these issues arises, the term is either abandoned or given a content that fails to isolate either specific sociosexual oppression generally or, particularly, the typical contemporary form of appropriation of woman-human power.

If we fail to clarify *that* something is transferred and *what* is extracted in the exploitative relationship, then we will most probably also fail to make clear that we are talking about an *interactive* relationship between certain groups of people. Social transactions where one party "takes unfair advantage" of the other presuppose active agents. It follows from this that *structural exploitation* is not a meaningless term as Elster (1980:12, and note 12) argues but that structure is produced by agents (under certain historical and social conditions). The agents are thus structurally formed and related through their own practical activity, but the system or structures cannot appropriate anything—only living agents can do this. The same principle applies broadly speaking to the sociosexual sphere as well as to the economic sphere.

The exploitation implicit in the relationship between capitalist and worker is structurally similar to the one between men and women.[21] In these two corresponding relationships an unequal transaction takes place involving goods or values—the capitalist extracts labor power over a longer period than that for which he pays wages and appropriates for himself control over the product of this extra labor. Men appropriate the caring and loving powers of women without giving back in kind. Moreover, this occurs under conditions that leave women unable to build up emotional reserves and authoritative social forces that can be used freely and "invested" for women's self-defined interests and for the good of all—as defined by women.

Form and Content

Earlier I used the expression "structurally similar" in a comparison between the sociosexual and the socioeconomic spheres. But here I do not mean, like Fredrik Engelstad (1978), that the notion of exploitation is applicable (or, if we wish, transferable from Marxism) primarily because of formal similarities between today's sex-gender and class relationships, though I agree for the most part with his ideas.[22] I also agree that sociosexual and class transactions should be treated as parallel issues in a more general social theory. My main point, however, is more a matter of content. That the term exploitation is applicable to the sex-gender relationship is a question of substance or materialist similarity (not substance identity), which also informs us of the compelling power by which the exploitation relationship is maintained. Individuals in a capitalistic society enter— both freely and compelled by economic forces—into economic exploitive relationships in order to maintain their independent existence; both in the literal, physical sense and as people who are forced by historical circumstances to produce their own identity and look after their interests. One is not born into either of these in the same way as before. It is therefore also correct to say that under bourgeois capitalism the "family unit is one of the most important cornerstones for individuals' sense of identity and cognitive stability" (Engelstad, 1978:356).

What is continuously overlooked by theorists, and is lost here in Engelstad, is the specific natural (socioculturally shaped, of course) compelling needs and power of the sex-gender itself. The existence of (privatized) individual beings, both in a narrow economic-material sense and in other wider meanings, is maintained in the (economic) work process. But the existence of the species as well as a very fundamental part or *current* in the social existence of individual persons presuppose sexuality as an active force. This is manifested, seen at its narrowest, in erotic links between people and a compelling erotic need for access to one another's body-and-mind. (I use hyphens when I write body-and-mind to indicate that I have adopted a nondualistic approach to the "mind-body problem.")[23] The production (and reproduction) of the human species is not a matter of nature in any pure sense. Sexuality is always practiced socially and thus in historically changing forms. Yet we are, at the same time, dealing with elements in human social life that most likely reach farthest into nature. If this is correct, it is not primarily art, as Raymond Williams asserts,[24] that, apart from work, expresses nature in man and his links with nature around him. Rather it would be people creating people—others and themselves—in the socially organized love process.

In my search for an appropriate term for the specific sociosexual practices, distinguishable in real life as well as in the world of concepts, I first used the term care.[25] But after a while I found that care alone was not sufficient. What was missing was a specifically erotic sexual element. *Care* can be seen as one of love's two main components or elements, while erotic *ecstasy* would be the other. Seen in this way, then, we can grasp love's internal contradictions. The way heterosexual love relations are institutionalized in contemporary society means that love's two elements—care and ecstasy—find themselves in continuous opposition (or contradiction). When (formal, legally free and equal) individual women and men *meet* as sexes, the societal/systemic conditions in which these *meetings* occur are not equal. Women are "forced" to commit themselves to loving care—so that men can be able to live/experience ecstasy. But it is not legitimate for women to practice ecstasy on their own terms, that is, as self-directed and self-assured sexual beings, who, in doing so, need men's caring. Men's systemic position, on the other hand, presses them to limitless desire for ecstasy (as a means of self-assuredness and personal expansion), while the practice of loving care in their relations to women is generally experienced as burdens and constraints, as a spending of time and energy that must be "economized." Thus, even if women do not "make do with the role of desired object," to borrow one of Barbara Sichtermann's many striking formulations, even if a woman has "a kind of *confidence in [herself] as*

the desirer (1986:11), the probability that she will be able to live/
realize this confidence is rather small.

Legitimate access to and practice of ecstatic experience seems to
be a precondition for dignity and worthiness in a society like ours,
the key characteristic of which is "growth" or, rather, "expansion-
ism." Ours is a society in which individuals are historically determined in such a way to force them to *make* themselves, so to speak,
and to *take* their social places and secure their positions in hierarchies by personal merits. Furthermore, it seems that sexual/erotic
self-assuredness, the effective ability to be a desiring individual, plays
an essential role in this mode of making or producing people. The
precondition, however, for this kind of expansionist sexual power to
be effectively maintained and to grow is that it be created and loaded
with value the ultimate source of which is care; loving care showed
to the desiring individual as a particular person. And in our social
and political (patriarchal) system men are in positions of control that
allow them access to this kind of empowerment and women generally are not.[26]

Sexual "Exploitation Proper": A Preliminary Typology

I conclude with a preliminary typology of sex/gender specific inequality or oppression. This typology isolates analytically men's particular kind of exploitation of women as women today and distinguishes it from other relations of inequality. I have found it
convenient to use as a starting point Elster's typology of injustice
(1980), partly because he uses "exploitation of women" to delineate
his types, but also because his view of exploitation coincides in part
with my own. It is of no decisive importance here, as we have seen,
whether the actual term exploitation is regarded as covering injustice
or whether this normative aspect is seen as a corollary.

Elster treats exploitation as a variant of distributive injustice. He
starts from a general definition of the concept exploitation: "taking

unfair advantage of someone," where one party *gains* something the other *loses*. Elster regards Marxist exploitation theory as one variant of this general proposition. Furthermore, according to Elster, the concept of exploitation in Marxist theory refers "properly" to only one type of relationship, namely, to economic injustice that is generated by economic circumstances. This is what typifies economic exploitation under capitalism. From Elster's text we could thus construct a typology with two dichotomous points of entry. He distinguishes between economic and noneconomic *causes* of injustice and also between injustice in the distribution of economic and noneconomic goods (1980:3). I illustrate this with a fourfold table (see Table 1). Elster defines his types more precisely in the following way:

> A causal chain is economic if it is made up only of materially self-interested and voluntary transactions, where by the latter I mean a transaction involving no threats beyond the withholding of offers. The definition excludes altruism and spite (as not self-interested), action out of the desire for salvation (as not materially self-interested) and coercion (as non-voluntary). A paradigm case of economic causation is the generation of injustice by means of economic power, e.g. private property of the means of production or just wealth. . . . A good is economic if it is scarce, alienable, not just a means to something else and either (1) is itself an object of consumption or (2) is used in the production of such objects. . . . The paradigm case of an economic good is of course material commodities bought for private consumption, but the notion also includes leisure, public goods, privately consumed services, labour-power and even persons (e.g. slaves who may be both objects of consumption and factors of production). (1980:3–4)

"Exploitation proper" for Elster thus belongs only in square E1. The open and direct coercive extraction of labor under slavery and

TABLE 1		Causes of injustice	
		economic	non-economic
Unfair distribution of goods	economic	E1	E2
	non-economic	E3	E4

feudalism belongs in square E2 (noneconomic causes of economic injustice). Elster describes this political and ideological type of extraction as extortion (a term that Marx also used although he did not qualify its use in the same manner as Elster). Extortion is also suitable, according to Elster, in cases where men gain "extra sexual favours from women by threatening to withhold promotion" (1980:10). In square E3 (economic causes of noneconomic injustice) Elster places, for example, the unequal distribution of such goods as knowledge and wants, but to square E4 he gives no content at all (1980:7).

As Elster sees it, women are exploited only in their capacity as workers, in the same way that men are. The purchasers of labor often employ women, he says, so that they may "pay them less than men for the same work, *because women have fewer employment alternatives or are unionized to a smaller extent*" (1980:10, emphasis added). But why do these situations occur? This and other comparable systematic inequalities between the sexes are what feminist theory seeks to explain.

It is my contention that what must be highlighted much more clearly and defined much more closely than hitherto, even within feminist research, are the actual relationships between men and women. The components of gender must be seen as a distinct (relatively independent) structure in society. And the agents in this structure and their activities represent a likewise distinct historical process. This means in turn that historical changes in the sex-gender relationships must in all probability be periodized according to a special classification that should only partly or indirectly be allied to an economically based periodization. I develop this further in Chapter 3.

It may seem self-evident that the empty square E4 in Elster's typology is just waiting to be filled with a content like that of gender inequality. But I do not think it fruitful to look on it in this way. Elster's typology is in fact limited to economic matters, despite the noneconomic variants. The political and ideological instruments of power (the noneconomic type of cause) that are taken as a possible cause of extortion are nevertheless completely saturated with economy, if we may express it so. The authority and possible monopoly of the legitimate physical exercise of force that extracts economic advantages are, just the same, based on man's economic-material production. And the noneconomic goods are also defined, if only negatively, in relation to economy. So instead of using the term noneconomic causes and goods, as Elster does, we could as well distinguish "economic (causes and goods) in a narrow sense" from the "economic in a wider sense"; or we could distinguish between "directly economic" and "indirectly economic" (causes and goods). The crux is that in the latter cases, independently of what words are chosen, economic power is *mediated* by external and overt coercion, while in the former, economic power is exerted through the covert or "silent pressure" of the economic relations themselves. It is important not to be misled by Elster's choice of terms when we apply these distinctions to the sexual process.

Anyway, sociosexual material production needs a separate dimension, a separate typology. The two typologies can possibly overlap by one square (see Table 2).

I suggest that we isolate analytically sociosexual power relations and sociosexual goods or values. Thus we can assume a specific (directly) sexual "causal chain,[27] relatively distinct from an indirectly sexual power relationship, and sexual goods as distinct from indirectly sexual goods/values. I mean in broad terms that all the requirements Elster lays down (see quotation above) with regard to the economic causal chain and economic goods apply here as well.

TABLE 2	Causes/sources of sociosexual inequality	
	sexual	indirectly sexual
Unequal distribution of sociosexual goods/values — sexual	S1	S2
Unequal distribution of sociosexual goods/values — indirectly sexual	S3	S4

The paradigm case (to use Elster's expression) of the sexual "cause" is thus the inequality—injustice if you will—that originates in men's specific, legitimate power both to give full expression to their sexuality and need of care, and to expect/demand of women that they provide the means for satisfying them. Today, in several countries, this power is not formalized as rights any longer but is supported ideologically everywhere. Most women, on the other hand, are in turn dependent on men for the expression of their sexuality: their need of care and desire for ecstatic pleasure. But their starting position is quite different. In the normal case, as stated above, a woman is "forced" in her relationship with a man to contribute more caring than he is, and on the whole to love in a way that he is not.

What above all characterizes sexual goods/values "proper"—in contrast to economic ones—is that they cannot be bought, and still less extracted by direct force, without a severe loss of effect or productivity. In this paradigm case, the essence of sexual goods is that they need to be *given* voluntarily, or rather that they are made available for use—without conditions. Hence their extreme vulnerability. Thus far square S1.

Let us now look briefly to the other types of advantage-taking and unequal distribution of sociosexual goods, which, in my view, must be placed outside the specific free sexual exploitation relationship. For instance jus primae noctis, the feudal overlord's and probably in certain cases even the priest's right to deflower the bride, belongs in square S2. Cases where Catholic priests take advantage of women's sexuality in the confessional situation also falls into this category, as does the sexual use made of housemaids by upperclass men and their sons. I would also place in the same category rape and even men's private use of women through pornography. Here we are dealing with direct, open force and cruelty—an extortion of sexual favors.

If we move on to square S3, sexual "causes" of indirectly sexual inequality, we enter a realm of distribution of goods that is easier to observe than the sexual in a narrower sense and that is often referred to (together with the economic) when we talk about the lack of equality between women and men. These, I suggest, are nevertheless secondary and derivatory in relation to the distribution of goods and its "causes" in square S1. Thus S3 includes the actual possibilities for action and power in the spheres outside the home (work and politics); purposefulness in life and demands on behalf of one's own interests as well as the division of work and use of time in the home sphere.

My square S4 may well coincide with the empty square in Elster's diagram. Here the "unfair advantage" taken of women by men is exerted by integrating male dominance with the coercive use of economic means. This embraces such things as sexual harassment at work with the help of economic sanctions. Here we may also include prostitution, both the pimp-prostitute relationship and the client-prostitute relationship. Pornography as a profit-making activity also belongs here. The two typologies could be linked (see Table 3), and we can thus distinguish between, on one hand, oppression (exploitation, etc.) of women (and men) as a class, and, on the other, oppression (exploitation, etc.) of women as women.

TABLE 3

Causes of economically based injustice

		economic	indirectly economic			
Unfair distribution of economically associated goods	economic	E1	E2			
	indirectly economic	E3	E/S4	S3	indirectly sexual	Unequal distribution of sociosexual goods or values
			S2	S1	sexual	
			indirectly sexual	sexual		

Causes/sources of sociosexual inequality

chapter 6

Her for Him—Him for the State: The Significance of Sex and Marriage in Hobbes's and Locke's Political Theories

> Men are so unconscionable and cruel against us, as they endeavour to Barr us all Sorts or kinds of Liberty, as not to suffer us Freely to associate amongst our own sex, but, would fain Bury us in their houses or Beds, as in a Grave; the truth is, we live like Bats or owls, Labour like Beasts, and Dye like worms.
>
> Margaret Lucas, Duchess of Newcastle, "Female Orations" (1662)

The main problem posed in this book concerns the form in which Western patriarchy of today exists and persists. This means to raise questions such as how the specific relations, practices, and power struggles between the sexes are institutionalized in the patriarchal present. Intimately connected with this theoretical side of the problem is the question of how and when in the historical process the fundamental precedents of contemporary patriarchal institutions emerged. One way to shed light on the historical circumstances is to look at how great theoreticians of the times in which we think the "how and when" should be located actually did deal with matters of sex.

In feminist theoretical literature, there are largely two different

A slightly different version of this chapter was published in Swedish in Eduards, 1983. Malcolm Forbes translated that version into English. It is reprinted here by permission of Gleerup Förlag.

approaches to that which I call the historical question. One is more narrowly economically oriented, while the other takes a more comprehensive, political view. One traces today's unequal conditions of women and men, through several phases, to the industrialization period in the nineteenth century. (Hartmann, for instance, takes this stance; see Chapter 4). The other approach localizes the societal conditions from which present patriarchy has developed, through various phases, to the period of great upheavals marking the breakthrough of capitalism and the nation-state; in other words, to the beginning of the modern period. For me, this second approach seems the more fruitful one.

In seventeenth-century England a great debate raged about how the fundamental societal relations—including those between women and men—should be understood and arranged. In this debate Sir Robert Filmer, the author of *Patriarcha*, and Thomas Hobbes and John Locke, the influential forefathers of liberalism, participated. All three dealt in a highly significant way with issues of sex. It is even possible to contend that the relationship between the sexes and the institution of marriage was at the center of their arguments. The winning argument, so to speak (that of Locke), was that the relations between the sexes, the specific "generative powers" of these relations and the "conjugal society" in which these matters were to be institutionalized, should be understood as "perfectly personal" and "only personal." At the same time these "personal" concerns were evaluated and defined from the point of view of utility to "political society." In this chapter I explore the writings of Thomas Hobbes and John Locke. They seem to have been very conscious about being involved in a "modern project" of reconstructing society. Let us look first, briefly, at the men and their work.

Thomas Hobbes was born in Malmesbury in 1588, the son of an Anglican clergyman. The family was of small means, but through the support of a wealthy relative Hobbes was sent to Oxford when he was 14. He was a boy of sharp intelligence, and soon he became critical of the Aristotelian scholasticism of his teachers. Later, in his books, he gave vent to withering condemnation of the universities and of "the schoolmen." A succession of biographers have followed Hobbes in asserting that "his nature was womanish, but his intrepid intellect was thoroughly masculine" (Laird, 1934:3).

After Oxford he became a tutor in the powerful Cavendish family and lived under their protection—part of the time in exile—for the greater part of his life. He spent several years on the Continent with them, and in France he spent a period as mathematics tutor to another refugee, the future Charles II.

Hobbes died in 1679 at the age of 91. The sources indicate that he had been moderate in the consumption of food and drink, of tobacco and of women. He never married, but he was "not a woman hater" and is said to have had a "natural daughter" (Laird, 1934:29–30).

Hobbes was a scientist and philosopher of the rank of Galileo and Descartes. Being aghast, though, at the civil strife and social disintegration in the country of his birth, he chose to devote himself to political philosophy, and in this field he has had an enduring influence. He saw it as his mission to describe the social order he thought best, and to demonstrate its superiority. His writings were as firebrands in the ideological conflicts of the seventeenth century, and it is said that he himself was—in return, as it were—threatened with being burned at the stake. His writings were in fact on the bonfire at Oxford on July 21, 1683, at the last burning of books in English history. During the same clamp-down John Locke was forced to give up the post he had held at the university for many years. But he had not published anything that could be used against him.

Hobbes's political philosophy is to be found for the most part in three works that are revisions and extensions of the same basic material. *Elements of Law* was published in 1640. Hobbes then fled to France, where in 1642 the second version of his political philosophy was printed, *Man and Citizen*. *Leviathan*, the final version, came in 1651. Hobbes wrote no work specifically on the subject of women, but women play a key role in the human power-relations on which his state-governed ideal society is founded.

John Locke was born in Somerset in 1632 and was given a strict upbringing by his Calvinist parents, who had recently come up in the ranks of the lower gentry. His paternal grandfather was one of many successful furnishers of working capital in the textile industry. His father was clerk of the local court and a captain in Cromwell's army. On his father's death in 1661 Locke inherited landed estate and a few mining assets. The Locke family was in the customary way under the protection of a considerably more powerful noble family whose support guaranteed John Locke's university career from when he was 20.

Locke twice lived abroad, 1675–79 in France and 1683–89 in exile in Holland. From 1691 to his death in 1704 he lodged with the Masham family outside London, and it was here that he found the closest friend he ever had, Lady Damaris Masham, who published anonymously and whose learning and brilliance he greatly admired. Locke never married.

Locke's active life can be divided into three periods. Until about 1667 he was teaching the philosophy of natural law—and also medicine—at Oxford. There was little that was controversial about his ideas. Nothing of what he wrote during this period was published. Formally he retained his position at Oxford, but beginning 1667 he was for about fifteen years employed as intellectual advisor to Lord Shaftesbury, a Whig who was one of the foremost political figures of the time.

Locke had to advise him about everything from affairs of state to the upbringing of the family's children, and he in fact was even given the task of choosing a wife for the son and heir, and also of seeing that this union in its turn produced an heir. It was during the period with Lord Shaftesbury that the essence of most of Locke's later writings was germinated. There was a mutual give-and-take between the withdrawn but potentially brilliant academic and the acute man of action, himself also interested in philosophy, whose life was one of political intrigue at the highest level. Locke is even said to have been directly involved in the attempts at a coup d'état at the beginning of the 1680s. Between 1690 and 1700, after the Glorious Revolution, Locke had a similar post with Lord Somers, the strongest member of the government. During these last years of his life Locke also acted independently as a highly regarded political advisor.

Locke wrote extensively on politics, economics, religion, education and epistemology, but none of his works was published before 1689, and then most of them came out anonymously. *Two Treatises of Government*, probably written during 1678–80, appeared in the autumn of 1689. Throughout his life Locke concealed the fact that he was the author of this work, even though the principles he set forth in it had won the day in England at the time of publication. It became one of the most influential political works in the history of Western civilisation. The only work of any significance that Locke acknowledged as his own was the one that set forth his empiricist theory of knowledge, *An Essay Concerning Human Understanding* (also published in 1689), which brought him immediate fame at home and abroad.

Like Hobbes, Locke wrote nothing separate on the subject of women. But as in Hobbes's theory, women were indispensable to Locke's theory concerning the foundations of "political society." Both men had a keen eye for the usefulness of the female sex in the new political order that was so dear to their hearts. Furthermore, the question of the relationship between the sexes was of decisive significance in the public philosophical discussion that Hobbes and Locke were both involved in. Hobbes considered that he had demonstrated "that the state of equality is the state of war, and that therefore inequality was introduced by a general consent" (1972:225). According to Locke inequality was introduced at the same time as money, and political society was founded by those who wanted to safeguard their economic rights. But did Hobbes's and Locke's evidence apply also to the relationship between women and men? This is the main question with which this chapter is concerned. We find, for instance, that women disappear without a trace from essential parts of Hobbes's theory when he lets the individuals leave the equal "state of nature" and establish society and the state. Locke, on the other hand, retains his grasp on women and assigns them to their rightful place—in the family, at a safe distance from politics.

The philosophy of Hobbes and Locke has to do with *social relations*: between men and women, parents and children, masters and servants, authorities and citizens. It has to do with the regulation of social relations—everything from foreign policy to sexual intercourse—in a specific way. Forming the basis of this philosophy is production—the production of new human beings as much as of life's necessities. In other words, it is a philosophy whose fundamental concern is with everything that has to do with practical life. But this concern is purely in terms of problems of order and control, that is, in terms of *power and rights*.

During the latter half of the sixteenth century, when Elizabeth was queen, England was relatively free from strife. It was a period of economic and cultural prosperity. Capitalist features which had first appeared in the economy as early as the thirteenth century, which had undergone an expansion that had become especially intense in the seventeenth century. A decisive change was the increasing shift of production from a household basis to a basis in the middle-class community. The new ownership and control relations in production were consolidated and assured of continued existence by the liberal constitutional state, the new type of state that had emerged from the civil conflict, and the political and religious upheaval, of the seventeenth century.

Historical research indicates that this process of change caused what in many ways was a worsening in the situation of women (compared with that of men) in all classes of society. The seventeenth century can be said to constitute a watershed in the history of women in England.[1] It had been the rule in the Middle Ages that the head of the family should be a man, and that women in every estate were formally subordinate to men, yet in practice women had a considerable degree of independence. Above all they had their own visible position—as women—in the social hierarchy and with regard to the distribution of labor, but also in the predominantly local decision-making. Married women were their husbands' helpmates, often legally competent substitutes for them—and their ordinary heirs too—on farm and estate, and as artisans and in other urban occupations.

But especially during the latter half of the seventeenth century there began to extend an order of affairs that caused women in the wealthy strata of society to become locked in the role of giving birth to lawful heirs and being status symbols for their husbands. More and more the wives of artisans became housewives without legal rights, and among the growing class of wage-earners the women suffered far greater need than did the men.

In seventeenth-century England there was a public discussion that came to have great historical significance. It was about power, about power in society, about what gave certain members of society lawful power over others. What was the real source of power in society? And given this source, how ought power relations to be regulated and maintained? The parties to this discussion can be divided roughly into two camps. On the one side were those who basically defended a medieval order of society, and on the other were the men of the new age who attempted to articulate the basis of a new order.

The first camp defended the cause of royal autocracy in the civil conflict of the time. Their philosophy of power was based on the conviction that an all-inclusive patriarchy should prevail in society. The king was considered the almighty father of the entire nation, and every father of a family was in turn considered a king who ruled over his family subjects. This absolute power of the father in the family and in the state was assumed to have been passed down directly from Adam, and to be a gift of God. A particular feature of this patriarchal philosophy (for that was what it was called) was that all power relations were considered identical. The state was the family writ large, and the King was the nation's father, at the same time as the father was a king; both were patriarchs by the grace of God. The Tories, who advocated this order of affairs, cherished the writings of Sir Robert Filmer as expressing their official ideas on the matter.[2]

The other camp differed among themselves. Some of them, including Hobbes, advocated royal power undivided (though bound by law), while others, including Locke and the rest of the Whigs, advocated that power be divided between king and Parliament, and still others, the Puritans, advocated rule by Parliament without the king. But these groups were united in the conviction that the ideas of their opponents concerning patriarchy were untenable, both with regard to the family and with regard to the state.

What this camp advocated instead was a completely new, and secularized, order of society, which they called *civil society* or *political society*. The power of the state was to be founded ultimately on the free consent of the members of society, and the family was regarded as separate from this society. In the Middle Ages, when production— and indeed human life in general—rested on a household basis, it would have appeared natural to look on all human dominance-relations as family relations. But times had changed, and the production process in England was getting further and further away from the household basis, was bursting the family framework, and was acquiring a social character quite unlike what had gone before. Those who opened their minds to this transformation and saw it as inevitable, perhaps even welcoming it, also saw how urgent it was to articulate new forms of power that suited the society that was coming into being. For the state of affairs where some had more power than others, where some worked for others, and where some existed virtually only for the benefit of others, remained as before, though under other forms. And it was a state of affairs that had to be explained and justified anew.

God, who during the Middle Ages had been a sufficient ground for both explanation and legitimation, had now to give way, or at least to move over and make room for a new and equally overwhelming ground—nature. The same purpose had been served by nature in classical antiquity. It was on the basis of nature that Aristotle explained inequality, explained why one person had more power than another. He did not have the God of the Bible, and any gods he did have were part of nature. But the exponents of the new order in seventeenth-century England, for instance Hobbes, attacked both Aristotle and the idea of the divinely appointed patriarchy.[3] Basic to the new world-view was *the belief that all men (all human beings) are born equal*. The men putting forward the new principles had different ideas about whether to include women and children—"the promiscuous multitude" in the initially equal human host (Butler, 1978:135, 139; Shanley, 1979:86).

But neither the relationship between man and woman, nor that between parents and children, was a side-issue. Indeed, the question of the "correct" nature of such relations, together with the question of their significance in the larger society, might reasonably be described as constituting the very heart of the discussion. Filmer had asserted that the source of all dominion, next after the Word of God, was Adam's capacity to beget children. Furthermore, God had granted the father in every family complete dominion over woman, children, and servants. Filmer thereby "set the terms of the argument" (Laslett, 1967:68). Locke made a direct attack on Filmer, and he was

> aware as others were not of the direction of social change. This is evident in the central issue of *Two Treatises*, which is primarily concerned with the structure of the family and its relevance to social and political authority. If ever men dealt with fundamentals, Filmer and Locke did in this polemic. (Laslett, 1967:44)

This discussion in England concerning power in society can be set against the background of the scientific revolution in seventeenth-century Europe. A mathematical-mechanical model was applied not only to the universe as a whole but also (and Hobbes was one of the first to do so) to society. God was replaced by nature as the ultimate source of all knowledge, and the Aristotelian thinking about ends was abandoned. The techno-utilitarian view of knowledge made its breakthrough. Hobbes, for example, thought that knowledge of human nature could and indeed ought to form the basis of the art of governing the state.

In the following exposition I start from two features of Hobbes's and Locke's treatment of women. In both men's disputation with opponents, women are used as a *device of argument*, only to be deftly shuffled out of sight once they have served their purpose. Also, an important aspect of the *substance* of both men's thinking (presented either openly or by implication) is certain utilitarian aspects of women and their bodies. The woman's body bears future soldiers (Hobbes) and heirs to property (Locke)—and is the only body that can do so. Women are also usable, together with men, for bringing up children to be obedient subjects (Hobbes) and respectful and economically capable citizens (Locke).

The liberal individualism for which Hobbes and Locke laid the foundations represented in several respects the removal of old fetters, yet at the same time contributed to the forging of new ones. The ideas of the two philosophers concerning women are charged with the same tension.

Thomas Hobbes

Thomas Hobbes constructed his political philosophy with the aid of geometry, physics, and, as he assumed, demonstrably true inferences concerning morality (the political order). He saw as the main issue the consolidation of the sovereignty of the state through scientific argument, in order to safeguard order in society. The most important feature of his argument—and one that set the problem of sovereignty in a new perspective—was his attempt to reconcile a model of society based on equal individuals, and the view that the equal individuals have to surrender their natural rights and freedoms to a strong state and let themselves be ruled by it.

How did Hobbes manage the reconciliation? He showed that it was equality itself that was the problem. The free and reasonable individuals themselves discovered that it was the uniform strength, the like needs and the unregulated equal rights, that were the root of the evil, of *the constant insecurity in relation to one another*, or in Hobbes's words "Warre of every man against every man." So the individuals joined together and voluntarily divested themselves of their own sovereignty through a *covenant* that was binding on all. They thereby formed the *commonwealth*, an artificial body whose head was the state authority. The equal rights of the individuals were surrendered to this authority, and to it was "transferred" (to use Hobbes's word) the strength of the members of society. Within the state authority the rights of individuals were transformed into public morality, law, and justice. Furthermore, what Hobbes calls artificial is in fact the "nature" of the commonwealth, and for this reason the laws of the state can without contradiction be described as laws of nature. Since justice is by definition a question of state-made law, injustice is a question of offending against the laws of the land, the natural laws. But offending against the state's justice is offending against oneself, against one's own voluntary act.

Even when it came to the state, Hobbes did not waver in his view of the equality of individuals. He rejected the old idea that certain persons were born to rule over the vast inadequate majority. No aristocrat, no chieftain—indeed virtually no man whatever—was born to political wisdom. Such wisdom was to be acquired only with the aid of training and experience. To assume the inequality of human beings, as Aristotle did, was "not only against reason; but also against experience. For there are very few so foolish, that had not rather governe themselves, than be governed by others" (Hobbes, 1968:211).

Hobbes's Model: The State of Nature

Thus Hobbes's political philosophy hangs on the division between a *state of nature*, or the fundamental conditions of human nature, and a *politically organized society* with many names.[4] Forming an unclear link between the state of nature (which is assumed to be populated by independent individuals) and the organized society is the *family*.

By "state of nature" Hobbes means several things, and his use of the idea can be divided into the following four areas or dimensions:

1 a basic mechanical model of society

2 conceptual analysis of human physical and mental characteristics

3 assumptions about social relations between men and women, with evidence drawn from history

4 a "historical/anthropological" concept covering all stateless forms of society

The state of nature constitutes Hobbes's ingenious theoretical model to explain political conditions.

Forming the foundations of the model are the basic principles of the new Galilean physics. The first postulate of Galilean physics is that the natural state of all matter is movement, not rest as Aristotelian physics proclaims. Human beings as "natural" persons are conceived of by Hobbes as bodies freely floating in a vacuum. They are more like than unlike, and they move freely, both by their own strength and because of the attraction to and from others, so long as there are no external obstacles. The equal strength, of body and of mind, means that all are equally capable of killing, but also that none finds it natural to suffer subjection. This is the most basic criterion of equality. Thus the constant motion of matter becomes in Hobbes a constant clash of interests. But human nature also harbors a need for peace, and to make peace possible Hobbes takes over from physics the law of inertia. If obstacles are all that can put a curb on the free movement, then social obstacles have to be created among the passionate and equal individuals. Thus Hobbes looks to a sociotechnical application of the law of inertia.

To qualify the basic mechanical model, Hobbes offers detailed conceptual definitions of the natural powers of the human body and mind, and also of the human being's acquired characteristics—though there is not always a clear distinction between the two. The powers of the body are chiefly of three sorts: *nutritive, motive,* and *generative.* Those of the mind are of two sorts: *cognitive* and *motive.* The motive, comprising the passions, is the most important in the present connection. The passions constitute the inner motive power, the person's will. The passions in motion are acts of free will, formed by previous experience and by reason (and reason is here a capacity for drawing inferences). What causes war in the state of nature is that no one can be sure of having his needs satisfied over a long uninterrupted period, or even be sure of staying alive. One thing in Hobbes that is not often noted is that he ascribes to the sex-drive, the drive to continue the species, a greater strength than the drive to seek food—ascribes to it, that is, a greater strength than the person's drive to preserve himself as an individual (1969:31).[5]

In the state of nature there are no laws and therefore no marriages, nor indeed any ownership relations whatever. But human beings do establish relations with one another through gifts or personal contracts. Thus, for instance, women and men regulate their sexual relations by means of freely made contracts.

Hobbes seems, finally, to use the state of nature as a designation of all social conditions where human beings live under an incompetent superior power or under no superior power. But in his evidence there are always families with members in ranking order, as a rule with the strictest patriarchy.

Now, how can this be reconciled with the central principle of the model, namely, that all have the same rights and none can successfully hold sway over others? It cannot, in fact, be reconciled at all *unless* the free and equal individuals who populate the state of nature are assumed to be *families* or, rather, the heads of families. There are places indeed where Hobbes spells it out that those who established the important social covenant were *fathers* of families.[6]

There are at this point a host of questions that one would like to put to the great pioneer of the individual-based theory of society. For instance, how were the dominance relations within the family instituted? Or, whence came the mandate of the fathers to alone found the state? Or, was there a generally binding marriage and family covenant before, and independent of, the entry of the fathers into a social covenant under the state?

In Hobbes the family consists of different relationships: man-wife, parents-children, and master-slave or master-servant. The only one of these relationships that does not receive serious treatment from Hobbes, and has been neglected in subsequent studies, is that between man and wife.

Let us now have a closer look at how Hobbes deals with women in relation to men and children in the state of nature, then as members of the family and citizens in the commonwealth, and finally as governing in the state.

Woman-Man-Child in the State of Nature

Hobbes asserts that men do not by nature possess other rights or a higher position of power than do women, and he supports this assertion with the same logical reasoning as in the general sections on the natural equality of human beings with regard to strength and wisdom. For reason indicates that "the inequality of their natural forces is not so great, that the man could get the dominion over the woman without war" (1972:213). Thus those who ascribe the natural dominion to the man as being a member of "the more excellent Sex" are wrong (1968:253).

But the entire argument has to do with who has the right to dominion over the children. Hobbes pays very little attention to the man's and the woman's rights with regard to each other and never takes the matter up as a subject on its own; it is just part of the important inquiry into dominion over the children. The children (or, rather, the sons) are the family subjects who are to be the future bearers of the commonwealth, subjects of the state, and in exceptional cases, monarchs.

The actual woman-man relationship in the state of nature is considered purely in the sexual sense: they are drawn to each other by natural desire, and from their coming together the species, along with the forms of power, is carried further. But power no longer resides in the semen. The patriarchal philosophers maintained that the divinely appointed royal power came in a direct line from Adam's potency as a father, but a main argument of Hobbes's against this was that man and woman have to cooperate in producing offspring, and therefore both of them—if this producing of offspring gives power—have the same claim to power. Thus the important basic principle of undivided power could not survive unless other arguments were found. Nor was it by any means obvious "that what is begotten by me is mine" (1972:212).

The seemingly most audacious blow that Hobbes directs against the old patriarchal philosophy is to say that if one of the parents is to be accorded dominion, then, since "every man by the law of nature, hath right or propriety to his own body, the child ought rather to be the propriety of the mother (of whose body it is part, till the time of separation) than of the father" (1969:131–32).

But in the long run Hobbes's most important deviation from the old philosophy was that he did not base parental right on birth itself but on "preservation." The person that has rightful power over a child is the person that from the time of the child's birth takes care of it and brings it up. Thus the mother loses her right if she chooses not to care for the child, and this right goes instead to any person who does care for the child.

But the mother's first-hand right with regard to the child is rooted in nature. In the first place it is only maternity that, biologically speaking, can be established with certainty in the state of nature. Then in the second place—and more important—the mother's power can more precisely be described as a sort of first-hand right of appropriation, which in Hobbes's state of nature is a natural right: "By the right therefore of *nature*, the dominion over the infant first belongs to him who first hath him in his power. But it is manifest that he who is newly born is in the *mother's* power before any others" (1972:212). For the fact is—and this is the weightiest argument— that the mother has a free choice with regard to every child she gives birth to: she can either take care of it or not. Her power thus resides in the fact that "she may rightly, and at her own will, either breed him up or adventure him to fortune" (1972:212). Where the mother does choose to take care of the child and bring it up, which in the state of nature is equivalent to saving its life, the child is bound to her by a debt of gratitude. Here Hobbes employs a special concept of the natural, a moral natural right. The law of nature, comprising binding ordinances with which we are furnished by reason, is fundamental in Hobbes. He in fact stipulates one basic natural law: the law according to which every person shall strive for peace. But if peace is not attained, a person has a right to defend himself

(1968:190). The law of gratitude is one that Hobbes derives from his basic law: a debt of gratitude arises when a person receives "Grace," or "Free-gift," from another (1968:209). This is what happens when the mother chooses to give the child life, that is, chooses to preserve its life. The same law comes into force when, for instance, a person who takes a slave chooses to let him live.

This law is very important for the entire Hobbesian order. It is a question of a psychological ordinance that has to be actively incorporated in every person so that society does not run the constant risk of relapsing into conflict. This special frame of mind in every individual is to guarantee that the state does not perpetually need to have recourse to violence and punishment. The children's debt of gratitude to the parents (or to the person who has provided for them) is of the same binding character as the duty of the subjects toward the state's justice that was established in and by the social covenant. Using modern terminology one might say that the duty of gratitude on the part of the children and of all other *dependent* persons toward the independent persons who have voluntarily accorded them grace, is calculated to *constantly recreate conditions of social dominance.* And Hobbes sees the dominance relations within the family and household as being of the same nature as the tie between the members of society and the state.

Why, though, should there be constant risk of conflict if the debt of gratitude were not established? Human nature seeks only what is best for itself, and therefore no human being would ever voluntarily help another, or even show any benevolence, if there were nothing to be gained by it. So "there will be no beginning of benevolence, or trust; nor consequently of mutuall help; nor of reconciliation of one man to another" (1968:209).

If the law of the debt of gratitude did not exist, the child would grow up to be its mother's equal, a person independent of her. And therein, says Hobbes, lies the risk of war. Obedience is necessary. "For else it would be wisdom in men, rather to let their children perish, while they are infants, than to live in their danger or subjection, when they are grown" (1969:132–33).

Equality is hazardous because it so easily leads to war. Receiving a benefit from an equal, especially a benefit that one does not think one can repay, disposes to hatred. "For benefits oblige; and obligation is thraldome; and unrequitable obligation, perpetuall thraldome." On the other hand, "to have received benefits from one, whom we acknowledge for superiour, enclines to love." The equal giving and taking of benefits can in itself dispose to love, but from it there arises a competition in benevolence, constantly involving victory and revenge (1968:162–63).

Thus the only true benevolence and the only orderly love are the benevolence shown by a superior and the love felt by an inferior. Here the debt constitutes no new burden but meets with "cheerfull acceptation." This is of central importance in Hobbes's political philosophy, especially in the light of the fact that all dominance relations—including those between parent and children—are assumed to be based on the voluntary act of the inferior person. Fundamentally, the point of this act is that the dominance shall not be broken. And the superior person can count on subjection as an enduring expected value.

But as far as women themselves are concerned, what is the real import of Hobbes's revaluation of the natural relationship between woman, man, and children? In direct contrast to prevalent ideology he set man and woman, as natural beings, on an equal footing. Furthermore—and this is very important—woman is freed of Biblical original sin. But what is to replace original sin and the divinely natural dominion of the man? Actually Hobbes ascribes to woman a new sort of original sin, of worldly type—or one might say that he imposes upon her an existential burden. As a natural being the mother is given sole right to and ultimate responsibility for the children's life and death. And from this natural right of hers derives the parents' necessary responsibility for shaping the children's wills in such a way as to insure the continuance of the inequality that in the name of peace was introduced through the social covenant. Furthermore Hobbes here defines the subordinate position and duty of gratitude of *those who are provided for.* This was later applied to women when such effective use began to be made of the one-sided concept of the family provider. Let us now have a closer look at Hobbes's conception of the relationship between the sexes and of the agreements between the free men and women concerning power over the children in the state of nature.

There are no marriage laws, and indeed no marriages. What happens is that women and men conclude various types of contract. Thus they can enter into the type of equal personal contract that Hobbes speaks of as possible in the state of nature. The problem with such contracts was that they were not universally binding, not regulated by law, and it was this that lay behind the lack of public order that made the social covenant necessary. What is odd, though, is that Hobbes does not say a word about constant conflict between women and men with regard to power over their offspring—conflict that would have required a universally binding *marriage covenant* corresponding to the social covenant. It does of course happen that persons take slaves or attach servants to themselves, and any offspring that come from such a relationship belong to the master. However, we shall not investigate these forms of relationship but concentrate instead on the contracts between equals.

Woman and man can form a union that can vary in scope.

> Of covenants that amount not to subjection between a man and a woman, there be some which are made for a time and some for life; and where they are for a time, they are covenants of cohabitation, or else of copulation only. . . . And covenants of cohabitation are either for society of bed, or for society of all things; if for society of bed only, then is the woman called a CONCU-BINE. . . . But if the covenants of cohabitation be for society of all things, it is necessary that but one of them govern and dispose of all that is common to them both; without which (as hath been often said before) society cannot last. (1969:133)

The different types of union involve different ways of regulating the right with regard to the children. If the agreement concerns "copulation only," there has to be a special covenant regarding the children. Hobbes mentions as an example of this the case of the Amazons: "And thus in the copulation of the Amazons with their neighbours, the fathers by covenant had the male children only, the mothers retaining the females" (p. 133). Even when cohabitation is "for society of bed only," there has to be special regulation regarding the dominion over the children. The concubinage in itself, says Hobbes, cannot involve the mother's being forced to give up her right with respect to a child. But if it is a question of "society of all things" no contract is required. Here the mother has simply to accept the loss of her right—in contrast, it may be said, to what is expected of the concubine: "And therefore the man, to whom for the most part the woman yieldeth the government, hath for the most part also the sole right and dominion over the children. And the man is called the HUSBAND, and the woman the WIFE" (p. 133). The question that now springs to mind is the following: Is Hobbes merely stating, on the basis of historical and contemporary experience, that the man's dominion in the unified family exists, or is he prescribing such dominion? The fact is, he does not take a clear stand on the matter.[7]

Equality in the sex-relationship in the state of nature is logically necessary to the new view of power—a view that Hobbes is so very careful to furnish with a scientific basis. The purpose of bringing women/mothers into the discussion is to support the argument concerning the fathers' "derived" right of dominion over the children/ sons—an argument that outdoes the medieval one based on "generation."

But the way Hobbes goes about embracing the undivided dominion of the *father* in the form of living together where everything is shared (where there is "society of all things"), goes directly against his philosophical conviction and scientific mode of working. That something is to be this way or that because it for the most part has been so in the past is not a valid inference in Hobbes's philosophy. On the contrary, the ultimate inferences concerning the order of society are not to be drawn directly on the basis of experience but only after meticulous and rational conceptual inquiry.

He does make a certain attempt at such analysis in the second book, *Man and Citizen*, where he enumerates four ways in which "dominion passes from the mother to others": if she chooses not to take care of the child, or if she is taken prisoner, or if she is a subject under a government, or if, finally, she "for society's sake give[s] herself to a man on this condition, that he shall bear the sway" (1972:213–14). But Hobbes offers no proper conceptual analysis here either. What does he mean by "give herself"? Or by "for society's sake"? In *Leviathan*, the third and last book version of his philosophy, the reasoning on the subject of this transferral of power has again become exceedingly meager.

What happens to the insufficiently investigated man-wife relationship is that the wife quite simply disappears, as can be seen from the way Hobbes's definition of "family" changes. In the first book, he writes that "the whole consisting of the father or mother, or both, and of the children, and of the servants, is called a FAMILY; wherein the father or master of the family is sovereign of the same; and the rest (both children and servants equally) subjects. (1969:135) The corresponding part of the second book reads: "A *father* with his sons and *servants*, grown into a civil person by virtue of his paternal jurisdiction, is called a *family*" (1972:217). Then, finally, in the third book we find that a family is defined as being made up of "a man and his children; or of a man and his servants; or of a man, and his children, and servants together: wherein the Father or Master is the Soveraign" (1968:257).

That the mothers should be completely gone from the picture may strike one as rather ironic in view of the fact that it is here that Hobbes says that one way for a family, "a little Monarchy," to grow strong is through an increase in the number of the children — strong enough "as not to be subdued without the hazard of war."

It is only in this type of context that the body's "power generative" finds entry into Hobbes's thinking. When he constructed his model on the basis of the natural powers of the body and mind, he left out the "power generative" and the "power nutritive," making use only of the third of the body's chief powers, the "power motive" (that is, physical strength). But, as we have seen, the "power generative" is in fact retained by implication, as a constant source of collective strength.

Hobbes's idea of the state of nature enabled him to eat his cake and have it too. He rejected the brutal old patriarchal philosophy where the father had the power of life and death over the other members of the family — had such power quite literally. For the purpose of this rejection "visible" mothers were needed, capable by nature of establishing power relations. But mothers and wives could disappear after they had been put to use as devices of philosophical argument. Bodies for the giving of birth to warriors — this is all that can be discerned of women when Hobbes defines the family, the regulated collective that links the state of nature with the commonwealth.

Woman-Man in the Commonwealth

What causes the lack of clarity in Hobbes's treatment of the woman as a member of the commonwealth is that there is a lack of clarity about the position of the family in his theories. The family both exists and does not exist in the state of nature and is then absorbed into the power relations of the body politic. We noted above how women disappeared when he dealt with the family. One reason for this disappearance may be that Hobbes's detailed definitions of the woman-man relationship in the state of nature were concerned first with dominion over the children. The parent-child relationship is then carried forward to become an important part of the theory of political society. But women are required anyway if there are to be any offspring — even in a well-ordered patriarchal society. And the chief structural element of Hobbes's basic model, namely, the equality of needs and strength, applied to women as well as to men. The point, though, is that when the absorption into the commonwealth occurred and the free fathers of families gave up to Leviathan (the impartial state will) their individual strength and their sovereign right in relation to one another, they at the same time insured themselves against the women with whom they shared "society of all things." Having said that in the state of nature the question about which parent was to have dominion over the children could not straightforwardly be determined without war, Hobbes adds:

> In Common-wealths, this controversie is decided by the Civill Law: and for the most part, tbut not alwayes) the sentence is in favour of the Father; because for the most part Common-wealths have been erected by the Fathers, not by the Mothers of families. (1968:253)

Here too, Hobbes refrains from taking up a position of principle or making any conceptual analysis worth the name. Once more he refers to what is usual and to a right that the fathers have acquired by founding the commonwealths.

That Hobbes does not prescribe patriarchy when it comes to the family in the commonwealth means—on the basis of his own thinking—that there is a way out of it. The relation of subjection remains in existence as long as it is constantly recreated, as long as the person in the subordinate position consents to it. It is ultimately a question of women's (free) choice whether they give up their natural sovereignty for the sake of public utility, or whether they subordinate themselves under the dominion of men. Neither nature nor God is at hand to settle conflicts between the sexes.

But on one point Hobbes does take up a position: a secular power that is difficult to overcome, namely, the power of the state, shall for preference be in the hands of men.

Woman-Man in the State

An Englishman of the seventeenth century could not fail to be aware that women are capable of being competent monarchs, and indeed not even the patriarchal philosophers denied it. In Hobbes's order of society the monarch, possibly with the assistance of a council, was responsible for all policy. In fact the only part of Hobbes's entire theory that he openly admitted was based not on firm scientific evidence but only on a judgment of possibility was that he preferred monarchy to aristocracy and democracy (1972:104).

Important in every form of government is what rules there are concerning succession to power. It was Hobbes's opinion that it was in a monarchy that it was most difficult to determine, and therefore also most important to regulate in detail, who had the right to ascend the throne when a monarch died. Hobbes did not completely dismiss female successors to the throne, but he did consistently relegate them to second place. Dismissing them would indeed have been an absurdity in his day, and furthermore would have offended both against his individualistic principles and against the important thesis that political wisdom is not dependent on which estate a person is born into, or on what property a person has. So why should the art of government be restricted to men? How does Hobbes argue this case?

Here too, the argument changes from book to book. Politically competent women are in the beginning regarded as exceptions that prove the rule: they know how to govern, and indeed have governed wisely on various occasions, but men are in general wiser and more courageous—and wisdom and courage are the qualities that protect all monarchies from dissolution (1969:136). In the second book the argument is different, becoming a mixture of conventionalism and a notion of historical development. With regard to the monarch's children,

> the males carry the pre-eminence; in the beginning perhaps, because for the most part, although not always, they are fitted for the administration of greater matters, but specially of wars; but afterwards, when it was grown a custom, because that custom was not contradicted. (1972:219)

Here, anyway, the rationalist Hobbes is in evidence: The weight of human custom can be removed by shoving against it. Even if women perhaps once upon a time had to withdraw from government because they were not as good generals as men were, it does not mean that they have to remain second-class beings even when conditions have changed. But custom rules if it is not resisted. Finally, in *Leviathan*, Hobbes spells it out that the heir to the throne shall be "rather a Male than a Female; because men, are naturally fitter than women, for actions of labour and danger" (1968:250). Hobbes has now come full circle and returned to the natural inequality he began by rejecting. The Hobbesian model of equality applied in the beginning to women too, but then the woman in the family was removed from sight, and now the woman's position in the state is undermined by means of argument quite alien to the rest of his thinking.

John Locke

John Locke is unlike Hobbes in that he does not attempt to use a strictly scientific method, and he defines very few of the concepts he uses (see Laslett, 1967:84). The first of his two treatises is an extended criticism of Filmer's philosophy of power. The second is a shorter work in which he expands his own ideas. His confrontation with Filmer is on the latter's own ground, in other words, with respect to the Bible.

As with Hobbes, the principal issue is the nature and continued existence of the state. Locke saw that the family as the source and framework of social power (class) relations was beginning to disintegrate, and he saw at the same time the importance of the family as a pillar of the new society. The family became in a new way a source of constant renewal of the power structure of society—not of the monarch's power as Filmer thought but of the politicoeconomic power relations. The family became a "natural" guarantee for the secure passing on of private property by way of blood-related sons. It was for this reason that it was a "main intention of Nature" that there should be "distinction of families, with the security of the marriage bed, as necessary thereunto" (Locke, 1978:41).

The family was for Locke a "conjugal society," beyond which the political society began. The latter comprised an organized joining together for the purpose of safeguarding property and of safeguarding the nation. The interested parties in this political society chose representatives who were to govern—for everyone's best. Conjugal society, though, was a union of man and woman, and its purpose (apart from enabling the married couple to support each other) was to produce heirs, to provide for them, to bring them up and to educate them until they were able to "shift for themselves" and pass on the inheritance. Thus, there was a connection between conjugal society, property, and political society. For Laslett, Locke employed "his property doctrine to give continuity to a political society, to join generation to generation" (Laslett, 1967:105).

Like Hobbes, Locke assumes that political society was preceded by a state of nature. But for Locke it was not the equal strength and the unbearable insecurity that caused the individuals to unite and embrace subjection to a state. Private property and a certain normative morality already existed in the state of nature. The direct cause of the founding of the state was the introduction of money and thereby of the desire to gain possession of more goods than were necessary to sustain life. When it was agreed that gold and silver should have a universal exchange value, it was also in effect agreed that there should be inequality (Locke, 1978:139–40). This in turn created states of war of Hobbes's type, and public laws and sanctions became necessary in order to restrain "evil doers" (p. 65).[8] The free and wealthy individual

> seeks out and is willing to join in society with others who are already united, or have a mind to unite for the mutual preservation of their lives, liberties and estates, which I call by the general name—property.
>
> The great and chief end, therefore, of men uniting into commonwealths, and putting themselves under government, is the preservation of their property. (pp. 179–80)

Woman-Man-Child-Property in "Nature"

Stretching the point a little, it can be said that Eve in Locke's first treatise (1978) corresponds to "the woman" in Hobbes's state of nature. Locke asserts Eve's rights with respect to the unconditional and all-embracing power of the father, which his opponent Filmer, on the basis of God's words in the Bible, ascribed to Adam and all his male heirs. But just as in the case of Hobbes's treatment of woman, it is more a question of a device of argument than of any intention of advocating an equal division of power between man and woman.

Locke starts his attack on Filmer with a general moral criticism. Filmer and others of like mind "have denied mankind a right to natural freedom," saying that "we are all born slaves"; "Life and thraldom we entered into together" (p. 4). The main criticism embraces two themes. One concerns Filmer's treatment of social power and rights, whereby according to Locke he mixes up two distinct areas. Dominion over the earth and its resources is one thing, dominion over human beings quite another. The former has to do with property rights, the latter with political power. The other main theme is that Adam (the father) has no exclusive right with regard to the earth's material resources—no right, that is, that excludes the grown-up sons from the same right. The whole of this discussion is in terms of Adam and Eve and their sons, and of Noah and his sons. On another plane it is of course a discussion about the possibility of freeing landed property and of the free accumulation of capital. But the rights of Eve (the wife/the woman) are sacrificed for the sake of asserting the economic competency of the sons (other male persons) with respect to the father (the state). Daughters play no part in the discussion.

According to Locke's presentation of the matter, Filmer's chief instrument for consolidating the origin of Adam's omnipotence with regard to human beings and the earth's resources was what God said when he gave Adam power over Eve:

> "And thy desire shall be to thy husband, and he shall rule over thee." "Here we have," says he, "the original grant of government," from whence he concludes, in the following part of the page, "that the supreme power is settled in the fatherhood, and limited to one kind of government—that is to monarchy." (p. 31)

Filmer then, according to Locke, distorted the Fifth Commandment: the children's duty to honor their parents was restricted to honoring the father. This was Filmer's most important Bible-derived support for his argument that the lack of legal rights of offspring and of subjects should remain.

Locke now attempts to bring Eve back into the picture in several respects. In the first place he corrects Filmer's one-sided exposition of the Fifth Commandment. He condemns—at least as fiercely as do modern scholars concerned with the position of women—Filmer's consistently distorted (in favor of the father, that is) use of the word "parents" (pp. 32–33, 44). There is no reason to believe, says Locke, that God does not follow the grammatical rules that prevail among human beings. It is a fact that the children were enjoined to honor their mother too. Locke sets out an argument extending over several pages, using a long series of quotations from the Bible, to demonstrate that the claim on the children's respect and obedience is the common right of both parents (pp. 41–51).

In the second place, when God said that mankind was granted possession of the world, "it could not be spoken to Adam till after Eve was made and brought to him" (p. 13). God spoke to Eve too. He blessed "them," and told "them" that they should have dominion. So "must not she, thereby, be lady, as well as he lord, of the world?" (p. 21).

But what was the purpose of this painstaking and long-winded defense of the mother in the Fifth Commandment?

> If therefore this command, "Honour thy father and thy mother," concern political dominion, it directly overthrows our author's monarchy, since it being to be paid by every child to his father, even in society, every father must necessarily have political dominion, and there will be as many sovereigns as there are fathers; besides that, the mother, too, hath her title, which destroys the sovereignty of one supreme monarch. But if "honour thy father and mother" mean something distinct from political power, as necessarily it must, it is besides our author's business, and serves nothing to his purpose. (pp. 45–46)

The sole purpose of Locke's defense of the mother was to demonstrate that the father's power has nothing to do with political power. It is especially effective to assert the mother's rights, because in this way the most important goal is attained, namely, that of toppling the all-inclusive sovereignty of a king. Locke is risking nothing of his own political doctrine in asserting the woman's rights as a mother, because parental power is at a safe distance from politics, from the power of the state. The duty of obedience that "we owe our natural parents" is distinct from "political obedience." And now suddenly the Fifth Commandment and the rights of the mother have become so unimportant that Locke himself forgets the equally divided parental rights and forgets too the linguistic rules that are shared by God and all human beings:

> For the person of a private *father* and a title to obedience due to the supreme magistrate, are things inconsistent, and therefore this command, which must necessarily comprehend the persons of our natural *fathers*, must mean a duty we owe them, distinct from our obedience to the magistrate, and from which the most absolute power of princes cannot absolve us. (p. 46; emphasis added)

What became of Eve's ownership rights with regard to the riches of the earth? Locke indicated that the "them" of the Bible did not have to refer to Adam and Eve. God had perhaps spoken to Adam about the riches of the earth before Eve was created. In that case "them" meant the entire "species of man," which is to say Adam and his children, or "man and the son of man" (p. 22). "Children," incidentally, is in the entire work synonymous with "sons." This interpretation inflicted a harder blow on Filmer than if Eve had been one of "them," thought Locke. Why? Other men's claim to a share of Adam's power would presumably make things more difficult. But if it was just a question of Eve—to whom is ascribed the possibility of (together with all her daughters) laying claim to property—it was less dangerous. Her it was easier to detach from ownership rights and political power. This Locke himself demonstrated, as I explain below.

In the England of the seventeenth century, according to Christopher Hill, the law of marriage was "almost the groundwork of the law of property."[9] It is easy to understand, against such a background, that Filmer should have regarded women as possible rivals of men for power in society. His works contain direct questions to the prophets of individualism, of contracts, and of free consent. What would it lead to if it were proclaimed that all persons—includ-

ing servants, women, and children, that is—were born free? He fore-
saw consequences that history to a large extent has indeed brought
into being. (See, e.g., Butler, 1978:140.)

What, though, does Locke do about the commandment that the
man shall have dominion over the woman—the commandment that
Filmer laid such emphasis on and thought of as the origin of the
man's patriarchal kingship? Yet another power relation must here,
according to Locke, be separated from political power. First it was
the parents' power over the children that had to be separated from
the right to political authority, then it was property rights, and now
it is the power of the husband over the wife. The words of God, says
Locke, have nothing to do with political authority. They were not
even addressed to Adam, he points out, but were "the curse of God
upon the woman for having been the first and forwardest in the
disobedience" (1978:31). And here Locke begins a somewhat remarkable line of argument. He passes judgments that intimate that
this sexual dominion is of scant importance compared with political
power. Then in the next breath he expresses what might be described
as ideas of liberation that are in woman's favor. Finally he comes to
the conclusion that the sexual dominion of the man is both natural
and in accord with human customs.

> Further, it is to be noted, that these words . . . were not spoken to Adam,
> neither, indeed, was there any grant in them made to Adam, but a punish-
> ment laid upon Eve; and if we will take them as they were directed in
> particular to her, or in her, as a representative, to all other women, they will
> at most concern the female sex only, and import no more but that subjec-
> tion they should ordinarily be in to their husbands. (p. 33)

But then suddenly Locke comes to the defense of women, which can
reasonably be supposed to intensify the challenge to Filmer.

> But there is here no more law to oblige a woman to such a subjection, if the
> circumstances either of her condition or contract with her husband should
> exempt her from it, than there is that she should bring forth her children
> in sorrow and pain if there could be found a remedy for it. (p. 33)

Nor does Locke believe that anyone except Filmer would imagine that this curse on "the weaker sex" was "a law" in the sense that women had a "duty not to endeavour to avoid it" (p. 33). This is directed against Filmer's patriarchal and royalist philosophy but of course at the same time constitutes challenge to all slavish adherence to the letter of the Bible, which contributes to the oppression of the female sex.[10] It is far from unlikely that Locke's argument was brought forth and put to use in the women's struggle of the nineteenth century.[11] But Locke does something else here. He distinguishes a new form of dominance relation between man and woman, a dominance relation that in part exists even today, namely, the form of marriage that suited the new society: man and woman as lawfully wed sexual partners living together, with the man as a private owner and the woman the property of the man and without legal rights. Here is how Locke puts it:

> God in this text . . . only foretells what should be the woman's lot, how by His Providence He would order it so that she should be subject to her husband, as we see that generally the laws of mankind and customs of nations have ordered it so, and there is, I grant, a foundation in Nature for it. . . . God . . . foretold what should *de facto* come to pass.
>
> But if these words here spoke to Eve must needs be understood as a law to bind her and all other women to subjection, it can be no other subjection than what every wife owes her husband. . . . If therefore these words give any power to Adam, it can be only a conjugal power, not political—the power that every husband hath to order the things of private concernment in his family, as proprietor of the goods and land there, and to have his will take place in all things of their common concernment before that of his wife; but not a political power of life and death over her, *much less* over anybody else. (pp. 33–34; the latter emphasis is mine)

Thus the order he sets forth is described as having "a foundation in Nature" and as being in accord with "the laws of mankind and customs of nations." One may wonder which is the heavier ideological burden—Filmer's Bible or his opponent's "Nature" and conventions. What remains of the subjection God decreed after the first human couple, on Eve's initiative, departed from Eden is "the subjection of the inferior ranks of creatures to mankind, and . . . the subjection that is due from a wife to her husband" (p. 35). Both these types of subjection, however, are "far enough from that which subjects owe the governors of political societies" (p. 35).

Who, then, have been freed from Filmer's "thraldom"? All of Adam's sons and their sons, especially those whose fathers were industrious enough to accumulate property to pass on. But those who did not inherit or who squandered their resources did at least get dominion over their wives.

Woman-Man in Civil Society

Locke (1978) has indicated that what the sons inherit from their fathers in civil society is "property" and not (political) "authority." No political right or position in the state goes with the economic inheritance. This is the right form of the new social order. All the more important, then, is the right of the first-born son and his brothers to inherit the father's property. But for this to function there have to be properly ordered marriages, and the sons have to be "sustained by those that got them till they are able to shift and provide for themselves" (p. 155). The lasting relationship of husband and wife fosters their effort "to make provision and lay up goods for their common issue, which uncertain mixture, or easy and frequent solutions of conjugal society, would mightily disturb" (p. 156).

Marriage is entered into "by a voluntary compact between man and woman" (p. 155). It becomes apparent that Locke was joining the ranks of those who were demanding the legal possibility of full divorce.[12] It ought to be possible to dissolve the compact between husband and wife just like any other voluntary compact, provided that "procreation and education are secured and inheritance taken care for" (p. 156). But for some reason the freedom and the will cannot be shared by the two parties to the voluntary compact. One has to reckon on husband and wife sometimes having different opinions and thereby also necessarily "different wills," says Locke. And now in reality he nullifies all the redress that the wife, by way of Eve, had received, in spite of all, with respect to the husband. For "different wills" cannot be permitted in a marriage under the order of civil society: "It therefore being necessary that the last determination (i.e., the rule) should be placed somewhere, it naturally falls to the man's share as the abler and the stronger" (p. 157).[13] The man's dominion is here a question of property and of the things that are of common interest, while the wife has "the full and true possession of what by contract is her peculiar right" (p. 157). But we are offered no example of what this "peculiar right" might refer to.

It has become clear that Locke denies the husband the legitimate power to kill the wife. Nor indeed shall the father have this ultimate power over any member of the family. Only the state in political society has such power. The state has no right, however, to interfere in the affairs of conjugal society but shall only decide any controversy that may arise between man and wife.

Unlike Hobbes (who set up rules for the succession to the throne), Locke offers no special discussion of woman as a political person. His contribution to discrimination against women in the state was more indirect.

Like Hobbes, Locke is of the opinion that the fathers of families (all men) have to give up much of their natural independence and freedom for the sake of the state's necessity. This they arrive at themselves, with the aid of reason and together. Reason, the man's own will, and public utility coincide. For women things are different. God has already decreed that every woman shall live under the power of a man. In Locke the wife does not (as in Hobbes) disappear when it comes to defining the family. Quite the contrary, indeed: she is expressly linked to the conjugal bed under the man's natural authority. But the woman enters into marriage of her own free will and should have the right to withdraw from it. Furthermore a mother shall be honored by her children, and she shares the responsibility for their upbringing.[14]

But Locke offers the wife no opportunity for equality with her husband in the marriage. He accepted God's judgment on Eve (though in a milder version than Filmer's) and turned to nature for additional support in justifying the man's being in the superior position.

Hobbes offered public utility as a reason for the woman to abandon dominion over her own body, to abandon her rights as a mother, and to subordinate herself to the man. It can also be mentioned that in the eighteenth century David Hume set forth purely utilitarian reasons for the subjection of women, opposing the use of nature as an argument (see Hernes, 1982:14–15; and Agonito, 1977:121–26). Hume was then in the process of toppling the entire edifice of the philosophy of natural rights.

The openly utilitarian reasoning with regard to the subjection of human beings offers the possibility of equally open resistance — of not letting oneself be used. But this of course requires that the human group in question does not itself consider that it was born first and foremost for the sake of being of use, because in such case the group has made a major contribution to its own oppression. At the same time it is important to remember that there is a difference between human beings using one another and human beings enjoying one another. The former involves a dominance relation, the latter requires equality and mutuality.

It tends to be difficult to get a proper grasp of the connection between philosophical ideas and historical development, nevertheless there is nothing unreasonable in maintaining that such ideas can, and do, have concrete effects, especially in times of social upheaval, and the seventeenth century was just such a time.

Both Hobbes and Locke prescribed that women should be subordinate to men, and they did so within the framework of an individualist philosophy. The only division into 'estates' which is clearly and openly put forward in this early individualism is the division between men (the higher estate) and women (the lower).

Filmer is the best-known patriarchal philosopher of the epoch, but research in recent decades indicates that Hobbes and Locke are worthy of equal renown in this respect.[15] That they were the most important forefathers of liberalism does not change this and is not itself changed by this either. But Filmer on one hand, and Hobbes and Locke on the other, were not patriarchal in the same sense. Filmer asserted that "human relationships were the natural outgrowths of the familial association and its paternal authority" (Schochet, 1975:55). Both Hobbes and Locke were of the opinion that subjection and the renunciation of rights were necessary to peace in a society. Subjection went furthest in "conjugal society." Eisenstein has characterized Locke's thinking as "patriarchal antipatriarchalism" (1981:33).

During the seventeenth century laws—as distinct from popular customs or the arbitrary decisions of the ruler—began increasingly to regulate the circumstances of people's lives. The bourgeois-liberal constitutional state gave the political economy an autonomous position protected by law. Private ownership rights prevailed, and this restricted the scope of state power. But the family developed into an extra private, or personal, sphere beyond the society of (privately owned) economic production. *The begetting of children*, "an act perfectly personal," and *marriage*, "which was only personal," came to be the specific and separate basis and superstructure of life's production.

In a work that came out in 1919 Alice Clark devotes part of her attention to the question of the effect on women of the extension of formal law. She writes:

> It must be remembered that the mass of the "common people" were little affected by "the law" before the seventeenth century. "Common law" was the law of the nobles, while farming people and artizans alike were chiefly regulated in their dealings with each other by customs depending for interpretation and sanction upon a public opinion which represented women as well as men. Therefore the changes which during the seventeenth century were abrogating customs in favour of common law, did in effect eliminate women from what was equivalent to a share in the custody and interpretation of law, which henceforward remained exclusively in the hands of men. (Clark, [1919] 1968:236–37)

Locke's exposition of the character of the married estate and of the family's separation from politics and state influenced legislation regarding the position of women. His distinctions were made use of to demonstrate women's incapacity as political beings (Hernes, 1982:16). These distinctions could also very easily be used to support the legalization of women's "civil death" upon entering into marriage. What marriage involved was that husband and wife became one person—the husband. During marriage "the very being or legal existence of woman is suspended."[16]

But a woman's being or existence is a question that goes beyond the legal. It may very reasonably be asked whether she does not still hazard parts of her existence in getting married—or, on the whole, in interacting with men.

Today, people continue to "deal with fundamentals" (as Laslett, quoted above, describes Filmer and Locke). Defenders of "conventional views"[17] in many disciplines are at pains to argue—against their feminist opponents—for theoretical definitions of society and the state that either ignore gender relations or openly state their "personal" and "highly particularized" (and, thus, nonsignificant) nature. Among political scientists this "defense" takes, for instance, the form of insisting upon that the central slogan of the women's movement, "the personal is political," is at best a truism that indicates nothing of interest to political science.[18]

In the following chapter I confront the question in what sense gendered interests are interesting, and what role interest theory should play in feminism.

chapter 7

The Concept of Interest, Women's Interests, and the Limitations of Interest Theory

The 'hard' political questions, such as war and peace, ecology and work, have always succeeded in mobilizing the public. The 'softer' questions, such as the critique of the family, children, sexuality and the relationship between the sexes, have either been swallowed up by the therapy movement or have disappeared behind a wall of nervous resignation. Only the women's movement continues to demand that the personal should be discussed politically.

Barbara Sichtermann, *Femininity: The Politics of the Personal*

Within feminist theory and research "interests" is a much-used but little-examined concept. This remains true despite—or perhaps because of—the fact that concepts like "interest(s)," "interest group," and so on, are among the most controversial within the field of scientific studies of politics.[1] Yet in everyday speech and strategic political discussions, the different connotations of "interest"—she is "interested in" women's issues; she "has an interest in" political work; or, it is "in the interest of" women that effective measures are taken against rape and battering—seem to be understood immediately.

The original Swedish version of this chapter was published under the title "Kvinnors intressen och andra värden," *Kvinnovetenskaplig tidskrift*, no. 2 (1985). Jan Teeland translated that text into English. A substantially reworked English version was printed in Jónas-dóttir and Jones, 1988. This chapter is a slightly revised version of that one and is reprinted by permission of Sage Publications.

Their meaning is understood by reference to the various contexts in which the terms are used.

Disagreement about terms may reflect an academic propensity for wordplay. But it may also reflect differing, often unarticulated, theoretical and metatheoretical approaches, that is, different conceptions of how social relationships and their histories are constituted, and how and to what extent we can obtain reliable information about these things. Yet, if we avoided using "contested concepts" altogether, we would not be able to study or relate to the realities of political life. Thus, when feminist researchers use expressions like "women's interests" we land in the middle of a scientific quagmire, suffused with contradictory meanings. Our analyses are affected by all the classical controversies, although, at the same time, our specific questions carry new conceptual challenges. These challenges have now propelled us into a special conflict situation.

Some feminist scholars argue, against traditional political thinking, that women as *women* should be considered a group with "representable interests." Other feminist researchers, who otherwise have differing views, question this argument; still others reject the concept of interest entirely. In this last view, the idea of interests, which since the Renaissance has constituted in one form or another a sort of backbone to almost all political theory, is thus declared to be something that feminist theory must transcend.

Women's Studies and Views on Interests

The aim of this chapter is to discuss the applicability of the concept of interest to women's concerns today. Two American articles from 1981 have focused particularly on this question: Virginia Sapiro's "When Are Interests Interesting? The Problem of Political Representation of Women," and Irene Diamond and Nancy Hartsock's discussion of Sapiro's article, "Beyond Interests in Politics." Sapiro's question is whether women today have representable political interests *because* they are women and not primarily independent of that fact.

She finds the former to be plausible, while Diamond and Hartsock criticize her very premises and reject interest theory altogether in favor of a theory of needs. In addition, traces of how and if interest terminology suits studies on women occur both explicitly and implicitly in several works. For example, in her book *Women and the Public Interest: An Essay on Policy and Protest* (1971), American sociology's grand dame, Jessie Bernard, anticipated the view of Diamond and Hartsock when she argued against using interest group theory as being inappropriate in studies of women and children. Instead, she recommends a view that proceeds from the traditional concept of common public interest, a perspective that Diamond/Hartsock do not discuss. They project a collective order where views of interests, in total, do not apply.

In two essays (1974, 1984) Jane Jaquette also questions the pertinence of the interest perspective to women's reality, the basis of which, according to her, is the home and the family. Politics does not take women's concerns into account nor do women feel at home in politics. Rosalind Pollack Petchesky (1980, 1983) makes a parallel argument when she questions the relevance of the concept of rights to the demands of women. Since "rights" are part of the framework of the theory of interests, her argument applies broadly. In a manner comparable to Sapiro, Helga Hernes (1982) considers various aspects of the problem of interests. She is concerned with making the theory of interests relevant to women. If democracy is to be really inclusive we need a shift from viewing women and women's organizations in traditional politics as a source of power for men to a view that acknowledges women's resources and women's organizations as a power basis of their own.

In addition to these primarily theoretical works, the conceptual problems around women's interests have been explored in empirical studies of political behaviour and of the concrete campaign issues of the women's movement. Abby Peterson (1981), for instance, provided a theoretical foundation for analyzing "women's issues" within voting studies, and Drude Dahlerup (1984) stipulates the right to vote as an objective interest of women, quite conscious of how inflammable that concept is. Arthur Miller, Anne Hildreth, and Grace Simmons (1988) distinguish between "gender identification" and "gender consciousness" and find that women (in the United States) are increasingly viewing their social situation in political terms as they have successively developed an awareness of shared interests.

This chapter considers the questions (and answers) that have been raised concerning the concept of interest, women's interests, and the limitations of interest theory. My main objective is to argue that the concept of interest is useful if redefined. Moreover, conceived of in a certain way, the concept is particularly significant in analyses of the society we actually live in. But it has its limitations. All the values that women strive for cannot be contained in the historically conditioned, utilitarian conception of interests. Thus my ambition is to attempt to transcend the either/or situation that the Diamond and Hartsock versus Sapiro debate suggests. At the same time I will indicate solutions to several of the problems concerning "interests" with which women's research grapples. I find that the concept of "needs," which Diamond and Hartsock suggest should take the place of "interests" as a conceptual core in feminist political theory, does not alone cover the dynamic essence of feminist political claims. On the other hand, taken together as two elements in a related whole, needs and interests lend a special historical significance to political theorizing about sex/gender in contemporary society.

For almost two decades women have been mobilizing in order to assert their interests as sexed and gendered persons which, in turn, has enabled them to begin to politicize their women-defined needs and the needs that arise out of their relatedness to other people and to nature. But to speak *politically*—that is, with reference to authoritative decisions—only in terms of needs leaves open who is to define what those needs are and who is to act on behalf of them. A crucial point, however, is that interests as an active counterpart to needs is not altogether salient when applied to the vast array of needs that exist in human beings and their relationships. Referring as it does to controlling situations, to instrumental agency, interest seems to claim its own opposite if some of our deepest needs—the needs for love and commitment—are to be fulfilled and developed.

In her essay Sapiro addresses a number of important issues. Yet her reasoning is weak since she seems to be unaware of the above-mentioned limitations of interest theory. Moreover, her notion of what kind of social oppositions make women as an interest category valid is far too narrow. The main question is not whether or not to politicize "the production of children"; the essential interested parties to be problematized here are not women versus the state. It is women versus men, that is, sex/gender versus sex/gender with all the complexity of that particular social structure.[2] The field of competing interests that is at the bottom of the problem in question is sexuality as a composite social process of generating, nurturing, and empowering people. How the sexuality process is related to the state, historically and theoretically, is a closely related question, but a distinct question.

Points of Conflict

The most heavily charged conflict about the concept of interest in modern times concerns the question of *objective and subjective interests.* How are objective interests determined? Is the concept scientifically meaningful at all, or are subjective interests, that is, an individual's conscious wishes and preferences, the only ones with which we actually can work?

The two main positions, which are also divided internally, have been designated pluralistic and Marxist (Balbus, 1971). Against the Marxists who assert objective class interests, the pluralists counter that what are considered to be a group's or individual's objective interests always rest upon the researcher's subjective values and thus are unscientific.[3] Within feminist research, the dilemma has much the same contours. Can we claim that women have certain objective interests regardless of what women themselves think?

Another controversy that has provoked extensive discussion concerns the presumed opposition between the *public interest and special or private interests*. Public interest in the sense of the state's external interests with respect to other states and internal interest with respect to various groups in the population constitutes the historical basis of the political concept of interests (Gunn, 1969). Quite early, during the eighteenth century and the French Revolution, it was claimed that public interest was a fiction. What did exist were the interests of separate social classes (defined in *Philosophisches Wörterbuch*, 1975b). During the twentieth century it has been claimed that the notion of public interest is both realistic and necessary. Writers like Pendleton Herring (1968:171) stress that public interest should not be seen as the result of negotiations between two or more parties—more or less like a labor market situation—but as "more than the sum of competing interests." Modern criticism of "public interest" has developed from two opposing perspectives, one Marxist and one libertarian/atomistic. The former sees public interest in a class society as reflecting the special interests of the ruling class. According to the latter, the concept of public interest is both scientifically meaningless and politically dangerous. Only the interests of rational individuals are able to be defined and represented and, thus, are real.

Another empirically and historically oriented view of interest groups and their bases takes a middle position between Marxists and pure atomists. This view takes into account certain, primarily economic, group interests; medieval rankings, merchant and craft guilds are supposed to have modern successors. Within this line of thinking the criterion for belonging to "the interest group universe" is to be "concerned with public policy," or in other words, to "have a stake in the political process" (Ehrmann, 1968:486).[4] Independently of how relevant this view could be, if re-formulated, from the point of view of feminist theory, one of Ehrmann's arguments should be underlined and expanded. He asserts on the question of the legitimacy of interest groups that "whether groups contribute to the operation of the political system or undermine it cannot be determined in the abstract" (1968:490). In much the same way we can claim that whether or not certain social groups (or groupings), for instance, women and children, do have group-specific interests or are concerned with public policy cannot be determined in the abstract or as a matter of principle. Theorizing in terms of interests (as all theory that aims at description and explanation of reality) must be historically and empirically informed.[5] Of course the question of what constitutes evidence is always a methodological problem. How, for instance, should we define a "stake" in politics or "concerns with public policy," or how do we measure impact on politics? In our case, for the time being, the pervasive mobilization of women in all areas of society would be a valid indicator for beginning such theorizing.

There has been less comprehensive discussion about a suitable classification system or *typology of interests*. One common way of doing this has been to differentiate between *material* interests, in the sense of economic, and *ideal* interests, in the sense of abstract support for a set of principles. It has been emphasized that this division is unclear since the economic and ideal aspects overlap each other, at least in part. Traditionally, the women's movement and its organizations have been included among the idealist types; they have been defined as "promoting a cause." According to this view, women *as women* (or men as men) are assumed not to have any common material interests. No social, historically relevant material interests based on sex/gender are supposed to exist. But the habit of reducing "material interests" to "economic interests" must be transcended.[6] According to the alternative feminist way of approaching society and history, which I propose in this book, sexuality (or the sex/gender relationship) can be seen as generating specific bio/social, material interests.

As soon as sexuality is posed as a basic category in the political theory of interests a new controversy enters the field of conceptual conflicts. In addition to the question of ascribing objective interests to women, regardless of their subjective consciousness, the problem has arisen whether *all women*, across all class and race lines, can be said to have *certain common interest*. Despite numerous deep divisions within feminist thinking, a majority of feminist students as well as activists are in agreement about maintaining some sort of minimal common denominators: the interest in not allowing oneself to be oppressed as a woman, or, in fighting patriarchy. Consequently, although there is dispute about the specific contours and contents of sex/gender interests, most feminist theorists support the premise that gender is a fundamental organizing principle of social life and of human consciousness.

The final conundrum in this debate about interest as a concept can be called the question of *female/male interests versus various role-based interests*. In these or similar terms we are confronted with questions about whether, for instance, promoting public care for children and the elderly are to be considered women's issues, while others, for example, those of economic policy or military concerns, are seen as men's issues.

History of the Concept of "Interest"

The origin of the concept of political interests[7] must be seen against the background of the rise and development in Europe of the national state, the capitalist system of production, and the emergence of the bourgeoisie. The term "interest" comes from the Latin "inter esse," meaning "to be" (*esse*) "among" or "between" (*inter*). The notion of "public interest" replaced some older ones with a similar function. In particular, ideas like "common good" and the "salus populi" were supplanted by this new notion.

The new revolutionary middle class demanded a place in the public sphere. They wanted "to be among" those who defined in the public interest. The social and political theory—classical liberalism—that directly or indirectly grew out of this social transformation heavily stressed the primacy of the individual's interests as well as the need for combining, consolidating, and literally fortifying these interests by means of the authority of the state. Defining the person as an individual who existed independent of society as a whole was a fundamental premise of this philosophy, and revolutionized thinking about state, society, and the nature of human existence. "Interests" were taken as an expression of the "natural" human being's unique qualities and capacities. An individual could determine his own life with the help of reason's and nature's measuring stick, independent of all spiritual and earthly despotic powers. By the seventeenth century the foundation had already been laid for a structural analysis of society and history that used interest as a key concept. Philosophers contended that social interests, class interests, group interests, and personal interests constituted those dynamic forces in the structure of society that created historical changes.

In addition to the broad political and social analytical significance that "interests" has had since the Renaissance, it also has had for a long time a much more narrow economic or financial meaning. The idea of profit as the result of exchange has increasingly permeated notions of what "inter esse" means. With the integration of utilitarianism in liberal social theory, especially under the pervasive influence of economic exchange theory, the broader political and philosophical concept of interest has focused largely on the dividend aspect. The demand to "be among" the state's actors was also motivated from the start by the idea of the individual's right to monitor the results of the political process since private individuals were affected by these results. This shift in focus has tended to obscure the controlling agency aspect in interests, that is, the aspect of who determines what the dividends should be and by what powers the political process is conditioned. This has fostered a type of theorizing that looks on interests "divorced from its sources."[8] The question is now whether we are moving into a new historical period where the emergence of conscious gendered interests and outlooks are undermining the validity of not only the liberal view of both public and private interests but also of the Marxist critique of that theory from a class point of view. Perhaps, as women enter the arenas of social and political struggles the very nature of their entrance will require a rethinking of the relevance of the categories of interest much in the same way as the "common good" was challenged earlier.

In sum, it can be said that the concept of interest has had, from the beginning, a double significance consisting of two connected, though often hidden, aspects: the *form aspect*—the demand to "be among," or the demand for participation in and control over society's public affairs—and the *content or result aspect*—concerning the question of those substantive values that politics puts into effect and distributes, including what this process results in related to various groups' needs, wishes, and demands.[9] Historically, this dynamic concept emerged as a politically relevant term in a period of rapid transformation: when new, innovative social groups (classes) and national states no longer accepted the existing political order or the characterization of general values as determined by an élite-defined "common good" or a scholastic "salus populi." A basic hypothesis in this chapter is that women as a group are now, in a historically new way, calling into question the ruling "salus populi masculini."

The Present Is Also History

The parties involved in the modern controversy over objective and subjective interests generally use the term "interests" as a synonym for words such as "needs," "wishes," "preferences," and "demands." Thus the stress is on *content*—what (values) people need, wish, or demand in order to be satisfied. The formal aspect, the claim to active participation, tends to disappear. The dynamic doubleness of the interest concept—the simultaneous stress on both form and content, both agency and substantial wants—then also disappears.

In political science, in system theory, for instance, concepts such as needs and wants are supposed to form a continuum extending from inchoate *needs*, through socially and politically articulated *wishes/preferences*, to politically linked (aggregated) *demands* on the political system. This is the ideal image of the representative democratic system. But an explosive issue lies embedded here. It is far from self-evident that the picture of citizens innovating and designing political issues is a valid one. Ever more important sources of "politics-production" are the top levels of the system where, to modify Schumpeter's ([1942] 1976:269) words, those "men sit who are to do the deciding." As Pitkin points out (1972:291–92), such a political system, though defined as a (methodical) democracy, is not necessarily a representative one. Thus, the fact that women vote in elections as much as men do does not guarantee representation for women as women, that is, as gendered persons. The active presence and positions within the "factory" of politics should be what counts as representation.[10]

There are strong reasons for maintaining a distinction between interest in the sense of actively "be/ing/among" on one hand, and interest as the satisfaction of needs and desires on the other; or, in other words, we should distinguish between *agency* and the *result of agency*. The main advantage of such a distinction is that it permits the resolution of the conflict surrounding objective and subjective interests. The concept's *formal aspect* becomes primary so that the content of needs and desires is, from the point of view of interest, an *open question*. In a certain way this means that only "subjective" interests exist; in other words, only human agents (or persons; see Connolly, 1983:69) have interests. This does not mean, though, that interests are determined by chance only. Understood historically, and seen as emerging from people's lived experiences,[11] interests about basic processes of social life are divided systematically between groups of people insofar as people's living conditions are systematically different. Thus, historically and socially defined, interests can be characterized as "objective." Unless we keep the form aspect of interest (and of politics in general) visible, we might come to believe that the history of political forms had come to an end. We might continue to think, as Lipset once claimed, and later Fukuyama (1992), that formally equal, liberal democracy is the culmination and completion of political history.

Ideas About Interests in Feminist Theory and Research

One of the points of conflict mentioned above concerns the unclear reasons for speaking about women's and men's interests, and women's and men's issues in politics. The question is whether and how we can differentiate general (human) interests, derived from individual historically determined positions and roles (people as parents, workers, etc.), and interests derived from the historically defined gendered reality of human existence. When we differentiate women's interests and men's interests, and women's and men's issues, we derive these distinctions partly from theoretical assumptions—often based on some variant of the theory of the division of labor based on gender—and partly on the basis of extensive empirical data. The main argument carried out in this book is that a theory of the division of *labor* based on gender is necessary but not sufficient for describing and explaining different—and partially opposed—sex/gender interests. What is needed, as a further foundation, is a historical theory of the gender division of *love*.

Studies of politics have shown unequivocally that the background variable of gender is one of the most, sometimes *the* most, differentiating factor in studies of political behavior (Fuchs Epstein and Laub-Coser, 1981; Halsaa-Albrektsen, 1977; Hernes, 1982; Lafferty, 1980; Milbrath and Goel, 1977; Putnam, 1976). And there is a clear pattern in this that is in total accord with both common sense and scientific hypotheses. Women, to a greater *degree* than men, and in different *ways*, initiate, pursue, and support issues concerning biosocial production and reproduction, that is, those questions having to do with control over, responsibility for, and care of people, and other natural resources (Edsall, 1984; Holmberg and Asp, 1984; Jonasson, 1985; Togeby, 1984; Walker, 1986).

Many authors of empirical studies are satisfied with statistically and typologically identifying certain feminist issues without making any attempt at theoretical deductions. Others explain results theoretically. According to Abby Peterson, a women's issue is defined through the value system of women's culture. It "originates . . . from those interests or demands which the reproductive sphere poses against the productive sphere, . . . from the fundamental levels in the family which all women in this society share—i.e. the *content* of their work in the family. In this sense a women's question is objective" (Peterson, 1981:6). Peterson further assumes that class membership, the different socioeconomic conditions of classes, explains attitudinal differences between different groups of women. She lists four features that characterize a feminist issue in politics: (1) women support the issue to a greater degree than do men, (2) the issue stands outside the traditional right/left scale, (3) the issue tends to be met with emotional reactions in the political arena, and (4) the issue lacks certified cultural authority or at least has an ambiguous political status (p. 9).

Looked at objectively, sex/gender–differentiated interests can thus be stated as those that pertain to women and men "being among" (compare "inter esse") different activities, working with different things, having different responsibilities, being involved with other people in different ways, What they are subjectively interested in, what their views are, and how they participate in other social matters "originates in" (nonmechanically) their respective sensuous practices. Understood in this way, the objective interest is neither mysterious nor difficult to work with. Nor is it totally separate from the subjective experience of it.[12] Aside from the bearing of children (and in a narrow sense the copulative sexual act itself), division of labor according to gender is not and has never been absolute, nor is the connection between experience and attitudes mechanically necessary. It is in this connection that the concept of gender is most important. Men who live and work in the "female" social sphere have all the opportunities for adopting a "female" consciousness. Likewise, women's political involvement is not a given, nor is it limited to so-called reproduction issues. For instance, in a Danish study of young people's political behavior, Lise Togeby (1984) shows that today's young women are very involved in employment issues. Thus the *historical character of gender interests* is actualized. Their changeability can be seen as a further dimension of the problem of the concept of interest.

Women and Men as Interest Groups

In "When Are Interests Interesting?" Sapiro sets out to demonstrate that women can demand gender interest–based representation in politics without going against generally agreed upon ideas about the bases of demands for group representation.[13] Sapiro claims that we are "accustomed to the idea that divisions of labor and stratification in public life define group interests in politics" (1981:704). Thus, she asserts, we can draw a parallel with the gender division of labor and stratification (power and status hierarchies) in private life, since the private sphere is affected and affects issues in public/political and policy debates. According to Sapiro, the ordinary indicators, that is, the socioeconomic differences in *public* life, also show that the politically relevant situations of men and women are very different. But despite these easily proven parallels it is politically and intellectually challenging to consider reproductive practices in private life as the foundation for conflicts of interest. For example, Sapiro refers to studies that show that women have lost in election campaigns when they define themselves as representatives of women or when they bring up women's or feminist issues (p. 711).

Sapiro discusses women as a group and representation in general. She does not distinguish between franchised (numerical) representation and resource-based (corporate) representation. Hernes (1982), on the other hand, deals in particular with the problem of corporate representation, and I would argue that it is here that analyses of sex/gender problems in terms of interests become really controversial within traditional political science. Dahlerup (1980:19) has offered the hypothesis that political parties have always tried to avoid a clear politicizing of the question of the position of women and have instead connected sex/gender conflicts with family politics or some other sub-issue. There is a parallel problem within scientific studies of politics, namely, one of resistance to conceiving sex/gender—women and men—as socially and politically relevant corporations or fundamental parties in society. In Western capitalist societies with their liberal democratic states, neither sex/gender groups nor sexuality as a field of activities is openly acknowledged as a politically relevant social basis for competing interests. Even many women's organizations are hesitant or unwilling to see society in these terms. Mainstream political science reflects this situation by being silent.

Besides the gender-based differences in traditional (electoral and public) as well as work-based politics (see Siltanen and Stanworth, 1984), studies show that men and women are forming groups based on the politics of housework, parenting, and sexuality. Many of these are taking the form of full-fledged interest organizations. Since the early 1970s women have, in a second historical wave, organized both more and less formally. They have come together in small groups as well as in large-scale organizations in order to be conscious of and protect themselves from patriarchal power in all its various forms, in addition to developing women-centered strength and strategies. Now even men seem to be moving toward a new phase of organizing relative to women. As in the history of classes, where the capitalists usually organized formally only after the laborers had unionized, men as men (i.e., as fathers and lovers) are now beginning to associate formally against what they see as the unfair advantages of women. A voluntary association for so-called weekend-fathers has started in Sweden. The aim of this organization is to influence the judicial procedures surrounding divorces, mainly the arrangements for judging parental fitness when determining child custody cases. It is also meant to be a forum where men can meet other men as fathers. In addition, a few male crisis-centers have existed for some years in Sweden.

Feminist Critique Rejecting Interest Theory

Diamond and Hartsock, in their evaluation of Sapiro, question whether views of, or ideas about interests should be "interesting" for women and feminist research. They claim that feminist theory must make a "clean break with the assumptions of the interest group framework" (1981:720). They criticize Sapiro for being at once too comprehensive and too narrow in her definition, as well as vague in her theoretical premises. They see a contradiction in Sapiro's claiming that the inclusion of women's demands in the political system constitutes a fundamental challenge to society, while still considering women as an interest group: "if the inclusion of women in politics threatens the most basic structures of society, one cannot fit their concerns into the framework of interests." They see Sapiro's inconsistency as an "inevitable consequence of trying to work within the conventional categories of political analysis" (1981:717). Her point of departure is in the "hidden and untested assumption that women's demands can be integrated into political systems." This, like the opposite assumption of "the inherent impenetrability of political life," must be made much more specific and studied empirically (1981:720). Diamond and Hartsock agree with Sapiro that women share common interests across class boundaries, and that the analyses of the power of the state and official policy must be expanded to include more than "social divisions of deriving from productive activity." But they must also account for the "profound implications of the social divisions deriving from *reproductive* activity." Thus, what remains, is a matter of studying the entire policy process and all the complexities of state power (1981:720).

According to Diamond and Hartsock, what argues against accepting interest theory and considering women as one interest group among many is that analyses according to these criteria become entangled in the dominant class and sexist patterns of society. They leave no room for regenerating demands, no openings for fundamental changes, and Diamond and Hartsock point out that, historically, ideas about interests reflect a view that society consists of rational, economic men seeking to maximize their satisfactions. "But," they continue, "human beings are moved by more than interests. The reduction of all human emotions to interests and interests to the rational search for gain reduces the human community to an instrumental, arbitrary, and deeply unstable alliance, one which rests on the private desires of isolated individuals" (1981:719). Such a view of social life is extremely partial. It is particularly difficult, for example, to imagine a mother's characteristically nurturing relationship to her children in terms of instrumental interests and individual gain (1981:719). For the more comprehensive categories of analysis that they seek, Diamond and Hartsock refer to the Canadian political scientist and philosopher Christian Bay, who has in various works advocated "needs" as an alternative to "interest" and "rights" (Bay, 1965, 1968, 1980).

This criticism is shared by Jane Jaquette (1974), who suggests that women have a lower rate of participation in politics because they do not have a "stake" in politics. And women do not have a stake in politics either because politics does not concern itself with what women find important or because it judges the engagement of women as naive, trivial, or even dangerous. Women are alienated in politics: they do not feel at home in the party apparatus, with its interest groups and its corruptions. What is often asserted to be "the true function of politics: that of brokerage among competing interests" does not appeal to women. Jaquette continues this theme of alienation in a later essay (1984), where she states that women's power, which is anchored in the home sphere, "is like a 'soft' currency in the international economy" (p. 23), that is, not "convertible" in the public sphere. She questions whether women's daily needs and goals are compatible with the usual view of politics as utility maximization and economically rational interest calculations.

Similarly, Rosalind Pollack Petchesky (1980) discusses the concept of rights and "women's right to choose" in connection with the goal of the women's movement—reproductive freedom. "Rights" are closely associated with interests; they are, in fact, part of the theory of interests. Petchesky rejects the concept of rights in favor of "social and individual need" as the key concept in the fundamental feminist-political analysis. She makes connections with certain branches of Marxism, for example, with Herbert Marcuse's ideas about the revolutionary potential in people living out their needs and assenting to their sensualism, as well as to Agnes Heller's theory of needs. In contrast to "rights," which are abstract and bound to a given social order, "needs" always refer to concrete, individual concerns, which can be seen as "part of a total revolutionary program," according to Petchesky (1980:670).

I agree that there *are* "difficulties of approaching the study of women and politics within the conventional categories of political analysis" (Diamond and Hartsock, 1981:717). I also agree that in order to develop new directions for theory and research where we spell out the radical implications of a sex/gender–based political representation, we need to transcend not only the result-oriented utilitarian notion of interest in its narrow sense but also Sapiro's theoretical frameworks. The important question, however, is *how* we cope with the conventional categories: from within themselves, or if "going beyond" just means ignoring or passing by. I claim that we must do it from within so that these categories, after being tried, can be put aside as unfitting. They will nevertheless have provided a given point of departure and, to some extent, a substance with which we must go further. Doing it the other way takes an outside view, one that refers to a reified version of reality rather than constructing valid indicators of reality, whereas it is only through valid indicators of existing reality that we are able to form alternatives and new visions.

Implications of This Rejection

Diamond and Hartsock's arguments are representative of the categorical rejection of interest theory. They fail to understand the point in Sapiro's assertion that including women as *women* into politics "tears at the most basic structures and conceptions of society." It is misleading to describe women as "simply another interest group" (Diamond and Hartsock, 1981:717). It is more constructive to see women as one part in an historically determined, antagonistic relationship to *men*. The point of seeing women as a group whose position has given rise to special interests is not the same as equating them with, for example, the National Association of Motorists or even pensioners' associations. It means to question from the aspect of sex/gender, the "individual" as *one*, and as an isolated unit, without throwing out the individual level as unimportant in social analyses. Besides implying a qualified criticism of the Marxist concept of class (as the one and only historically and theoretically relevant basic social category), the view of women as a group with certain shared basic interests means that the individual—the one—of liberal theory does not in fact exist.[14] And that alone is a challenge to a society that both practically and ideologically atomizes and individualizes people more and more. The definition of the determining set of social relationship—"ensemble of social relations"—that an individual is, in Marxist theory, nonetheless remains an incomplete task. This task can be completed only by introducing a new basic unit of analysis: that of the sexually and generically related individual.

Diamond and Hartsock also give too one-sided a picture of the theory of interest. Ever since this idea appeared it has been linked with values other than merely economic and economically colored profit motives. It could apply to the right to practice religion according to one's own beliefs, and the demand to be acknowledged as a full subject—politically, judicially, and in every other way. To argue that all such other practices only reflect the class-divided economy would be to lock oneself into a sterile deterministic way of thinking. Moreover, we cannot dismiss in advance the relationship between mother and child as having nothing to do with interest, even in the sense of interest as a narrow utility-maximizing category. The mother-child relationship includes many different dimensions all of which are socially and historically molded (and are thus, for instance class-divided and culturally different), but one essential in this multiple relationship is nurturing and care in one form of another. Yet even a superficial look—not to speak of one's own experiences—at everyday practices makes it plausible that the parties in these relations are to some extent rational beings "seeking to maximize their satisfactions" (Diamond and Hartsock, 1981:719). The character of the mother-child relationship must, like all other social relations, be investigated empirically and not be determined on principle. If we do not base our conceptual definitions on how this relationship manifests itself and develops in various real social contexts, and during various phases of life, we run the risk of returning to the "myth of the good mother"[15]—albeit in new guises. This is not to say that we should return to the myth of the omnipotent/evil mother either.

There is a final point about the difference between applying an interest perspective and a needs perspective in political studies. Diamond and Hartsock, as well as Petchesky, make the general claim that the theory of interests cannot reveal human desires, needs, and aims. To support this claim they cite, for example, Christian Bay, who says that precisely this character of interest theory implies a vindication of the "right of the strong to prevail in every contest" (Diamond and Hartsock, 1981:719). This must be modified. The idea that human needs should constitute the point of departure for political analyses and considerations means that those affected do not necessarily need to be where the lines are drawn and decisions taken in society (compare "inter esse"). Various weak groups should, for example, be able to have their needs met without first having to overcome their weakness and fight for their own positions of influence. Those groups poor in resources should not be penalized for their weakness. A society where this view is implemented as a general political principle is of course more humane than one where it is not implemented, or one where it is practiced within the framework of private charity.

One fundamental difference, in politics and political theory, between the point of view of interest and that of needs is that the former is necessarily a view taken from below as far as individuals and groups are concerned. The core of this perspective is the demand to "be among"—the demand to be present, literally (physically), or with ones own wants represented. This is central to the theory of participatory democracy. Political thinking in terms of needs involves a perspective from above, the perspective of socially engaged experts, of the political elite and administrators, the perspective of anticipation and of service democracy. Strictly speaking, the needs perspective, if applied separately from an interest perspective, does not require the existence of any channels of influence from below other than for positive or negative responses to decisions and policies.[16]

Another Theory of Interest

The concept of interest has some relevance for feminist theory. Studies containing a feminist-political premise of "offensive solidarity"

(Haavind, 1982:413), namely, women's conscious acting as a group, require analysis in terms of interest. My remarks in this section are based on a modified reading of Robert Q. Parks's essay "Interests and the Politics of Choice" (1982).

Parks's primary aim is to loosen the opposition between subjective and objective interests. He asserts that all types of "interest speech" have the same "speech-act meaning" or "point." "Interest" always refer to control over *conditions* of choice, rather than to the consequences of choice.[17] The function of arguing in terms of interest in the real world of politics "is to allow us to persuade, to assert, and to deny claims that an action or policy increases one's control over the conditions of choice . . . instead of functioning as a standard of what is beneficial to or good for someone (which is assumed by definitions of interests in terms of outcomes) (Parks, 1982:549, 552).

Parks understands interests 'as "that which increases my *control* over the range of options or conditions of choice, or [that which increases] my capacity to choose." But interests do not "involve merely *any* increase in the range of options or choices available." An increase, for instance, in the number of toothpastes or soaps on the market from twenty to one hundred could hardly be taken as in my interest under ordinary circumstances, according to Parks (1982:557). The promotion of our interests, that is, increased control over conditions of choice, relates, on one hand, to increasing our real possibilities to determine what values become the objects of choice, and, on the other, to increasing our abilities to see alternative choices clearly, free from distorted feelings, and aided by adequate concepts and sufficient information (Parks, 1982:550).

Furthermore, he treats interests, explicitly, as a historically specific concept. In our society, "with its politics of choice," interest talk has its appropriate place: "Our society has seen an unprecedented proliferation of choices thrust on the individual without any corresponding increase in our individual or collective ability to control the range or type of choices with which we must deal" (1982:549, 563). We are living in a society where, in more and more spheres of existence, everyone is forced to make choices constantly—whether about work, education, living quarters, sexuality, living partner, having or not having children, or merely between different types of soap. Under such circumstances it is the "being among," the attention to, and the undistorted insight into those societal conditions that form our lives, that comprise the relevant point of interest. Thus Parks focuses on what I have chosen to call the formal aspect of the interest concept. To evaluate the consequences or satisfaction of choice—the content of the values we desire—does not require the concept of interest. For this the concept of needs, the satisfaction of needs, desires, and preferences is more appropriate.

In the next sections I expound more fully on the following points:

1   The concept of interest is historically conditioned. It comprises the key to a particular theory of society, and it implies a particular view of humankind. These features are connected with the normative character of the concept of interest, or, in Parks's words, its "value slope." "Interest" ascribes to people in a certain form of society the norm of participating, the motivating power to try to expand their control over the conditions of choice.

2   The historical determination contained in point 1 implies that, of the two main aspects of the concept of interest, form and content (or conditions for and consequences of choice), form is the aspect that is fit for being *theoretically* determined, while content must be conceptualized as empirically open. Regarding the content aspect: people's valuations and preferences are and will remain the object of conflicts, discussions, and compromises. But discussions of content are expressed best in terms of needs, wants, and desires, and not in terms of interests.

3   By focusing on the formal aspect, the subjective and objective dimensions of interest can be linked. "Interest" always relates to some sort of *controlling attendance confronting conditions of choice* (more than what gains one receives from a choice, or an increased number of alternatives to choose between). This means either "be/ing among" those creating the alternatives, or knowing, by means of information, concrete thinking, and clear vision, what one chooses and has to choose between. This approach also implies an integration of the prevailing fragmented view of humanity. By focusing on conditions of choice and not just on the contents of those choices, people as producers/creators of their life conditions are seen as united with people as consumers/choosers of ready-made packages.

4 Yet, the concept of interest has a limited area of application. For certain of the most intensive human needs, especially those of love and caring for others, the concept of interest as outlined above is irrelevant. Many of the most important choices in life, such as choosing one's work, choosing one's partner, or choosing to have a child, are hardly involved with increasing control over future choices. Instead, these choices are primarily about assuming responsibilities and committing oneself, giving up one's options. Of course, a utilitarian dimension is not altogether absent. Even so the concept of "interest" need not be rejected: its limitations should be recognized, as should the sort of landscape that lies, and should lie, beyond these limits. Involvement in relationships of mutuality and trust, and the commitment they foster, may create possibilities of choice that could not have been otherwise obtained (Parks, 1982:562).

In agreement with Parks, we can differentiate interest and choice on one hand, and commitment on the other. Assuming there are values that authorize a limitation in the control over possibilities of choice, we must weigh and compare the arguments we deduce from such values and those related to interest. Parks thinks that the contrast between controlled choice and committed engagement is unavoidable in any type of society; but he assumes that larger conflicts between choice and commitment in important areas of life ordinarily need not arise. Applied to gender, this last point in Parks's argument is a weak one. There is reason to believe that such conflict situations are more difficult and arise in significantly more areas for women than they do for men. Women are, for instance, caught in the oppressive contradiction between the home and the sphere outside the home in a way that men usually are not. In most industrialized countries women, even if they have to work outside the home for economic reasons, are still forced ideologically to "choose" whether or not to do so. Therefore it is also "their choice" who is to take care of the children, how to make the household work, and so on. Moreover, women seem to found their choices on motivational bases that differ from those of men (cf. Gilligan, 1982).

The Historical Character of the Concept of Interest

In her essay from 1984 on the earlier women's movement's difficulties in placing the demand for women's franchise on the "public agenda," Dahlerup cautiously takes up the problem of *objective interests*.

> If we want to understand the suppression of issues, we must start from the assumption of *objective interests*. If we do not, we cannot grasp the most important form of issue-suppression, that of preventing issues from being raised at all. As [Matthew A.] Crenson starts with the assumption that people want to avoid being intoxicated by pollution, so the following case starts with the assumption that women as well as other disenfranchised groups have an objective interest in achieving the right to vote. But there is no reason to try to hide the fact that the question of objective interests is very delicate. (Dahlerup, 1984:40–41)

The problem Dahlerup faces when relating her study to Crenson's is that the assumption that women (or other groups) have an objective interest in political participation is far from being as obviously valid as the assumption underlying Crenson's study.[18] Crenson connects interest to objectively measurable living conditions of (more or less intoxicated) people as biophysical bodies. Dahlerup writes about the societal conditions of people as free-willed human beings.

If we conceive of the concept of interest as a historical category, we should be able to support the proposition that the right to vote is an objective interest in another way than just making an analogy with Crenson. We can see "interests" as a categorical element in political theory about the historical development of Western society. Our argument would be more or less the following: the objectivity in women's relation to the right to vote (and eligibility) derived from the fact that the form of society that actualized the issue was based increasingly on the will of "the many," that is, internally competing group's choices of action alternatives. People's actions were no longer justified or vindicated by appeals to rigid traditions, or by offers from an absolute ruler. A real political society had grown in Europe, replacing the old regime.[19]

In a political structure where an increasing number of groups are affected by situations of choice, where more and more areas become a matter of choice, the force of people's circumstances becomes to "be there" where choices are made. This is especially true in a society divided and dominated by class and gender; there it is part of the conditions of social life that people are driven to try to expand control over those spheres that encompass choice. Further, this historical process is a process of concrete social struggle that can not be seen as steps in a mechanic order, or as derivatives of rational logic. In Chapters 6 and 8 we see, for instance, that the classical philosophers who wrote of individual rights and individual autonomy did not extend their reasoning "automatically" to women. In our society now, however, women's objective political interests no longer concern being individuals in the formal system. (Women attained that position gradually; Swiss women finally got the right to vote in 1972). Women's objective political interests today concern building up and controlling *as sex/gender* a concrete presence or attendance in this system. This historical political situation—the development of sex/gender into a specific, historically relevant "cleavage basis" in society—has come about through those practical life struggles with which women are involved.[20] It is reflected in the gap between their formally equal rights and the oppressive and exploitative social realities in which they live and work. For instance, with a public policy that increasingly intervenes in family and other so-called personal matters, and more and more family care and housework being taken over and organized by agencies outside the home, the potential of conflicting interests between women and men has increasingly been unfolded and shaped.

Women should be able to act on the strength of being women and not mainly despite being women. They must be visible politically as women and be empowered to act in that capacity, because there is the continual possibility (not necessity) that they may have needs and attitudes on vital issues that differ from those of men. This does not imply that women have no needs and preferences in common with men. Nor does it imply that these differences reflect only biological distinctions. But it does imply, as extensive facts in contemporary Western societies also indicate, that women and men are beginning to constitute themselves as two basic societal corporations. These developments, which have their origins in the second wave of the women's movement and its ensuing mobilization of women, can be found more or less within every area of social life. This means, further, that the sex/gender structure must be analytically conceptualized independently of class structure and race relations, and such.

Interests as Controlling Presence

As Dahlerup shows, the right to vote was preceded by lengthy attempts to get the issue present and noticed on the public agenda, to give it "public attention." Parks uses the word "attend" as an underlying and distinguishing feature of the concept of interests. "Attend" and "attention" have the double meaning of actual/physical presence and subjective notice or consciousness.

One type of structural barrier that hinders women's issues from reaching the public agenda is the fact that women have been excluded, and to a large extent still are absent, from those institutions that create these agendas, for example, the mass media, political organizations (in a broad sense), literature, public meetings (Dahlerup, 1984:44–45). But the reverse situation applies also now: from well within such institutions women now seek space and an attention in the public debate in order not to be pushed aside *within* the institutional contexts. Today women have the simple legal right to be present in, for example, political and union organizations, and they have increased their numbers, sometimes significantly. But if they conceive of themselves or act as a gender interest group, that is, when they try to control their attendance in order to be able to shape those conditions that they live under in their capacity as human beings who are women, they run into obstacles. Women active in unions have written about how they are forced to start public discussions in order to bring attention to and prevent their issues and demands from being pushed aside or choked within the unions.[21]

In the early 1960s the Swedish essayist and journalist Eva Moberg used the expression "conditional liberation" to describe the circumstances of women. They were allowed to be wage earners, and otherwise active outside the home—as long as they took care of "their" domestic chores too. One could similarly speak of women's "conditional membership" in political parties and unions. Research from several different countries shows how women's presence and participation in these organizations are accepted as long as they do not express themselves or act from sex/gender-based interests.[22] This way of applying the concept of interest as form and this notion of form differentiating between the *simple* and the *controlling* presence (or between the legal right and the active practicing of shaping social reality) takes us right into the complicated question of objective circumstances and the subjective consciousness of these circumstances. It takes us into the "first and most serious problem" for the women's movement to overcome (Dahlerup, 1984:43): women's own lack of consciousness of oppression—a lack that is easy to understand.

In the light of my proposal that women are exploited by men and, further, that this exploitative relationship comprises the most vital mechanism for keeping contemporary patriarchy going, the elaboration of the concept of interest and of interest theory made here, takes us also "beyond oppression" (see Chapter 5). The most serious problem is, then, not just a question of *women's lack of consciousness*. Rather—not to say, "on the contrary"—it is also a question of most women's *awareness of the risks* they take by challenging "the rules" of patriarchy. Presumably, the risks are at times overemphasized. But taking them can, at other times, result in unendurable consequences. And the risks that individual women take must be seen in connection with the obstacles, referred to above, that they run up against when they organize or when they articulate their collective interests as women.

The "conditional status of equality" that is women's status with respect to men, makes it inevitable for women to take continual risks—not only the risk of losing control over their circumstances, but also the right of attendance itself if they consciously act in terms of gendered interests. Women take similar risks in love relationships if they start conflicts, if they argue that male dominance in the relationship must be a question to be discussed and answered, or if they merely take control themselves of their shared life conditions. Examples of this could be women's claims to financial autonomy, or to full insight into the couple's common finances; demands that men take their emotional responsibilities as fathers; and not considering it self-evident that men's chances of getting work or pursuing a career should one-sidedly determine the family's place of residence or its life-style. Even *being interested in* and seeking knowledge about women's lives and the different conditions of the sexes can be considered threatening. Women are often left in the end without either partners or success.

The essence of the problem of the sexes is even more about the body-and-the-soul of concrete, socially related *individual people* than is the problem of class and race. In the struggle of the sexes even more areas of life and values are affected, and in different ways. The striving to "be among" and, in the capacity of sex/gender group, to control this presence also demands that each individual person as far as possible gains perspective of his or her own actions and powers to exist and function as precisely sexed/gendered persons. This in turn presumes unity among women and mutually supportive alliances with sympathetic men as well.

One important strategic question is how far it is reasonable to consider agreement when it comes to common needs, values, and demands. With reference to the question of organization, perhaps large (offensive) women-only organizations can have no other function than to organize women's "collective discontent" (Hernes, 1980:265) and protect and promote general positions of equality.

The longer-range women's struggle, strategy development, and goals must necessarily be fragmented and cultivated both formally and informally within all the various areas and contexts of social life, even within all intimate relationships. Because of the deep social cleavages of class, race, or ethnicity among women, I suppose it is realistic not to presume genuine *sisterhood* among all women, or even *solidarity. Alliance* on certain issues is perhaps the only realistic kind of large-scale unitedness. Sisterhood, conceived as a bond of relatively deep affection, of friendship and sometimes love, is presumably only possible between *few.* Solidarity, understood as a relatedness that does not necessarily presume personal friendship but when practiced involves sacrifices and sharing of burdens, should be possible among *many.* Limited alliances, both offensive and defensive, could be seen as the minimum of necessary unitedness among *all* women.

Limitations of the View of Interests

All the authors mentioned above who reject the theory of interests share the view that the issues of reproduction by their very nature do not lend themselves to utilitarian interest arguments. All of them take up the birth of children and love and caring in mother-child relationships as particularly incomprehensible in terms of interests. Considering, however, all the conflicts and power struggles—not only for "standing" (control) but even about the distribution of many limited resources, for example, time and money—that are constantly waged openly and covertly between parents and children, it seems to be more realistic to assert the composite notion of both utility and care, both control and commitment. And I refer not only to oppressive or to purely exploitative relationships but also to those containing "good conflicts," to use Jean Baker Miller's (1978) expression.

What, on the other hand, clearly sets aside the traditional view of interest is that the parents' vocation according to this planet's life program is to promote their offsprings' interests beside their *own* (cf. Ruddick, 1980). According to the idea of interest that I argue for here, this would mean that parents should help their children successfully overcome their dependency on the parents and on parental authority. Children must learn as relatively autonomous persons to take control over their own conditions of choice, without the self-denial of parents. This is difficult, especially perhaps for women, who from infancy are taught altruism: women learn "to be something for others," to identify themselves with other people's problems, particularly those of husband and children, and to make the well-being of the latter their own, often at the expense of their own presence. One result of this is that conflicts of interest in relation to others become problematic to articulate and work on (cf. Ve, 1982:418–19; Ve, 1984:133; Gilligan, 1982).

The satisfaction of many values in life presumes that one loses, or restricts considerably, control over future conditions of choice— being pregnant and giving birth to children, for example. Does the bodily part of motherhood, then, stand in opposition to a woman's interests? Strictly speaking, yes, according to the idea of interest outlined above. We also can formulate it so that by bearing children women involve themselves in promoting "mankind's [and in extension also the state's and capital's] interest." Pregnancy carries us into a union with nature (which always varies with different social forms); we enter into a process the course of which we can influence ourselves only to a minimal degree (and of course this degree differs socially and historically); we run risks to life and health both during and after pregnancy and birth; and to all this are added the ties and responsibilities during the child's upbringing and for the rest of his or her life. But the value of bearing life and helping it to be is so enormous that many happily restrict their own autonomy for its sake. What promotes women's interests in this context is to safeguard the very real possibilities of being able to decide whether or not we want children, under what conditions we want to give birth to them, and within what parenting pattern and with what expectations we will raise them.

The theory of interests is particularistic by nature. The essence of this theory is that each party in a community or an association strives to ensure his or her autonomy in the community and his or her voice in those policy processes that shape the development of the community as a whole. Thus the idea of interests issues from the view that social contrapositions and conflicts are both unavoidable and potentially fruitful. The notion of interest developed here that emphasizes its formal (as relatively distinct from the content) aspect is essentially more appropriate as a core concept in a theory of broadly based participatory democracy than is the concept of needs (the content) taken separately. These two related concepts should not be viewed as exchangeable but rather as referring to two different layers of social existence: agency and the needs/desires that give strength and meaning to agency. As a core concept in (a participatory democratic) political theory, needs must be mediated by interests. In no developed country have women reached the stage where they can give up the struggle for a real and controllable attendance as an identifiable group within the various groupings of society. Even within relationships of love and care this struggle is necessary in order to have a worthwhile life, a life with woman-human dignity.

Sapiro asks the question "Why is an individual's relationship to the production of children not commonly accepted as a matter of political interest while one's relationship to other forms of production is?" (1981:713). Put this way the question becomes rather misleading. In all welfare states, including the socialist ones, this relation is indeed accepted as being of political interest. Childbirth has always been of concern to the state, as an issue of population growth or decline, and has thus made motherhood a concern of the state (this is actually suggested by Sapiro herself). The problem is not whether to politicize the production of children (of course, from women's point of view, what is of decisive importance is *how* it is politicized); the crucial issue is the politicization of the gender/sexual relations themselves. Women and men are obviously the producers of children and responsible for them, but women and men, or rather, people as sexual beings, are also the primary parties in the reproduction of themselves and each other as persons who have special human, natural/social, capacities for sexual love. Regardless of how the forms of society may change—for example, in the direction of less "compulsory heterosexuality" (Rich, 1980)—perhaps we will never avoid a certain struggle of interests in this matter. We will perhaps never cease to exist in a delicate balance between surrender, leaping into situations where control and reflective choice stand in direct opposition to what is valued highest—profound love—and a compelling need to monitor interest, control, and responsibility.[23] What can and must be changed is that women are affected and damaged much more and so differently from men in this basic process in social life.

chapter 8

Does Sex Matter to Democracy?

The personal sphere is something directly political for women because it refuses to leave them alone, because they cannot rid themselves of responsibility for personal matters. Women who want more than family life make the personal political—even without intending to directly—with every step they take away from the home. A woman in parliament or on a political platform is tantamount to making public something as personal as a female mouth or the hem of a skirt.

Barbara Sichtermann, *Femininity: The Politics of the Personal*

The main question to be addressed in this chapter is how citizenship, individuality, and sexuality are connected in the contemporary Western social context; that is, how the undividable/the individual—and yet divided into man and woman—human being is, and could be, related to democratic citizenship. By "could be," I mean: What would a "free, equal, and secure" (the three classical justifying criteria of liberal democracy) membership for women in a democratic society be like? Naturally, the second part of this question cannot be answered in any detail.

As the social inequality between women and men has been increasingly considered in practice as well as in theory during the past

The first and considerably longer version of this chapter was presented as a paper titled "Does Sex Matter to Democracy If Democracy Wants to Be Global?" in a mini-plenary session on political theory, 14th World Congress of the International Political Science Association (IPSA), Washington, D.C., August 1988. A shorter version was published in *Scandinavian Political Studies* 11(4) (1988): 299–322, and is reprinted here, with some revisions, by permission of Scandinavian University Press.

twenty to twenty-five years, the flagrant difference in political power positions between the sexes has also become highlighted. Recently, feminist scholars have begun to raise questions about sexually differentiated citizenship, and about women and men having different kinds of relationships to the state at large. This difference has taken on new forms under the welfare state and has become accentuated and easier to observe. What mainly characterizes this difference is that women, to a much greater extent than men, are dependent on the state, as employees, and as clients and consumers of the state's services—which also means that women and men are socially vulnerable in different ways. It means, too, that women as voters are more favorable to a large public sector (Gilljam and Nilsson, 1985). But at the same time women are far less influential, and have far less authority, in the state than men have, whether through individual citizenship or through corporate organizational life. Thus, one of the ironies of history is that, at present, although most Western democratic governments carry out comprehensively backed-up sexual equality programs, at the same time, more women in proportion to men are victims of the undermining of the welfare state that goes on in most Western countries.[1]

Feminist state theory is very much in its infancy; still less has been done by feminists in democratic theory,[2] in part because in feminist scholarship liberating conditions for women generally have more often been discussed and investigated in other terms (such as equality, freedom, autonomy, power) than the more specified political-theoretical terms of democracy. And this, surely, reflects another fact, namely, the dearth of women in general, and of feminist scholars in particular, among "disciplined" students of politics and political theory.

As a critical point of departure for the problems raised in this chapter, I relate mainly to work by Carole Pateman (1983a, 1983b, 1985b), in particular to her questions and answers concerning the difficulties and possibilities for women as women to be full and equal citizens. With the help of this reference point, I want to extend, into the field of democratic theory, the lines of theoretical reasoning for understanding contemporary male authority, and women's interests, in formally/legally equal societies, which I develop in the previous chapters.

Patriarchy in formally/legally equal societies should be basically defined as a historically specific, *political* sexual power structure; definitions in terms of socioeconomic, psychological, or ideological power are not fully satisfying. In this particular power structure I conceived women *as women,* and men *as men,* as constitutive. And this power structure, my argument goes, conditions or influences the relations between women and men in all other social contexts, for instance their activities as public persons.

What, then, is meant by "women as *women*"? Is there anything left when we have defined women as "workers," as "mothers," and as "citizens" (Siim, 1988)? And also, directly related to the state, as "employees," "clients," and "consumers" (Hernes, 1984)? Are there any more roles that are relevant to a theoretical analysis of women's political situation today? What about women as (in D. H. Lawrence's words quoted at the end of Chapter 2) "real human being[s] of the female sex," women as "individual persons"?[3] This last question hints at the opinion, widely and for a long time taken for given, that this creature, "human being" or the "individual" in general, is irrelevant; particularly with regard to a political theory, which claims to be guided by principles of historical materialist method.

Carole Pateman argues that "that great question that now faces us" is whether a form of "democratic citizenship is possible that includes women *as women*" (1985a:3:4). She claims also that: "We need a conception of universal, participatory citizenship that is grounded in the recognition of sexual difference, so that women, to become full citizens, do not have to attempt to become pale reflections of men, but can actively participate *as women*" (1985a:2:14). According to Pateman, this would be the only solution to the oppressive and degrading fact that "women have never been and still are not admitted as full and equal members and citizens in any country known as a 'democracy' " (1983a:204). On the contrary, she asserts that: " 'The' individual is sexually particular and liberal democratic

values, practices, and institutions accordingly reflect masculine attributes" (1985a:3:3). This means, from Pateman's point of view, that
the social barriers restraining women's status as citizens must be
sought and combated not just in the public sphere itself, or simply
in women's double-burdened and ambiguous work situation; rather,
"women's status as workers is as uncertain and ambiguous as our
status as citizens and both reflect the more fundamental problem of
our status as 'individuals' " (1983a:215). All this results in her claim
that: "The assumptions and practices which govern the everyday,
personal lives of women and men, including their sexual lives, can
no longer be treated as matters remote from political life and the
concerns of democratic theorists" (1983a:213).

What exactly does Pateman mean by "women *as women*"? And
how does she interpret "individuality" in its prevailing masculine
form and as potentially feminine and human/universal? What is the
"fundamental problem" of, and the political relevance of, the difference in women's and men's status as "individuals"? Furthermore,
what content or capacity does she select from the, obviously multiple, womanhood that would—and should—function as the vital
condition for developing a truly universal democratic society? *Is*
there something beyond the role-set listed in the 1986 ECPR workshop, a role (I would say a position or capacity) that is relevant to the
solving of the—to quote Pateman again—"fundamental problem" of
individuality and, therefore, important to conceive of theoretically?
Does Pateman's solution cover this "role," or does it not?

Women as women, for Pateman, seem to be split into two separate figures with no obvious connections between them: women as
victims of male, sexual, and political coercion, and women as potentially dignified civil mothers. Furthermore, her concept of sexually
differentiated individuality is grounded on assumptions about feminine and masculine identities, derived from more than three-cen-
turies-old patriarchal convictions and practices, prevailing today, by
which women are claimed to be subject and inferior to men by
nature.

She does not think, however, that the way to a better future for women should lead us to still more appeals for a masculinist defined reason of nature (as many liberal feminists have done since at least 1650) or even to the ideal of *sameness*. Nor does she perceive a way through a new confirmation of *separate spheres*, the ideal that many feminists and suffragists in the nineteenth century shared with anti-feminists and antisuffragists. She believes that conditions for a third approach now prevail, although she is rather pessimistic about the possibilities of its realization in practice and even in theory.

In short, what has to be done, according to Pateman, is to transform the current separation between the personal and the public spheres, without necessarily breaking down everything that distinguishes each of these spheres. Furthermore, women should be accepted in political theory and practice as concrete individuals who differ from men primarily on one crucial ground, that of the ability to give birth. Therefore, Pateman thinks that the way to a truly universal democracy must be redirected and completed by women in virtue of motherhood. In the following I question and discuss some of Pateman's central points.

This chapter is organized around three main themes. First, If women's citizenship has been and still is constrained by individuality, how should this be understood and explained? Second, What is the explanative value of the concept of "difference," now so popular among feminist writers? and How far is (different) "individuality" politically relevant for feminism? Third, In the light of the prevailing confusing views on Western society and democracy, what do women want? If it is equality, what kind of equality? If a new kind of different citizen status, on what capacity should that status be founded?

My main conclusions are that Pateman's thesis about the appeals to reason of nature being the most powerful of the antifeminist arguments since the seventeenth century has to be modified. What was the most treacherous in antifeminism, which had already begun in the late seventeenth century and that was definitely established in the eighteenth century, was rather the appeals to *utility*; women's place being defined by the good they should do to the thrift of private property, to the order and stability of the state, and to the pleasure of men. Furthermore, while I see it as an advantage that Pateman refers to sexuality, and not only to work, to explain the contemporary social barriers to women's full and equal membership in political society, I believe she falls into a radical-feminist fallacy when viewing sexual violence as essential for such explanation. The fundamental sexual conflict concerns freely given, and taken, love.

Like many other feminist writers, I believe that the concept of "difference" and differentiated individuality is both theoretically and politically important. But the deepest layers of our present social reality we can only capture with a processual and relational way of thinking, that is, by a kind of thinking that conceives these relationships as a flow or a process rather than as connections between discrete units (or items). Concerning individuality versus collectivity, a nonoppressive integration of these states of social being is, perhaps, the most important political goal of feminism. Finally, my conviction is that women have to demand citizen status simply as womankind, if we are to be able to act for our own purposes.

Women's Citizenship as Constrained by Individuality

In what way does individuality, as the basis for liberal citizenship, constitute a hindrance for women? What does it mean to say, as for instance Pateman does, that the "individual/citizen" has always been a male category, and that citizenship still is sexually particular, not universal in any true sense? What exactly is it about individuality *today,* in the formally/legally free and equal society, that restrains women from becoming "full and equal citizens and members" of this society?

One way to answer these questions is, of course, to look at the empirically based explanations of women's, still prevailing, subordinated social and political status, especially the explanations delivered by contemporary feminist theory; and, if found insufficient, to attempt to develop this theory further. Another way to answer the questions above is to look at the various philosophical arguments that have been used historically against women's equal public status with men. Such arguments have flourished abundantly and intensely from the very beginning of Western political thinking. They reached their modern heyday during the revolutionary period of the eighteenth and early nineteenth centuries; at the time of the Enlightenment, when freedom, equality, and brotherhood (protected or not protected by a state) were demanded for all "men". Moreover, in some countries, during the period of struggle for women's suffrage the bearers of antifeminist arguments united and organized to oppose women's becoming full and equal members of political society (Harrison, 1978).

The antifeminist arguments so forcefully carried on in political history are interesting not only as an antiquated curiosity (even if they often *are* curious) but for other reasons too. First, they functioned as operative principles in jurisprudence and were carried out in practice without mercy, when put to the test, as was often the case. And, presumably, as many feminist students of law assert, there is still much in the making and practice of law that, more or less nonintentionally, functions oppressively for women. Second, the deep-rooted devaluation of women might continue to function as ideological power, as so-called historical rests, and thus continue to influence the attitudinal structures of people today, even after the disappearance of the legal foundation of this devaluation. Or, as Hume wrote in his *Treatise on Human Nature*, when a convention or a general rule "is once establish'd, men are apt to extend it beyond those principles, from which it first arose" (quoted in Agonito, 1977:126).

Third, there were many women among the antisuffragists, women who obviously thought that equality between women and men in public life would be destructive for women. Understanding the motives of these women might help to answer the tricky question, actualized today, whether or why the barriers to equality with men are partly produced by ourselves. Fourth, as Pateman (1985) interestingly underlines, perhaps overemphasizes, the arguments of the antisuffragists and the arguments of suffragists themselves over-lapped on a fundamental point, although the two antagonist parties drew different conclusions from it. The point of unanimity between antisuffragists and at least the social- or cultural-feminist part of the suffragists was to underline the importance of *difference* between women and men. It was different needs and interests that should be protected (by men in the one case, by women themselves through the state in the other); and men and women were supposed to have different capacities and values with which they should enrich their own family and marriage *or* the whole society. As is well known, sameness versus difference is still a problematic pair in feminist debate.

"Nature" and "Utility" in the Legacy of Antifeminism

A growing literature of feminist research shows more and more de-tails and unsolved problems in the history of philosophical antifemi-nism and its feminist challenges. Pateman argues that "after three centuries of controversy about individualism, women and citizen-ship [the fundamental question that remains unanswered] is: what exactly is the political relevance of sexual difference?" (Pateman, 1985:1:15). In her own search for an answer, she asserts: "To under-stand why, in the 1980s, there are special difficulties about women and democratic citizenship, and to understand what form these dif-ficulties take, it is necessary to see how the problems developed out of the first feminist challenge to the new individualism of the seven-teenth century, and in the feminist reaction to Rousseau's participa-tory but patriarchal arguments of the eighteenth century" (p. 2). Ac-cording to her, "the anti-suffragists' arsenal of arguments consisted largely of recapitulations and elaborations of arguments used since the seventeenth century to maintain the sexual particularity of citi-zenship." And, she continues, "the arguments ultimately came down to the claim that women, by virtue of their *nature*, lacked the capaci-ties required of free and equal individuals and citizens and so posed a threat to the state" (p. 8; emphasis added). She also claims

(1983a:212) that the conviction that wives are inferior to their husbands by nature prevails today.

I fully agree with Pateman on all but the last points, which I think have to be modified. Already in the late seventeenth century, and definitely in the eighteenth and the nineteenth centuries, the general dominating ideology, used by some people to keep other people down, shifted; from a stance where applications to the *reason of (differentiated) nature* were central to a stance that justified itself by applying to various aspects of *social utility*.[4] My point is that antifeminism, although resting on its own grounds, also was transformed in this direction.[5] In another context (see Chapter 6) I argue that already in Hobbes's and Locke's analyses of the true nature of power relations in the various spheres of society, a utility view of women's subordination becomes clear; and that this utilitarian embryo became fully developed and extremely honestly delivered in Hume's arguing for the sake of "the interest of society."

Even if many antifeminists continued to refer to women's inferior nature, and feminists, beginning with Mary Astell (see Pateman, 1985), steadily had this ideological construction of women's nature as a target (still today, we find ourselves sometimes involved in mostly confusing disputes over the social consequences of sex-differentiated nature), it was increasingly the utilitarian kind of arguments that set the terms of the combat. And this, I believe, is at least a part of the reason why the otherwise so surprising overlap of standpoints emerged between antisuffragists and suffragists in the nineteenth century, both parties asserting sexual difference and separate spheres as fundamental in their arguments.

Assertions about inferior female nature could in principle be falsified on the grounds of rational thinking and empirical evidence. This was what Hobbes did; and this was, of course, what both Mary Astell and Mary Wollstonecraft did. And for Hume, the conviction that women being deviant "had no foundation in nature" was "so obvious a subject" that, as he writes: "I believe I may spare myself the trouble of insisting on [it]" (from *A Treatise of Human Nature*, bk. 3, pt. 2, sect. 12; quoted in Agonito, 1977:123). For Hume it was as perfectly clear as it was for Astell and Wollstonecraft, that "such notions [about women's inferior nature] arise from education, from the voluntary conventions of men, and from the interest of society" (p. 124). The arguments about women's inferior nature were problems of true or untrue claims, which were relatively easy to solve, particularly in this period when people turned from God and the Bible to Nature and their own rational thinking for founding truth. Moreover, it was relatively easy for women to get furious at such ideas and to reject them, in theory as well as in practice, in an era of widespread beliefs in individual equality and of revolt against all unjust masters and their oppressive ideas.[6]

The utilitarian masculinist arguments about the necessity of keeping women in private enclosures were not in the same clear-cut way possible to test against a truth-value. As such notions became more elaborated (which does not necessarily mean more logically clear), they became a treacherous mixture of a seemingly pro-women ideology that emphasized the value of women's specific capacities and virtues, *and* degrading definitions of the powers of womanhood as being politically destructive if let free. So the "peculiarly feminine," which was explicitly defined as "inherently subversive" of social order and the state if willed freely and aptly by women with a purpose of their own, was also declared to be the absolutely necessary creative and recreative source to the existence and well-being of the modern equivalent to Divinity, that is, to Humanity.[7]

It is not easy to keep clear boundaries in a debate in which the empowered party is telling the subordinated party that what is wrong with them is precisely the same as that which is necessary for doing good to others—and therefore also to themselves. Such ideas were degrading for women given the new standard of dignified Humanity, which, following Harold Berman (1983:31–32), implied a kind of "religious . . . belief [not] in God but . . . in Man, individual Man, his Nature, his Reason, his Rights." According to Berman, this belief in Man, which emerged as a conscious notion with Lutheranism and which was embraced by the "great revolutionary minds [of] men like Rousseau or Jefferson" (pp. 31–32), was also the guiding principle for the transformation of the Western law system brought about beginning in the sixteenth century. So what was characteristic of the new "esprit de lois" was the concept of "the power of the individual, by God's grace, to change nature and to create new social relations through the exercise of his will . . . and intent" (pp. 29–30).

During the period when "the world [was] turned upside down" two lines of reasoning concerning women emerged, which, if viewed logically, flagrantly contradicted each other. But, what is logical is not always sociological. Thus, in the seventeenth and the eighteenth centuries, women were conceived, by some of the most influential philosophers and political theorists ever, to be men's equals; and if there was a difference in the gifts of nature, women rather than men were endowed with more vital powers (cf. Hobbes). The same theorists, however, declared that women had to be kept under men's sovereignty and molded for this status from infancy to old age. Hume and several others made this point extremely clear (see, for example, Thomas, 1959).

Thus women were philosophically and judicially, that is, in theory as well as in practice, moved out of the new sanctified concept of Man, out of Humanity, out of—perhaps we could say—the new "great chain of being."[8] The different links in this chain, or the states of this new being, each with its own peculiar unit of being, were Humanity and its Man, Society and its Individual, and the State and its Citizen. Women were, together with the rest of God's creation, expelled to a status exclusively of use- and exchange-value to be harnessed by Humanity. In the previous, medieval and less abstract hierarchical chain of being the various links of the chain had been the different species of God's creation—mankind, the animals, the plants—each placed after the ordering principle of closeness to God's image. Now, all the links are instead different aspects of the human being itself; and as soon as these links are concretized and made socially valid, they are all male or masculine. To be sure, even in the older worldview the male part of mankind had been standing closest to God. But a fundamental difference is that the female part had its own place in being that was not so totally dependent of the arbitrary will of individual men. Men had to negotiate with God for the control over women and were subjected under his judgment. Now, when Man was sovereign, and dignified by God "to change nature and to create new social relations through the exercise of his will," not only nature—as Berman points out—but also women "became property" and as such liable to men's use and regulation.[9]

The core of my argument is that what was so effectively oppressive of women in the new powerful metaphor of modernity was the unrestrained utilitarian rights men entitled themselves to with respect to women, and that definitions of natural, female inferiority were of secondary importance. This double-faced understanding of the early modern antifeminism—which later on became idealized and romanticized, and thus more opaque, in its continental variants—is more important as a background for perceiving the ideological conditions today than only to maintain the "appeals to nature." The crucial point is that it did not really matter whether women were seen—in the state of nature—as being equal or inferior to men; the specific capacities of women's sexuality and love were thought by "the great revolutionary minds" to be uniquely valuable as a *useful resource of nature* and, therefore, self-evidently to be exploited.

If we look at the pro-equality arguments today in public policy documents, I guess that the most usual kind still implies a utilitarian view of women. This should be revealed and criticized by feminists.

Since women became citizens, the male-dominated political philosophy, theory, and science have been ambivalent to women and sex-related questions. Issues that hinted that Man (and Man was "the goal" of science, according to "the great revolutionary minds" of the behavioralist era) was also Woman, and that this sometimes made things complicated, tended to be seen more as *troubles* than as *problems*. And as troubles they were to be settled with as little costs as possible, rather than invested in with serious interest.

Contemporary Explanations of Women's Inferior Citizenship

According to Pateman, feminist critics have shown that "post-war political science has largely ignored women as citizens; [and] when women have been mentioned, their presence has been noted through empirically unsupported and male supremacist assumptions" (Pateman, 1985:2:1). She contends that the connection between women's position in public life and their social situation was ignored by political scientists until feminist scholars themselves began to question this connection.

Even given Pateman's reservations, this is not so simple. It is true that women were ignored at large in the discipline. But women *were* considered as voters, and their behavior as voters *was* related to social conditions. They were also considered as presumptive voters in socialization studies. The inadequacy in most political science research in the behavioralist era was that social conditions as an explanatory context were not sufficiently elaborated theoretically.[10] And—precisely as Pateman herself certifies—democratic theory, whether revisionist or critical/participatory, did nothing to change this inadequacy for the better. On the contrary, the silence about women in democratic theory, since Berelson, Lazarsfeld, and McPhee (1954) in an influential chapter had declared sex to be almost "a-priori meaningless," legitimized the frequent abuse of the sex-role explanations in voting studies and socialization studies. Before 1970 there did not exist any sex-concerned parallel to Marxist class-analysis or to the analyses of the social conditions of the working class, a problem which, compared to the sex problem, was given much more interest especially in critical democratic theory. Nor were women self-evidently noticed within stratification theory.[11] While women were noticed in voting studies and in socialization studies, the absence of women within the political authorities—to use David Easton's vocabulary—was almost totally ignored. And what is not questioned does not require explaining.

If the questions posed and the explanatory frameworks used by conventional political scientists before 1970 left much to be done, feminist scholars, since the late 1960s, have done immeasureably more to deepen and broaden the empirical as well as the theoretical knowledge about how the social conditions of women influence their political situation. This deepening and broadening of explanations has, very much been limited to already conventional factors or fields. Let us begin with a summing up of the conventional arsenal of explanations.

Discussion about the different nature of men's and women's ways of exercising, or not exercising, their citizenship most often assumes an insufficiency in women; in formal education, in socialization, or in practical training in other contexts supposed to foster political competence. This is what was often summed up in the formula: the social sex role determines the political sex role (see, for example, Campbell et al., 1960). Second, at least after publication of Lipset's *Political Man* (1960), *situational hindrances,* which meant women were too busy with housework and children, became a given. A third explanatory framework came into use in empirical voting and participation studies in connection with the more general shift, or displacement of weight, within the discipline from so-called deterministic (i.e., socioeconomic) to intentional or *rational choice* explanations. Thus, for instance, the absence of women in bodies of political power, if not ignored, could be explained simply as reflecting women's choices.

I want to underline very strongly that all these kinds of explanations are or have been more or less valid. But, even when used seriously, they are limited. For example: Nobody, after Gosnell in his *Democracy: The Threshold of Freedom* ([1948] 1977), until some exceptional studies in the 1970s, asked about the conditions, in political life, for women who, by evidence, *were not* less competent in any obvious sense of that word, who *were not* hampered by either housework or children, and who *had chosen* to exercise their citizenship actively and visibly in public arenas side by side with men (see Chapter 7, note 22).

Feminist studies have approached the social conditions of political women both much more and otherwise than before. But still, when it comes to questioning and explaining or interpreting the prevailing *sex-specific* difficulties for women, an overwhelming weight of interest is still directed to the same background fields and background variables as before, let alone broadened and deepened. Thus, explanations of the type *work-situational hindrances*—now broadened to encompass the gender division of work both at home and at work outside the home—are still those by far the most usual. And, I want to underline again, working conditions *are* important restraining social realities. The *rational choice* explanation is also highly tenable, given the often very unbalanced division of work burden between women and men. It is not only that women work more than men, and more often at inconvenient hours. They have also less free or uncontingent leisure time, and they more often work in places or situations where it is extremely hard to leave for political meetings or otherwise to practical political obligations; just to mention a few points.

It is in the area of *competence* that perhaps the most important new things have happened. Feminist scholars, as well as—and this is crucial, of course—women citizens themselves, question more and more consciously the one-sidedly posed lack-of-competence view. They contend, instead, that the competence of women, for some reason or another, tends to be different from the competence of men. But it *is* competence, and competence that is not more incomplete than men's in any simple sense. Perhaps it is not better either in any simple meaning of the word. This "different voice" expresses itself in the so-called gender gap among voters,[12] in what women politicians are engaged in and how they handle their tasks, how they speak, and, at the extreme, in the fact that women have begun to shift for themselves, so to speak, in the political party system.[13]

In connection with the challenging of the lack-of-competence view, feminist scholars also report that women politicians criticize the characteristic sound of the dominant voice; as, for instance, the lack of pertinent political discussions and how such serious discussions are steadily substituted by more or less empty rhetoric.[14]

What about questioning and explaining situations as that mentioned above, when no lack of competence, no work barriers, and no choice is in the way, and still women citizens do not manage, compared to men? In other words, what about "the unexplained variance" of the "sex variable" in such situations? As far as I can see, feminist scholars have not isolated this kind of question clearly enough and perhaps, therefore, not pushed themselves strongly enough to take issue with the sex variable—or sexuality—itself, as an explanatory context.

Sexuality as a Social Condition

Sexuality is a field that has to be addressed more consciously in political theory, if we want to answer the kind of questions that arise as soon as we realize that the conventional variables, even when scrutinized and revised by feminists, do not explain the whole variance in men's and women's political behavior. Furthermore, arriving so far, we have to confront the possibility that such theoretical explanations have to be developed on more than one level; so that the most abstract explanation might not be *immediately* applicable in a language of variable concepts or even *directly* testable. My point is, however, that such "deep-theoretical" analysis, where the men/women relationship is isolated, is necessary if we want to make progress, and to satisfy demands from women to interpret situations where less obvious barriers than housework and children or lack of competence are at work. In the next section, I come back to the question of abstraction levels and different modes of conceiving reality.

Sexuality, as a multifaceted social relationship and a process of production of people, has been almost invisible in that part of feminist theory that has aimed at comprehensive, historically and empirically oriented explanations and interpretations of women's situation and of male dominance. Essay after essay, book after book has been written searching for specific grounds for the oppression of women, without ascribing any decisive weight to sexuality. This has only very recently and very slowly begun to change. Therefore, it is an advantage when Pateman contends that there is something peculiar about the "individual" that runs behind both the "citizen" and the "worker," and that this something concerns sexuality as practiced and interpreted in our society. Particularly interesting is her investigation of *consent*, how this holy principle of liberal theory loses its very meaning when applied to women within marriage and in sexual relationships with men. What is also plausible in her approach is that she focuses on women and men as agents in a specific authority structure, that is, the structure of sexual relations in general and the institution of marriage in particular. And, for her, it is urgent that the "connection between the structure of sexual relations and problems of democratic citizenship" (Pateman, 1985:3:7) shall be identified and investigated. From my perspective, however, she misses the point.

The real problem is not that *no* feminists have written about sexuality but that the work has been compartmentalized and one-sided. After the first years of the second wave of the women's movement and the beginning of the new feminist scholarship, sexuality as a field of experience and a context of discovery has more and more appeared to consist of nothing but violence and coercion or, at best, of lesbian friendship or love. Normal (simply statistically, if in no other sense normal) heterosexual relationship, not to speak about love, has so effectively been thrown out with the male-chauvinist-smelling bathwater, that we have to go to a male, sex-role sociologist from the late 1950s to encounter a scholar who raises questions about, for instance, "the theoretical importance of love" (Goode, 1959). The only relations between ordinary women and men that seem to be theoretically relevant for empirically oriented feminist scholars are relations of work; sexual power relations are reduced to questions of economic dependence or needs of capitalism, and when not, they are reduced to sexual violence: rape, sexual harassment, pornography, and so on. The closest to "ordinary" sexuality that feminist theory has come is in its socialization theories, that is, the theories of gender construction that reveal—and often very strikingly—how females and males are formed into different units of gender.

Thus, when Pateman identifies a central mechanism in the sexual relations that she assumes exerts a vital influence on individuality and citizenship, she sees only coercive sexuality, namely, rape. According to her, democratic theorists must pay attention to "the practice of rape and the interpretation of consent and non-consent which define it as a criminal offence." And, she continues: "The facts about rape are *central to the social realities which are reflected in and partly constituted by our use of the term "individual"* (Pateman, 1983:212). I agree that the sociosexual authority structure, and in particular, the institution of marriage (see Chapters 3 and 9), must be focused on. But we should not put rape in the centrum of that focus. I think that it is the "freely given"—and taken—love that should be centered (see Chapters 5 and 9). It is the "freely contracted" empowering care and ecstatic experiences in intimate love relations; and it is the "free exchange" of socio-existential, that is, personal, generic confirmation, at work and in other public contexts, that *now* are "central to the social realities which are reflected in and partly constituted by our use of the term 'individual.' " It is in these "free" affairs of transactions of existential power, power that creates and recreates individual identity and strength for agency, that men tend to exploit women. And women, we let ourselves be exploited, because we love; that is, not only "in the name of love" as if this process were only question of a "false consciousness," or a lack of (the right kind of) "desire." We know we are doing good to others and that does good to us.

Of course it is true that men's abuse of women's consent is most glaring in cases of rape. It is also true that women, especially in sexual relations, often "find that their speech is persistently and systematically invalidated [and that such] invalidation would be incomprehensible if the two sexes actually shared the same status as 'individuals' " (Pateman, 1983:213). I also think that the exposure of and the struggle against the widespread practice of sexual violence in all its various forms and social surroundings is one of the most important achievements of the women's movement. But, still, direct and open coercion or violence cannot be taken for the vital mechanism of the sexual authority structure prevailing in the formally free and equal, contemporary societies. Assuredly, in these societies, where women also now, in principle at least, are economically independent of individual men, sexual coercion and violence occur often, and, moreover, incredibly often also end in murder. But violence cannot be seen as *constitutive* of the historical form of sexual relationship that is characteristic for the type of society described above. This does not contradict the salience of the assumption that legitimate or illegitimate physical force is a steadily present possibility, even in this formally free, equal, and protected society. However, coercion and violence is as little or as much central as a vital cause in the reproduction of today's liberal male authority as it is in the reproduction of liberally embedded capitalism.

Pateman is not quite correct when she thinks that the assumption still prevails that wives are inferior and subject to their husbands by nature. To the extent it still does prevail, it is giving way to other more complicated beliefs.[15] The legal right of husbands to rape their wives has also been banned in many states and is under attack in still more. Even after this legal right is suspended, and since old-fashioned attitudes about female natural inferiority have essentially given way: the last struggle is still here—to put it a little poetically. This is the struggle over the creation and confirmation of a self-evident authority of women; a struggle for and against the self-evidence of a woman/human status as what women are—both similar to and different from men—as embodied humans, as "incarnate subjects."

My reason for bringing in this Merleau-Pontyan concept, without being able to account for it any further in this chapter, is that the utmost argument for equality, that holds for concretization, has to be established on the level of ontology. And the sociomaterial ontology of Merleau-Ponty seems to be in tune with the other theoretical views that I attempt to apply to women and men being in the (formally free and equal) world. This does not mean that ontology comes instead of empirical, historical social anlyses. Those are necessary if we want to know how the sexually differentiated *and related* humanity—women and men—continuously "change [their ontological] nature," and how they steadily "create [the] social relations" between them.

The Relevance of "Difference" and "Individuality"

Let us look a little closer at the concepts of "difference" and "individuality." Pateman, for instance, claims that democratic theory must reject a unitary (that is, masculine) conception of the individual and be grounded in a conception that recognizes sexual difference (1985, vol. 3, p. 4).

Whereas *sameness* was the ideal and the goal in the sex-role debate in the early 1960s, a new women-centered *separateness* characterized much of the feminist discussions in the 1970s. In the 1980s the notion of difference seemed to take over as a loosely uniting basis of the various branches of feminist thinking. "Difference" is a theoretically and empirically as well as politically important concept, and I have argued for this especially in my work on women and interest theory (Jónasdóttir 1985, and Chapter 7 above). But I do not share the belief, which is so widespread today, that this category is the utmost deliverer of conceptual clarifications. The main advantage for feminist studies of paying special attention to difference seems to be that it promises to help to transcend implausible dualisms concerning the men-women relations and to get away from an oversimplifying homogeneous perceptions of women and men as groups. In other words, taking difference into consideration in theory promises to guarantee that empirical diversity is not made intellectually (or paradigmatically) invisible by a priori closed categories. For me (see Chapters 3, 4, and 9), this is fully consistent with the claim that we should—*at a basic theoretical level*—conceptualize women and men as just two separate sociosexual groups; as such groups they comprise the main parties in the (historically varying) patriarchal structure.

I have also argued elsewhere (Chapter 7), from the point of view of *historically structured* sex/gender, that feminist critique of the liberal notion of "individuality" as well as of the Marxist notion of "class" challenges some very important theoretical and historical fundamentals in the prevailing view of modern society. We have to introduce into our conception of society a new basic analytical level: that of the sexually and genderically related individual. This last statement implies that it is not enough to recognize sexual "difference". If we want to *explain* the different power positions in which women and men tend to be situated, the character of the structured *relations* between the sexes has to be revealed theoretically. And for this project the usefulness of "difference" as a core concept is limited.

In the first section above, I contend that it is not primarily on the strength of defining women as *different* that the anti-feminist philosophy of the early modernity contributed to enforce male sovereignty over women. It was primarily by legitimating, by scientific confirmation, a new form of oppressive *relationship* between the sexes. What constituted this relationship was thought to be that women's essence as well as existence *was in the world to be used* by the new state-society in general and by men in particular. To follow this up in the study of women and men today it is important to make explicit a similar distinction between "difference" and "relationship."

The Importance and Limits of Different "Differences"

There are so many different ways of using "difference" that concepts that should be kept apart are easily confused. In an article about the concept of "difference," Michèle Barrett (1987) distinguishes three particular uses of the term in feminist writing and debate. She stresses that "sexual difference, positional difference and experiental diversity are best identified separately" (p. 39).

In a comment on essays from the *Signs* special issue on feminist theory (Spring 1982), Judith Kegan Gardiner (1983) is worried by the ubiquitous use of the conceptual triangle: *power—desire—difference*. Even if clearly useful words for her, they are also problematic: "In particular, our ideas about both power and desire are hampered by the dualistic and polarizing thinking connected with the concept of difference" (p. 735). And she quotes both French (Kristeva and Cixous) and American (MacKinnon) feminists on this critical point.

According to Gardiner, the category difference conflates three logically separate kinds of difference that it is important not to equate or
confuse. First, there is the kind of present/absent; as for instance
being male or not, having white skin or not, being competitive or
not being competitive. Second, difference can mean one extreme/
another extreme; as for instance powerful/powerless or competitive/
cooperative. And third, difference refers to "items selected out of an
indefinite series, as in competitive [cooperative] solitary" (p. 737).

Gardiner claims that the main deficiency of some of the most
popular feminist theories today is that they "have absorbed a polarized male view of sexual difference as present/absent as the one
model of difference," or they perceive women and men exclusively
as opposing extremes. What is worse, they often equate these two
different kinds of difference with the consequence that woman "is
always the empty chair." But, as Gardiner puts it, the effects of being
enslaved or oppressed may be very different from the effects of being
absent (1983:736–37). She seems to think that everything is said
and done about the usefulness and fallacies of "difference" as soon
as we cease to confuse or to equate the various aspects of this very
notion, and especially when we learn to be aware of the third kind
of difference, "items from an indefinite series."

As I state above, "difference," whether or not distinguished into
dissimilar concepts, does not capture the essentialities of all the levels of abstraction that feminist theory has to develop. To be sure, it
is important not to be locked into simplistic binary thinking of difference. In observations of directly, empirically accessible reality, experiential diversity as well as other kinds of difference between women
and men have to be accounted for.

I doubt whether this mode of thinking of which the notion of
"difference" is the core (perhaps we can call this mode the logic of
variable concepts) is at all fit to capture the mechanisms that produce
and reproduce the inequality between the sexes. Certainly, to say
"inequality" is to speak about differences, in some sense or another.
But if we want to explain these socially and politically relevant differences between women and men, we have to reveal the sources of

power that produce them. And for this we need the help of another mode of thinking that we might call processual thinking. Instead of variable concepts we have to apply relational concepts. Furthermore, this way of a basic-level theorizing about the relational processes in question seems to be meaningful only within the context of a materialist view of reality, and a realist view of power and causality (Sayer, 1984; Isaac, 1987).

To sum up: it is not enough to be conscious of the limitations of binary, present/absent thinking—"the logic of the digital computer" as Gardiner (1983:737) points out. The usefulness of thinking in "an indefinite series" is also limited. Not only the logic of the computer but also the conceptual logic of variables as such is insufficient when it comes to the question of conceiving, qualitatively, the process by which empowered human agents relate to one another through materially substantial, transactional practices.

This is also the reason why it is necessary to handle the explanations of women's (and men's) political behavior more seriously than has conventional political science; that is, if students of politics are interested in any knowledge other than "positive" descriptions and probable prescriptions. For example, if we are to know when it is the differences between women and men and when it is the similarities that are the most interesting outcome of a survey of, for instance, political behavior, we have to relate the issues in question to a different kind of theory. This has to be a theory about the, historically understood, social mechanisms of sexuality; that is, the social processes through which women and men produce the socioexistential conditions of each other as well as of themselves. Furthermore, the crucial feature of this composite relationship, as it tends to be practiced in Western societies today, is an inherent conflict between love and authority.

Individuality Compared to Collectivity

Given some theoretical relevance of acknowledging the sexual difference within a problematic individuality, what about the relevance of individuality itself, constrained or not? Should we not question concentration on individuality on both theoretical and political grounds? Does it not lead only, in theory, to hopeless attempts either to legitimate women's status by establishing a similar abstract "Womanity" hierarchy of being, as that which has served "(Hu)Manity," or to still more hopeless trials to get a place in the masculinist one? (Compare, for instance, Diamond and Hartsocks's criticism of individualist thinking that I deal with in Chapter 7.)

Another objection, which for instance Nancy Fraser (1986) actualizes by directing it against Seyla Benhabib (1986), is that focusing on individuality implies that the political relevance of the analysis is essentially reduced. For Fraser, it means to concentrate on the intimate voices of individual women without necessarily reflecting the collective voice of women. Fraser's critique is fruitful to a certain extent. But, for me, it also expresses a tendency to reproduce that kind of Marxist way of viewing things that was developed in connection with class and the economy, without really reflecting on whether it also fits questions related to sex. It reminds me, for instance, of how David Held interprets Marx on human nature, freedom, individuality and collectivity in his *Models of Democracy* (1987). He writes: "For Marx, it is not the single human being who is active in the historical process; rather, it is the creative interplay of collectivities in the context of society: human nature is, above all, social. By 'species being' Marx referred to the distinctive characteristics of humans, as compared with other animals" (p. 122). *Perhaps* this is plausible as long as the "class-question" alone is in focus. On the other hand, still following historical materialism but shifting the fundamental theoretical point of view so that the problematique is founded on the "sex-question," the individual becomes relevant in a different way than before. The individual actualizes itself—not as an atom—but as the needy and potentially creative, social existence she or he necessarily is, enmeshed in relations with other individuals.

One of the problems for feminism and the women's movement is that women's collectivity is steadily objected to in politics, on theoretical or practical grounds (Jónasdóttir, 1985; Chapter 7 this volume; see also Eduards, 1992). There is, at present, no other realistic way for women than to keep on striving for what they are already seeking, namely, that women and men somehow should be acknowledged as interested parties in the long since established corporate democracy. But this does not contradict the belief of mine that one of the most important things feminism has to say and do is to make clear and effective the perception of reality that collectivism and individualism need not and must not exclude each other. To be sure, several voices of socialism have asserted, too, such a perception of reality. But to the extent these voices have been allowed to be heard, they have, more often than not, come to mean only the collectivity of individual brothers.

Sexual Equality and Women-Worthy Society

Many people think today that we are in the middle of a fundamental transformation from "modern times" to something postmodern, and that this transformation includes the whole Western/modern legal tradition, the modern state, church, philosophy, university, literature, "and much else that is modern" (Berman, 1983:4). If this is right, it means both an end of an era and a beginning of a new, and the most difficult problem in such a transitory period is the future (cf. Halsaa, 1988). Against such a background there is an endless number of questions to be asked about women's situation as citizens.

What happens with women's position as the basic institutional pillars of society change; institutions such as Monogamy, Family (status of parents and children), Private Property, Inheritance, Contract—to follow Brecht's definition (1959:148–49)? What are the new and becoming "specific social tasks" to be performed? What values are to be backed with what power (cf. Berman's [1983:5] and Stinchcombe's [1968:182] definitions of "institution")?

A key concept of value and one of the main sources of law in the Western legal tradition is *equity*—defined initially as "reason and conscience" (Berman, 1983:11). The multiple meaning of this word today—"fairness" referring to substantial values as well as formal "disinterestedness" and "justice" in general—shows that it has framed itself after the changing needs of the time. What, then, would the postmodern kind of justice or equity be like? Equity also connotes equality. If equality is what women want, what kind of equality would be realistic—given the changing social context—*and* what kind of equality would be women-worthy? In Sweden "equal rights" and "equal results" are often put as the two possible alternatives; the first seen as reflecting the liberal, the other as the social-democratic ideal types of equality. "Unlike but equally valued" is a well-known sex-role maxim that has long been shared in many ideological camps. In the West, we seem to be leaving behind us all these entries into the equality question as not being fully satisfying. What else could there be? What do women want? Or, rather, what is relevant for women and for feminism in the existing views of the present and future of democracy?

In her article "Private Rights and Public Virtues: Women, the Family, and Democracy," Carol Gould (1983:6) argues that freedom, meaning self-development, reciprocity, and democracy, should build the value framework for feminism. Reciprocity, the most highly developed form of which is mutuality, presupposes and goes beyond equality "in that it involves the recognition by each agent of the differences of the other, in terms of the other's own projects and goals"; and in the mutual form of reciprocal relations "each agent consciously endeavors to act in such a way as to enhance the agency of the other." And, according to Gould, for these values to be effective, both material and social conditions must be available through which agents can achieve their purposes (Gould, 1983:5).

Sharing Gould's arguments in general, I am developing a thesis that goes one step further than hers concerning how the material and social conditions should be politically structured. Women (and even men) are already demanding an active presence in politics *as women* (and *as men*). This means that demands not only for particular material issues but for a shift in "the requirements for the system" (Berelson et al., 1954) are being addressed to the gate-keepers of

Western political democracy. This means to demand that sexuality be acknowledged at the side of economy as a fundamental generative, material source of society, a nutritive "trade and industry" that, for centuries, as is the case with economy, has been organized on a cleavage basis. This means to demand that the participatory membership of women and men in society somehow be arranged— openly and consciously—with sex as one of the main bases of interest.

In what specific capacity should women claim to be an interested party in organizing, leading, and governing society? In their capacity of motherhood seems to be the most usual feminist answer (see, for instance, Halsaa, 1988). This answer is at least partly founded on the fact that the ability to give birth is the most obvious point of difference between the sexes; and because motherhood obviously also implies a kind of vital power, not to mention all its positive values, this answer appears to be very plausible. I share Ruddick's (1980) case for "maternal reason" and agree that this reason has to be voiced largely in the women-worthy society, but I do not think this is precisely the way. Demanding a new form of citizenship for women as mothers would be to claim space in the public communicative action for still only one aspect of womanhood, albeit a concrete one. This is why I think we have to conceive of "women *as women*" as sexed beings, as simply the human womankind. Sex itself is the only capacity that relates *all* women to one another, even if this relation is often weak. And, perhaps the most important argument: since the dawn of patriarchy, until its change into its prevailing free and equal form, women have been excluded from equal standing with mankind, not in any particular aspect but *as such.* Moreover, the social conditions of many competent, not work-hindered, choice-potent women, ever since the so-called breakthrough of democracy, indicate that what, still, is wrong with women is—that they are women.

Women have too long been used oppressively—for their own good. Now women are mobilizing all over the world to use their own powers—for their own purpose.

chapter 9

Taking Sex Seriously

A substantial part of my work in this book consists of a critical examination of feminist theory, especially its socialist feminist variant, which I consider to be both promising and unsatisfactory. The outcome, however, of my critical analysis is an attempt to develop an alternative approach to patriarchy as a theoretical problem. In the preceding chapters criticism and constructive thinking are largely interwoven, and in this critical/constructive web I sketch three distinct but related theories. First, I propose an alternative feminist materialist conception of history that forms a "distinct theoretical project," or perhaps better still, a specific "research tradition."[1] Second, and based on this alternative metatheoretical conception, I outline a historically specific theory of contemporary patriarchy in the formally/legally equal Western societies. Third, I take a step toward the development of a normatively oriented theory of women's interests and the preconditions for a democratic, women-worthy society.

In this last chapter I wish to summarize my critical assessments as well as my attempts at formulating an alternative, constructive thesis concerning the conceptualization, explanation, and elimination of contemporary patriarchy. I say "thesis" rather than theory because there is still much left to be done to move feminist historical materialist analysis of patriarchy in a new direction.

The Impasse of Socialist Feminist Theory: A Radical Critique

I agree with Josephine Donovan in her criticism of the indiscriminate deconstruction of certain core concepts in feminist theory. She states that "the future of feminist theory lies in a rapproachement with Marxism" (Donovan, 1985:214). For me, this presupposes a *radical shift* in the fundamentals of that extensive branch of feminist thinking that from the start grounded its analysis in Marxist method. By its followers, socialist feminism is assumed to constitute a "distinct theoretical project" (Jaggar, 1983:118). But given its present status, socialist feminist analysis cannot answer its most basic question about why women are, have been, and continue to be the *sex* that is systematically dominated.

Socialist feminism embarked on a program aimed at developing a "theory and practice that will synthesize the best insights of radical feminism and of the Marxist tradition and that simultaneously will escape the problems associated with each" (Jaggar, 1983:123). In their theoretical practice, however, socialist feminists never took really seriously the questions that the radical feminists had raised. And despite all their declarations about the necessity of transcending conventional Marxism, increasing numbers of socialist feminists adopted the Marxist viewpoint of the problems "associated with" radical feminism. This "loyalty" came to mean that socialist feminists saw as their main task the working out of solutions to many of the problems generally associated with classical Marxism, such as the need to develop further a theory of how ideological forces under capitalism form the consciousness of individual subjects, and the need to make class theory more concrete. Furthermore, an influential strand of socialist feminist thought saw it as their role to deliver an all-embracing or total theoretical solution to all systems of domination (cf. Jaggar, 1983:125–26).

Initially, the general subject matter of socialist feminist analysis seemed relatively clear. In short, it was the new or re-actualized "feminist questions," particularly those of radical feminism. The questions raised by radical feminists in the late 1960s and 1970s revealed "new" research areas that needed new theories. Their questions dealt with sexuality (heterosexuality as well as homosexuality and lesbianism), with motherhood, love, housework, the marriage contract, and even the entire male-dominated culture (see, e.g., Hole and Levine, 1974). Later, sociosexual evils such as abuse of women, rape, incest, increasingly misogynist pornography, and harassment of women at work, were drawn out of the "dark closet" of personal matters. When old and new "women's issues" were included (the conditions of women working outside the home, daycare facilities, issues of health and social security, wage equality, access to power positions, and so on), the scope of feminist subject matter, in theory as well as practice, extended over every segment of society. On the whole, feminist inquiry today, radical or not, addresses the circumstances in which women and men as social sexes exist, produce, organize, and govern society, now as well as in the past.

Socialist feminist theorizing developed in such a way, however, that it obstructed the detection of a specific sociosexual dimension in society and history. This in turn became an obstacle in utilizing Marxist method to its fullest potential, which was the second part of their "theoretical project."[2]

Critical Theses

Work Fixation

Almost from the beginning socialist feminism got stuck in the basic problematique of Marxism, the domain of political economy. The new theoretical program came to center on the concept of "work" (or "social labor"). The everlasting centrality within historical materialism of "work/labor" as the basic concept of social practice is never questioned. It is used regardless of what kind of human activity is to be understood. Alison Jaggar's (1983) thorough account of socialist feminist theory exhibits clearly this unreflective adherence to the fundamentals of the classical Marxist research tradition. She sees nothing strange in, for example, writing about "women's *sexual labor*" (p. 305) or that "the means to satisfy the needs for children and for sexual and emotional satisfaction [are] produced through human *labor*" (p. 135). The following quotation from Jaggar's account reveals in a nutshell the impasse in socialist feminist analysis: "Radical feminists have identified sexuality and procreation as areas of human activity that are susceptible to political analysis. Socialist feminists claim that these practices *fall within the domain of political economy*" (p. 135; italics added in all three quotations).

Although lately some socialist feminists have raised their voices against the limitations of the "paradigm of production"[3] none of them has actually departed from conventional Marxist understanding of historical materialism. This is why their often deplored inability to conceptualize and explain patriarchy as being relatively independent of capitalism (or other forms of economic systems) persists.

Confusions About the Theoretical Status of "Men"

From the start, socialist feminists have hesitated to ascribe any theoretical significance whatsoever to "men" (see, e.g., Eisenstein, 1981:8–9). Rather than viewing this as a result of recent deconstructionism (in which collective concepts like "women" and "men" are problematized in a special way; see, e.g., Riley, 1988), it should be seen in the more general context of the long-standing confusion over the relationship between agents and structures. If our aim is to build a structural theory, then what status—if any—do individual agents or collective agents have in this theory? But to exclude men from explanatory frameworks, and at the same time claim that patriarchy or male-dominated structures continue to prevail, results in something of a paradox. This, in turn, becomes an obstacle in the quest for more precise questions about *the sociosexual relational activities that are supposed to be the operative mechanisms that hold together a particular societal structure.* It becomes difficult to pose questions that deal more exactly with *what* is being done to us, to paraphrase Juliet Mitchell (1986:92), and by whom. And, if (the) male power (that feminists speak of) does not emanate solely from economic arrangements, then what are its other sources and what is it made up of more specifically? Furthermore, in the absence of questions that deal with such aspects of male power, it seems unnecessary to analyze in more depth the notions commonly used to designate "the traffic in women," the concept of "oppression," for example. In particular, men's traffic in women remains vaguely conceptualized.

My criticism is not intended to reduce the importance of the great number of excellent empirical studies that reveal women's oppressive experiences and the numerous ways that they actively cope with or create an existence of relative dignity for themselves. Nor do I claim that prevailing socialist feminist theory is worthless. The aim of my critique is to argue that there still exists a vital *theoretical* lacuna in socialist feminism. There is no *feminist* historical materialist theory of *social being*, or *social existence* (as distinct from *consciousness*). This statement presupposes that the materialist concept of "social being" *must be defined distinctively in the feminist problematique.* There is something more being done to women *as women* than the shaping of our consciousness through the gendered division of labor and the effects of the social apparatus as a whole.

No Theory of Sexuality

Socialist feminism lacks a theory of sexuality *as a field of specific relational practices* because of its failure to recognize a theoretically significant sex/gender dimension in social reality that is relatively independent of work and economy. It lacks a theory that can approach historically and explain structurally the changing patriarchal relations between women and men *as sexes.*

This deficiency is all the more remarkable if we consider that sexuality as a specific field of productive human activity is not only identified as being of central importance by radical feminists but also explicitly included as one of the "first premises of materialist method" by its founders. Sexuality is seen as being one of the (four) "fundamental conditions" of history, a "circumstance which, from the very outset, enters into historical development" (Marx and Engels, 1970:42–52).

Moreover, and perhaps "surprisingly," as Shlomo Avineri (1968:89) puts it, Marx (in the *Economic and Philosophic Manuscripts of 1844,* 1977b:89–90) "discovers [the] paradigm of the [fully humanized] future in the relationship between the sexes."

> According to Marx [to quote Avineri further] the unique pattern of these relations has a systematic significance which makes it possible to project them as a general model for the structure of human relations in socialist society. Sexual relations are at once necessary and spontaneous; they are also other-oriented *par excellence.* Man's need for a partner in the sexual relationship makes his own satisfaction depend upon another person's satisfaction. By definition, sexual relations are reciprocal. If they are unilateral they cease to be a relationship, degrading the other person to the status of a mere object, rather than a co-equal subject. (p. 89)

Surely, and this is extremely important, the point is not that "the good society" should be, or could be constructed like a family or a love relationship. That would be a romantic illusion and a reductionistic fallacy. The point is, rather, as Avineri also emphasizes, that:

> For Marx the family and sexual relations can be a paradigm only so far as they point to the possibility of other-oriented relations. The whole problem is to avoid romanticizing the family (or sex) and to reach at the same time a solution that will make the basic structural principle of sexual relations into a universal principle of social organization. (p. 91)

Even if other Marxists hitherto have largely ignored this alternative way of theorizing change, feminists could have been expected to take it seriously and put it to the test. As far as I know, however, the sole feminist piece of work that deals with this theme is an article by Virginia Held from 1976.

What socialist feminism does have is a theory, or rather theories, of *femininity* (and masculinity). Apart from studying women in the social labor process (wage work as well as housework) and what positions women have in the "occupational hierarchy" (see Chapter 4), socialist feminists have hitherto concentrated almost exclusively on *socialization theory*. For them the important thing is to find out how "a systematic social apparatus . . . takes up females as raw materials and fashions domesticated women as products" (Rubin, 1975:158); how children are formed into different genders by mothers who are present and fathers who are absent; how women develop a specific consciousness by performing specific types of work and thus, why women choose or are allotted certain gendered "places" in the class hierarchy. This has been brought about with the help of anthropological structuralism, various strands of psychoanalytic theory, Marxist theory of ideology, and, more recently, poststructuralist theory; all of them more or less revised for feminist purposes.

All this is valuable but insufficient in fulfilling the aim of the socialist feminist theoretical program. Theories of socialization and the attempts to concreticize class theory by gender do not create the need for a departure from the domain of political economy; but this is what must be done.

One important reason why socialist feminists are unable to actually transcend conventional Marxism and reorientate historical materialism is that men are for the most part absent in socialist feminist analyses. With very few exceptions (see Chapter 4), men are either ignored or perceived as theoretically irrelevant in the analysis of women's oppression. When men *are* seen as theoretically significant it is only as economic beings and not as a sex.

The Total Ambition's Detrimental Implications

A characterizing feature of much of socialist feminist theory is the idea that all social systems of domination (class, gender, race, age, and others) should or could be accounted for in one theory. For me this is an untenable total ambition *with regard to basic theory*, while it is highly plausible with regard to empirical research and political activities. (I deal with this at some length in Chapters 3 and 4.)[4] Related to this problem is the fact that feminist theorists seldom distinguish clearly between different levels of analytical abstraction. Many writers seem to remain unclear about which concepts and assumptions are appropriate at different levels. This lack of clarity is the cause of many fruitless debates about key concepts, such as "patriarchy," the very conception of "women" and "men" as groups, and the question of what is "common" and what is "different" in the oppression or the interests of women.

To take an example from historical materialism, it is of vital importance to be clear about whether we are moving around in the dizzy heights of such diluted creatures as "commodity" and "money" or whether we are talking about concrete people divided into social classes. In the first case our analysis is on a very abstract, although historically specific, level where "labor-in-general" meets its structural counterpart "capitalist power." Here the concept of "class (relationship)" is used in the abstracted sense, in order to show analytically how the appropriation of surplus value takes place and, thus, how the accumulation of capital is possible, When, on the other hand, we talk about class in the sense of the division of people in the labor process, or in the sense of grouping people according to wages, education, and so on, we are operating on quite a different level of concretization.

My point is that socialist feminists have not been sufficiently aware of the analytical problem of different levels of abstraction. This has resulted in unnecessary confusion about some of feminism's most central concepts. The concept of "patriarchy," for instance, is as useful as the concept of "class society" is in Marxism, roughly speaking. In neither case do these rather abstract concepts give any detailed information about any specific historical form of society, and still less about this or that concrete society or about particular groups within various societies.

Lacking Elements Needed for a Basic Theory

Socialist feminists' fixation on the concept of work, their reluctance to take sexuality and men seriously theoretically, and the confusion that has arisen because of their ambition to cover in one and the same *theory* all systems of domination, has been detrimental to their analytical goal. They *cannot identify clearly any of the main elements needed for the very theory they called for initially.*[5] They have yet to identify a specific and "essential" sex/gender *relationship*, one that generates sex/gender specific *practice* or creative *activity*, a specific human development capacity or *power* over the use and control of which certain groups of people struggle. Therefore no sex/gender specific *structure on the basic level of social being* has been distinguished. Nor have they been able to determine which specific *institution(s)* is/are more central than others in the reproduction of patriarchy. These elements are a necessary minimum in order to build a distinct feminist materialist conception of history, and a theory of contemporary patriarchy appropriate to that conception.

Lacking Gender-Specific Agency-Structure Mechanisms

Another way of displaying the analytical shortcomings of socialist feminists is to ask *which means or mechanisms of social control (over women) they pay attention to* in their theoretical construction and which they do not. Central among such mechanisms are (1) the legal system, (2) the cultural or ideological climate (in a society as well as in groups within a society), (3) the socialization process, (4) social interaction in direct person-to-person relationships, and, as a continuous outcome of all this, (5) the prevailing social structures.

A vital flaw in socialist feminist basic theory is that the *social interactions between women and men in direct person-to-person relations* are consistently overlooked. These interactions occur constantly, not only within the family or in intimate relations, but throughout society as a whole. But socialist feminist theorists seem to have lost, or have never really grasped, "the idea of *personal interactions as a political arena*, a brilliant concept brought most sharply into focus for feminists by Kate Millett's analysis of sexual politics."[6]

A further consequence of this is that the fifth way, mentioned above, of focusing mechanisms of control, namely, by identifying certain social structures, remains unclear. Thus we cannot identify *what actually constitutes patriarchy as a structure* as distinct from the structural elements of class or something else (cf. the deadend of Hartmann's theory, discussed in Chapter 4).

A theory of what goes on interactively between the sexes at the level of social existence must be framed as an internal, or "intrinsic," theory of the sociosexual process itself,[7] that is, the sociosexual process must be conceived as being able to explain itself. My answer to the question "What is being done to us" as women, in the free and equal, yet still patriarchal, Western society? is that men exploit a certain power resource in women, namely, the power of love. That is, basically, what the contemporary, Western sex-struggle is about.

Toward a Reorientated Feminist Materialist Analysis

The aim of applying Marxism as method is to be able to conceptualize and explain patriarchy. It is important to identify different aspects of patriarchy as a theoretical problem. In Chapter 2 I list three main aspects of the question how to explain patriarchy: (1) the anthropological question (the question of the earliest origins of patriarchy); (2) the historical question (the question of various phases of and transitions in patriarchy including the question of the historical genesis of contemporary Western patriarchy), and (3) the theoretical question (the question of how contemporary patriarchy is structured and how it is reproduced).

In addition, a fourth aspect may be distinguished (see Chapter 3). Here we are concerned with the level at which it is at least phenomenologically meaningful[8] to raise questions about the essentials of human social existence, such as, What characterizes human labor or human love as types of activity? The ontological question about what labor is, or what love is, must be kept distinct from the question of what counts as work (or labor) and what counts as love in certain historical periods and in particular societies and cultures.

My primary emphasis has been on the third question, how patriarchy in today's formally/legally equal Western society is structured
and reproduced. But in order to come to grips with this problem, it
was necessary to embark on a reevaluation of the methodological, or
ontological, fundamentals of historical materialism. A slightly different way of describing what I have done is to apply the metatheoretical vocabulary of Larry Laudan, which centers on the concept of
"research tradition."

According to Laudan (1977), a research tradition is, in short, *"a
set of general assumptions about the* [ontological] *entities and processes
in a domain of study, and about the appropriate method to be used for
investigating the problems and constructing the theories in that domain"*
(p. 81). Thus, "a research tradition provides a set of guidelines for
the development of specific theories [belonging to that tradition]."
But research traditions, unlike the theories belonging to them, *"are
neither explanatory, nor predictive, nor directly testable"* (pp. 79, 81).
Furthermore, the fruitfulness of a research tradition depends on the
specific theories it spawns; that is, on "those theories' ability to allow
for the posing and solving of puzzles and problems arising within
that tradition" (Ball, 1987:29). Thus, *"a successful research tradition is
one which leads, via its component theories, to the adequate solution of
an increasing range of empirical and conceptual problems"* (Laudan,
1977:82; italics original in all citations above). Examples of research
traditions in the field of social or human sciences are behavioralism,
historical materialism/Marxism, psychoanalytic theory, linguistically
grounded structuralism, and others.

A research tradition thus comprises two distinct but, according
to Laudan, "often intimately related" (p. 80) components, an ontological one and a methodological one. A research tradition can be
reduced to what I elsewhere simply call "method". Laudan's conception enables us in a simple and lucid fashion to distinguish between
the two main metatheoretical components without losing sight of
the fact that the two are more or less closely intertwined. It also
differentiates clearly between empirically and normatively oriented
theories on one hand and the general assumptions about what consti-

tutes society and what makes history (the "core ontological entities and processes") on the other.

By using this conceptual framework to conclude my critique I show that the prevailing socialist feminist analysis has failed to work out a plausible historical-materialist theory of contemporary patriarchy because it lacks the main ontological "entities and processes" as well as "the appropriate methods" needed for the construction of such a theory. Consequently, the socialist feminist theory lacks the appropriate conceptual framework needed for a feminist theory of change as well as for a feminist analysis of politics. Here I refer mainly to the socialist feminists' use of "need" (or collective needs) as a core analytical concept in political analyses. The use of the concept "need" has led many socialist feminists to abandon the concepts "interests" and "rights," which have been defined as being too bourgeois, or not at all appropriate for the concerns of women. I will return to the question of interests versus needs as the last point in my list of constructive theses.

As I remark in Chapter 1, the shortcomings in socialist feminist theory accounted for above have not been compensated for in radical feminism. In neither case are the general assumptions or the specific theories tenable, when evaluated from the perspective chosen here—a feminist realist variant of the historical materialist research tradition. Furthermore, the impasse in radical feminism was traced to the break (in the latter half of the 1970s) with the kind of approach begun (or restored) by Kate Millett and Shulamith Firestone.

Firestone (1971) traces the causes of women's oppression to the burden of childbearing and recommends artificial reproduction of the species as the number one solution to the tyranny of nature.[9] I will not comment on this here, yet it does seem rather remarkable that no one has noticed or found it interesting that Firestone *also* states in her otherwise frequently acclaimed chapter on love that "love, perhaps even more than childbearing, is the pivot of women's oppression today" (p. 126).

This duality in Firestone's analysis regarding the main site of women's oppression is worth a thorough study. But my reason for bringing her in at this point is to show that Firestone actually furnishes us with something that a socially and historically significant analysis of patriarchy cannot do without. Despite her ambiguities and the preliminary character of her theorizing she points to a sex/gender specific *activity*, a *transformative power*, of such great importance to societal organization that even its analysis seems to "threaten the very structure of culture" (p. 126). This is the social potency of love.

Firestone did not complete a tenable theory, nor, surely, will I. I believe, however, that a viable point of departure is one where the construction of a distinctive ontology (in the Laudanian sense) seriously takes into consideration what Firestone calls "an untried third alternative," namely, "a materialist view of history based on sex itself" (p. 5). The element to start with, then (recalling the "appropriate methods" given by historical materialism), for such an ontology cannot be the concept of "sexuality," coercive or noncoercive, but the practical activity/power and the social relationships that *constitute sexuality* as a distinct current in human social life. The "practice of love" or the "social organization of love", and "sociosexual relations", must be the starting point. These "entities and processes" must displace "labor" and "socioeconomic relations" so that they limit the application of the domain of labor, within a more developed materialist research tradition.[10]

Constructive Theses

In the following I elaborate on six of my constructive theses. Inevitably, these include more or less of a mixture of both general assumptions (on the ontological level of a research tradition) and elements thought to be constitutive for a historically specific theory about why men continue to be empowered as men.

The Essential Relationship

The social relationship that constitutes the structural basis of contemporary partiarchy is the power relation between women and men *as sexes.* According to this view, patriarchy does *not* refer *primarily* to relations between men or to relations in which women are oppressively entangled with other structures, or systems, such as the economic system or the state. Nor does patriarchy refer primarily to symbolic systems of gender or to gendered linguistic signs, and thus theoretically interesting/significant only insofar as they signify other power relations (economic, political, cultural).[11]

I do not mean to say that relations of solidarity (and competition) between men are not a constitutive part of patriarchy. They are necessary in the same manner that relations of solidarity and competition between capitalists are a necessary part of capitalism. This component, however, cannot replace the relationship between labor and capital, the very structure in which the social work-process is brought about and framed. Similarly, if women are defined as a nonactive party in patriarchy's basic structure, and seen only as a resource acted upon and used by men, then women are, by definition, abandoned as vital agents in social construction and as their own liberators as well.

This thesis does not say that women are not oppressed by and dependent on capital and the state. Obviously they are, although differently than men, and the question of utmost importance for feminist theory is, Why differently? This, in turn, makes it imperative to get beyond the use of "difference" as a basic theoretical concept (see Chapter 8).

To view patriarchally structured sexuality as both necessary and sufficient for explaining the continuation of male dominance is about as unrealistic as to think that class-societies are held together and reproduced exclusively by economic means or restricted to the work process (see the last section in Chapter 4). So what this thesis does *not* say is that sexuality is the sole site of women's oppression.

This thesis does not, however, rule out the importance of understanding how gendered codes of meaning are liable to signify hierarchical power relations in the most varying social contexts. But to understand oppressively organized sex/gender systems on the level of cultural meanings/signs is not enough. Structured sociosexual relations are, here, claimed to be historically significant in and of themselves. Therefore they must be theoretically conceived, above all, on the level of the actual social being or social existence.

This thesis *does* say that a vital element of patriarchy, operative in maintaining sex/gender inequality, especially in the formally-legally equal societies of today, is embedded in a specific kind of productive, or creative,[12] process, a continuous and interactive process that goes on between women and men as socially moulded sexes. This is the process of creation and recreation of people as social existences. What happens in this process varies both historically and culturally; we could even speak about various *modes of production—or creation—of people.*

In the specific form of society that is in focus here, the forces inherent in this process are such that people need to be raised and replenished (or created/recreated) as individual and autonomous agents, or persons. At the same time the means for satisfying these needs presupposes a specific kind of intercourse that in turn threatens the possibilities for the maintenance and growth of the desired value: that is, individuality and personal autonomy. This type of social intercourse goes on continuously in every sphere of society and must be identified and understood as a relatively independent feature or dimension of society.

Why focus especially on *women* and *men* as sexes? Doesn't that mean that the heterosexual organization of society is somehow taken for granted? How can we account for homosexual relations when using this approach? The answer is that the patriarchal organization of heterosexuality is crucial since it is the dominant form of sexual organization. As such it functions oppressively both internally and with respect to people who engage in other forms of sexual encounters. Therefore, heterosexuality must be the pivotal axis in this substantive empirically oriented theory.

To propose that women and men are the main parties in a feminist analysis of society does not mean—and this is extremely important—that I conceive of them simply as biological entities, and even less as universal, static categories. I view women and men in a historical, materialist, and *realist* way. Women and men as "enminded bod-ies"[13] are always formed/form themselves under certain historical, sociosexual circumstances. The sociosexual circumstances, in turn, influence, and are influenced by, other social circumstances, such as those prevailing in the economy and state. In the particular kind of society in question here, women and men *are* the kinds of people they are, *historically*, at present.

To speak of what women and men are is, thus, actually to speak about the social conditions in and on which they act. Thus, the at-tempt to conceptualize what women and men are and what they do as sexes does not necessarily imply any kind of mysterious essential-ism or biological reductionism.[14] But it is not solely social-construc-tivism either. On the contrary, the realist, historical-materialist mode of thinking opposes, and goes beyond these views. It displaces the "human essence" in the romantic/idealist as well as the biologistic sense. It displaces also the philosophical structuralist universalism, which rejects "human essence" only to re-establish it as a "thought object" (be it in linguistic terms or others). Moreover, the realist way of thinking replaces the, likewise denaturalized, sociological social-constructivist view of human nature which, as Kate Soper (1979) writes, only "give[s] us again a dumb generality in which all individ-uals participate. . . . The human essence is no more always [or, per-haps better: no more *exclusively*] the essence of its particular time than it is the essence of all time" (p. 99).[15]

Why then speak about the sex/gender relationship as an "essen-tial relationship"? By characterizing a particular feature of social life as "essential" I mean that it, at a minimum, must fulfill two different but related criteria: that it is *insubstitutable* and, that it is *imbued with causal power* in the realist sense (see below). Sexuality is such an essential feature because it is an organic source of society, it is the realization of humankind. People cannot "make . . . their [own] kind" (Marx and Engels, 1970:49) from wood or metals, by rational decisions or administration alone, or solely by means of an ever so developed technology. The raw materia and the means of production with which people make people are, and cannot be other than, the enminded sexed human bodies. This insubstitutability implies that people as sociosexual beings are endowed with a certain power, a certain creative and, thus, transformative capacity that—when exerted—may not only result in the making of new people literally but also continuously makes and remakes people, both children and adults.

In the search for a term that could denote precisely this human capacity, this "practical, human sensuous activity", a term that could distinguish it both from the power of labor or work,[16] and from the capacity to act in administration and government, I initially used the concept "care" (see Chapter 5). Soon, however, I came to believe that "love" is the best term available if "care" and "erotic ecstacy" are incorporated as its two main elements. To focus on sexual love—in the sense of interactive practices relating people actually and potentially as sexes—implies that the way sexual love is practiced influences significantly not only the way other love relations are practiced, for instance, those between parents and children, but also the way people tend to practice person-to-person relations in other social contexts.

Love: A Causal Power in History

Love is a specific kind of alienable and causally potent human power, the social organization of which is the basis of contemporary Western patriarchy. Love refers to human beings' capacities (powers) to make—and remake—"their kind," not only literally in the procreation and socialization of children but also in the creation and recreation of adult people as socio-sexual *individuated* and *personified* existences.

Following the realist view, I use a naturalist, nonmechanistic (or non-Humean) notion of "power" and "causality."[17] Fundamentally, the various forms of social power are human capacities, powers or forces ("powers" or "forces" in Hobbes's, "Krafte" in Marx's vocabulary). In everyday language we speak about labor power and labor force, about the force of someone's intellect and the like. Social powers are productive or creative human capacities of various kinds that people "alienate"—as, for instance, Locke and Marx put it—and fuse with external objects resulting in the transformation of these objects. This means that when we act upon objects, people, or nonhuman materia, we exert power in the sense that transformative or causal forces are brought into use. Human societies and history are both the intended and the unintended consequences of people's enjoying/using the various powers of their specifically human enminded bodies. The basis of human social life is that people, related in one way or another to each other, use their powers to act upon nature. Nature is the absolute source of life, and for people nature has two sides, the environmental and the human side.

What is crucial is that throughout recorded history the essential human powers have been employed in social circumstances where certain groups of people systematically, and entitled by various forms of legitimacy, control and use the powers of other groups.

But what powers are "essential" in the sense that they are of consequence for historical movement? In other words, what powers are theoretically significant in order to understand historical change, and, thus also, for discussions of purposively willed social development?

The ability of human beings to exert their individual, free will (power) to make rational choices would be a contemporary liberal theoretician's typical answer. The classical Marxist answer would go further and include human labor power, meaning the ability of human beings to combine rational thinking and practice into an effective force with the objective of creating new "things." (Both sides would then include something about unintended consequences.)[18]

In my second thesis I thus propose that love, or socially organized love (as an interhuman, creative, and practical activity), is in fact a third main kind of power that moves history, and that it should, therefore, be seen as theoretically significant and be taken seriously as such.

Thus, as human capacity to act wilfully and rationally for collective purposes is controlled (appropriated and protected) by the state, and human labor power is harnessed (extorted and enabled to develop) by ruling classes, so also human love power is used (taken rightfully and let free to flow) largely for male-determined purposes.

A thesis on love as a causal power in history can, and must, be grounded in at least two, or perhaps three, ways: methodologically (the ontological level included); by means of historical, empirical evidence; and in political-theoretical, or normatively oriented, terms. This means that a theory centered on historical, sociosexual relationships and the love process would develop as a theory of and for social change.

My presupposition is that in our society human love has, especially during the last half of this century, attained an alienated status comparable to that of human labor in the eighteenth century. The organization of freely bought and sold labor power was at that time crucial as a historical precondition to the development of Western capitalism.

Love Power Versus Male Authority

The form of the sociosexual relationship that dominates today is the one where women's love power, freely given, is *exploited* by men.

It is not enough to say that women are oppressed when we want to characterize today's patriarchal power relationship between the sexes. If the analysis ends at the level of abstraction where the use of the concept of "oppression" belongs, then we only know that something occurs systematically that upholds sociosexual inequality. But we do not know what happens or how.

What occurs can and should be understood as an exploitative transference, from women to men, of a specific sociosexual capacity, love power. The expression "women who love too much" has been used in particular to characterize relations where battered women stay with husbands or lovers despite repeated abuse. Irrespective of why women stay in such relations, the expression itself is indeed a more appropriate description of the "normal" nonabusive man/ woman relation today. It is in this typical relationship—built on some sort of partial equality but where nevertheless, in the end, the result is constant inequality—that women love too much in the first place.

This is possible—without any visible coercion—because of the different situational conditions on which women and men meet and interact precisely as sexes. My usage of the terms "meeting" and "interaction in meetings," in person-to-person, giving and taking relations, should be seen as a parallel to (and thus also distinct from) the buying and selling in markets. So the "persons" who meet in this drama are "Woman" and "Man."

"Woman" comes to this meeting and is, so to speak, the owner of her capacity to love, which she can give of her own free will. No law or other formal rules can force her into a relationship with "man." And still there are forces in these circumstances. "Woman" needs to love and to be loved in order to be socioexistentially empowered, in order to be a person. But she is without effective control over how or in what forms she can legitimately use her capacity; she lacks the authority to determine the conditions of love in society and what its products should be like.

"Man," on the other hand, comes to this meeting, not so much in order to love but in order "to let me love him [and] . . . to let him through me love himself" (Hermodsson, 1980:36). Already when coming to the meeting, "Man" is entitled and authorized to make use of his entire range of existing and potential capacities as a person. "Man" is thus empowered as a person, a situation that is quite different from that of "Woman." Yet in order to maintain this empowerment, he is dependent on having access to "Woman"'s particular creative powers. Those who meet are, in short, women as sexual beings and men as personal authorities. This means that men, in a different way than women, can act independently in particular sociosexual meetings. Men are not, in the way that women are, circumstantially "forced" to award their sexual capacity to the other sex, if they dislike the conditions offered. Men can stand off temporarily; they are less dependent on a particular woman than women are on a particular man.

The assumption that there is a social process where the power *of* love and the power *over* love are systematically divided in such a way that women are exploited by men must be understood as a historical necessity or contingent force. As the capitalist must exploit the laborer in order to remain a capitalist, men today are dependent on an exploitative "traffic in women" if they are to remain the kind of men that historical circumstances force them to be. In neither case does this structural force exclude the possibility for other kinds of socioeconomic and sociosexual arrangements to exist as nondominating modes of economic and sex/gender production, respectively.

The consequence of today's exploitation of love power (alienated as sexual goods) is that men's effective possibilities to operate in society as the self-evidently worthy and able (hu)Man(kind) is steadily produced and reproduced (although not stated explicitly in legal terms any more), so that they can bring about the generally (hegemonically) valued goals of Man in ever increasing volumes. This means that in those cases when men lack human worth and socially produced power of agency, it is not because of their sex but because of other more or less fundamental circumstances (class, race/ethnicity, or other "handicaps"). But compared to women within all social strata men are the effectively worthy kind.

The consequence of the exploitative love process is for most women a continuous struggle on the boundaries of "poverty" in terms of their possibilities to operate in society as self-assured and self-evidently worthy people exerting their capacities effectively and legitimately. Statistical evidence of a sex/gender hierarchy in all areas of society indicates this state of affairs. Another can be found in the main type of arguments used in public debates to support equality between women and men. After decades of legal equality women are still forced to motivate their active presence and participation in community affairs by maintaining that they should be seen as a useful complement to men. It is men, the self-evident humankind, who have the power to judge the vitality of this proposition, whereas the burden of evidence rests with women.

Thus when men request an increase in the number of women in

an organization or enterprise it is usually related to changes within these bodies that reveal the need for women's complementary experiences—on men's conditions. (Seldom has this phenomenon been as obvious as recently in Sweden where an intense recruitment of women to management [especially middle-level management] in the public administration sector coincided with a policy of cutbacks in public spending.) The saying "where power is, women are not" does not, as is sometimes claimed, necessarily indicate a functionalist fallacy. The relations between women and power should not, of course, be thought as if they followed some kind of an a priori, universal law. Rather, the tendency expressed in the phrase above, noticed in one historical context after the other, should be seen as the result of structural changes and, thus, also as a result of historically conditioned political struggle between the sexes.[19]

This is why feminist strategies for change must be built primarily on analyses of women's interests (including needs and wants as defined by women themselves) instead of gender complementarity, which tends to underestimate the power relations involved. After all, the law of equality between women and men is written in terms of equal rights and possibilities and not in terms of women's conditional usefulness as defined by men. The exploitative relationship will not end until women are collectively able to form the conditions on which they live personally as well as publicly.[20]

Exploitation of human capacities in contemporary Western societies are, commonly, not of a plain and simple repressive kind. Rather, it presupposes stimulation of life and desire.[21] Male power today, thus, keeps women down, to be sure, but it is also a stimulating force that simultaneously makes women's creative powers useful and enjoyable. It forces them into conditions of "equality" and "freedom" that are measured by the standard of the very male power arrangements that they (women) steadily replenish at the cost of their own persistent subordination. In Chapter 8, I discuss the peculiar role of utilitarianism as an ideological force that backs up modern patriarchy. Many leading male philosophers since the seventeenth century stipulate that women should be kept subordinated and only contingently free and equal because their subjection is *useful* to men, to private property and the state. Even those who explicitly reject that women and men are unequal by nature (as a matter of fact, especially these philosophers), formulate this utilitarian rationale. I take the standpoint that the utility argument is far more crucial today as a means of oppression, enforcing patriarchy in the individuated society, than the older type of argument that assigned women an *inferior nature.*[22] An undermining of men's power to decide when women are useful or not in the various contexts and instances of society would be a necessary precondition for the realization of a *women-worthy society.*

The surplus worthiness invested in men endows them with male *authority* (as distinguished from "influence," which is the less effective, not necessarily legitimate form of power); and this authority has the appearance of being not male but generally human and generated from individually achieved merits exclusively. In other words, male power is also a form of hegemony. The creation of surplus worthiness and the reproduction of male authority is far from merely a question of subjective ideas dwelling more or less intensely in the heads of individual people. It must also be understood as an objective and ongoing process whether or not individual people are conscious of what is going on. This means that the agents, women and men, are stuck in a structure of opposing interests, a process in and through which male authority (and women's relative powerlessness) is produced and materialized. But being held together basically by a unique human activity (the practice of love), which by definition (or by nature) is transformative, this structure should, at the same time, be changeable.

Political Sexuality

The typical relation between women and men as sexes is today specifically a political power relation. The institution of marriage is the most decisive structural arrangement that holds this power relation together as well as connecting it to the state. Marriage is thus seen as a set of institutionalized norms concerning possessiveness in sexual goods and in gendered persons. These norms operate in men-women relations throughout all of society, and not only between particular married couples.

In my work I use the concept "sexuality" both in its narrow everyday meaning and as a structural concept. I use it in a way that is analogous, approximately, to the concept "economy". In their broader meanings economy refers to the social process of the production of the means of life while sexuality refers to the social process of the production of life itself, or the process in which people create people. Sexuality as a structural relationship is an organized process of human intercourse in which people enjoy and create people (others and themselves), in which they give and take/receive, use and produce sociosexual goods.

Sexuality, as it is typically organized today in Western societies, is political not simply because it persists as a relation of dominance or because of the conflicts that occur between women and men over scarce resources, even if both these ways of using the concept "political" are feasible. It is political above all because its form is shaped in accordance with the mode by which the liberal state operates in (civil) society, in that it affirms and fortifies essential social relations and distinctions between groups of people. This particular "mode" is a historically specific combination of individual freedoms and circumscribing forces. In it all "wills" are entitled to have a voice in personal as well as in public concerns, while the state, simultaneously, seeks to uphold its authority structures. To put it somewhat Nietzschean, the will-to-power has become legitimate for anyone, a general virtue, even a necessity. Yet at the same time the social circumstances within which the individual wills are supposed to operate are systematically biased to benefit certain groups.

It is common, in nonfeminist social theory, to distinguish two such basic authority structures, namely, political economy and the state. The feminist argument pursued here is that these basic structures are three: the socioeconomic class structure centered on private property and control over the means of production; the patriarchal sociosexual structure centered on the marriage institution, which regulates the possessions in sexed persons as being the means of production of live and living; and the state-political structure, which regulates the relations between the governors and the governed in the production and reproduction of state power, and which is centered on institutions that maintain the legitimacy of state power.

My point is, thus, to propose as a thesis that the basis on which contemporary Western patriarchy should be defined as a type is in fact this historically unique combination of freedom and monopolized force that characterizes both the capitalist economy and the liberal state. Today's patriarchy is thus structurally *similar* (not identical and not simply in symbiosis) with capitalism and the state; but it is also relatively autonomous because, as argued above, it is made of and moved by its own relational *power*, the dynamic of which is regulated by specific institutions.

These three structures are not only both distinct and similar, they are also organically conjoined with each other. Just as private property is the key institution linking the liberal state and capitalism, marriage, or the conjugal possession in gendered sexual persons is central among the institutions linking patriarchy with the state. The usual feminist way of connecting patriarchy with capitalism is to point to the common interests between men and capital in the control of women's labor power. To the extent sexuality is at all considered in this context, it is done so in terms of capital's need for women to give birth to heirs to private property or to fresh labor power.

Based on a tentative analysis of how capitalism and patriarchy are fused in today's highly developed countries, I propose instead that capital is becoming more and more dependent on recreative (as distinct from procreative) love power; and on conditioning people to use and invest their energy (that which is built up by the use of love power) to serve, directly, or indirectly, continued economic growth.

From "Patriarchy" to "Marriage Society"

The concept of "marriage society" should be tested as a partial successor to "patriarchy." How useful is the concept of "patriarchy"? In the 1970s and early 1980s the concept of patriarchy was criticized mainly with arguments taken from Marxism, which were directed against radical feminists for overemphasizing sexuality, biology, and the active role of men in the oppression of women. The idea that sexual matters might have an importance of its own seemed untenable to many. Now "patriarchy" is mainly questioned in terms that are more or less explicitly influenced by postmodernist thinking. This contested concept is said to hide experiental differences and is, therefore, considered to be useless, more or less, in feminist analysis and politics. But "patriarchy" is also strongly defended as a useful concept.

Three different standpoints can be distinguished in today's discussions of the concept of patriarchy. One rejects the concept altogether. A second, and in opposition to the first, claims that if patriarchy is abandoned, then "feminist political theory would . . . be without the only concept that refers specifically to the subjection of women, that singles out the form of political right that all men exercise by virtue of being men" (Pateman, 1988:20). The third is the somewhat ambiguous middle position, which claims that "patriarchy" should be "moved from stage center to the background of analysis and politics," not because the pervasiveness of male dominance has decreased, but because it is said to presuppose "coherent 'pure' identities of political agents and knowers" (Harding, 1988:13).

In a certain sense Sandra Harding is correct when she claims that the concept of "patriarchy" should be placed in the analytical and political background. But this does not mean that the concept is misleading, or that it necessarily presupposes coherent or "pure" political identities in people, as Harding pursues. In fact, to the extent that this is the case it is a weakness that is specific for the so-called feminist-standpoint theory that originated in Canada and the United States[23] rather than a flaw in all feminist theory in which "patriarchy" is used. Relying on Lukácsian consciousness theory this kind of feminist analysis has constructed a "pure" standpoint (of/for women) in terms of a directly politically adequate epistemology, rather than considering women and men in an empirically sensitive (sensitive for situational and experiential differences) social theory.

The concept of patriarchy is theoretically adequate only on the most general level of theory. In this it is comparable to the concept of class society. The theoretical importance of such historically general concepts is not that they alone spell out the details of concrete reality but that they give particular clues of *how to approach* a complex and endlessly detailed social reality.

I agree with Carole Pateman that feminist theory needs a specific concept that singles out the subjection of women as women and the rights men exercise as men. I also think that the term "patriarchy" has been and still is useful with reference to the notion that the sociosexual dimension (as distinguished from the economic, political, and cultural dimensions that society, conventionally, is thought to comprise) holds a position of its own in society and in history. But to what extent is it useful in the analysis of this dimension? As used by early radical feminists and some socialist feminists, "patriarchy" connotes at least three important features of a feminist view of social reality. It says that the supremacy of men and the subjection of women is *systematic* and not dependent on individual cases alone; that this systematic supremacy/subjection consists of a particular social and political *relationship of dominance* and is not the biologically determined estate of women and men; and, finally, that *men* are held to be actively involved in the exercise and in the maintenance of this systematic subjection of women.

With this we have perhaps reached the limits of the theoretical significance of the concept of patriarchy. It gives no exact guidance to a further analysis of political sexuality, that is, of the systematic power struggles (which need not be open conflicts or violence) that go on between women and men. It does not enable us to distinguish clearly enough the particular, historically changing, essential relationship between women and men *as sexes*. This is connected with the fact that the concept of patriarchy does not specify which sexual-political institution is more central than others in legitimizing and maintaining sociosexual inequality. Usually the family or some family-related "values backed with power,"[24] such as the family wage system or women's unpaid housework and care for dependants, are pointed to as key institutions. But these are not inherent to patriarchy as a conceptual entity.

Focusing exclusively on the family becomes an obstacle to further analytical clarity, because the family consists of several different types of relations of power and dependency. Husband and wife, parents and children, and other relatives are related through both love and work, erotically, in caring, as well as in educative/upbringing and laboring practices and obligations. Following Marxist method (starting in present social circumstances and from this looking at history in reverse order; see, e.g., Hobsbawm, 1984:41) it is tenable to argue that it is the institution of marriage rather than the family that should be the analytical focal point. This has become all the more evident when we consider that the systematic oppression and subjection of women as a sex continues even in circumstances of economic and social security and even in situations where household and childcaring chores are equally divided or do not exist as a problem at all.

There is an additional advantage in focusing on the institution of marriage besides the fact that it singles out the possessive sexual man-woman relation within the family or in the household. This is that it enables us to transcend the family/household as a limited sociogeographical sphere; a limitation that localizes women's oppression to a particular place that in turn leaves an unclear conceptualization of how the subjection of women as women is institutionalized outside the family.

The history of the institution of monogamous, heterosexual marriage since the twelfth century (beginning with the formation of the Western national state) reveals that not only are relations between married couples, living together, with or without children regulated. The institution of marriage regulates both directly and indirectly the relations between women and men as sexes throughout society as well. The definition of marriage as an institution can roughly be stated as those norms or values that formally or informally prescribe different possessive rights and obligations to the sexes concerning the access to vital powers in other people's person. These norms and values are backed with regulating power that resides in the male collective and with the state. Women's counterpower (influence) is of a different nature. It continues to be yielding and defensive.

Taking the vantage point, then, that society consists of women and men as groups and individuals who relate to one another in a whole set or system of distinct relations, the conjugal relationship can be seen as being the determinative feature for all of them and, thus (given our vantage point) as a relation that structures all of society. Whether we look at the political party system or private and public corporations we can see manifestations of the dominating conjugal pattern, a kind of a secondary or derived marital order.

A Feminist Theory of Interests

A historically located and empirically sensitive feminist theory of interests would, rather than a one-sided theory of women's needs, link political analyses appropriately with feminist theories of contemporary Western, patriarchal society.

A central purpose with my work on interest theory is to create a theoretical space for *differences* in women's varying needs and preferences. This is done by making this very space categorically open; that is, detailed theoretical determinants are absent. In other words, such "determinants" do rest in and emerge from women's concrete experiences and must be formulated, primarily, in practical-political terms. But what I assume to be of common interest to Western women today, namely, to appropriate an authorized[25] presence as women and to hold power equally with men in all the formative instances of society, is not and cannot be grounded ultimately in a theory centered on the concept of difference. Instead it should be based on a historically specific theoretical idea of the character of the society that is at issue here. One way of characterizing Western society rather generally is to see it as a "society of choice." (This is done and discussed in Chapter 7.) But behind the rather vague notion of a "society of choice," I trace the common denominator of women's interests today to a relational theory (summarized in the preceding theses) that deals with the system of the production of collective male power; a type of production where some of women's capacities are alienated and exploited.

Let me sum up briefly my preference for a reworked interest theory rather than a separate theory of needs.

1 In political analyses the concept of interest has a certain historical relevance that the concept of need, when isolated, does not have. Of course, following historical materialism, people's needs are not static but change and are even created historically. But as a political category on a socioexistential, or decision-making level, only the concept of "interest" is able to capture individual and collective choices in contemporary society. In medieval societies, for instance, with their fixed traditions and authoritative ideology, the necessity of making choices and decisions was not in the same way inherent in the force of circumstances.

2 Normatively, the concept of interest is impregnated with a social "logic" that is consistent with theories and practices of participatory democracy. Political theories where needs alone function as the core concept are in quite another way compatible with the real suppression of people's control over what they think is important in life. The concept of "needs," if separated from "interest," does not imply the demand of a controlling presence on behalf of the affected parties, which the concept of interest does, historically and etymologically.

3 The last point is based on an assumption of mine that "interests" and "needs" are not really comparable or interchangable. They refer to two different levels of reality, whether social, personal, or political, and thus do not, after all, compete with each other analytically. The concept of interest works on the level of human agency and autonomy, whereas the concept of needs works on the level the content of which is, so to speak, the object for human agency.

There are many other controversies that surround the concept of interest, both in political studies in general and in feminist studies. The most heavily charged conflict is the one that deals with the question of *objective and subjective* interests. In addition there is the controversy that has arisen in feminism over whether or not *all women*, independent of social and cultural cleavages, can be said to have certain common interests.

By reworking interest theory in a way that makes it inclusive of not only the content or the dividends of politics but also its form, I claim to offer a certain solution to both of these conflicts.

If Sex Were Taken Seriously

What would be the consequences of taking sex seriously for political thinking and political analysis generally? Roughly, every crucial notion in political theory seems to be liable to a more or less radical rethinking from a sex/gender perspective. Some central points would be: the status of "man"/the "individual citizen," what political democracy is and should be about, what social and political interests constitute the institutional pillars on which Western political communities rest, and thus, what politics is and where it takes place. Moreover, taking sex seriously would mean that in contemporary history the sex/gender dimension would be seen as highly significant for the development of modern capitalism. It would therefore become an increasingly integrated part of various recent attempts to formulate noneconomistic theories of capitalist society.[26]

Regarding the application of sex/gender relevant theory in political research, taking sex seriously implies a definite relativization of the theoretical status of sex as a variable. Let me now single out (from the points above) three issues for a brief discussion: the status of *man/the individual*, the status of the *sex variable* in political research, and the notion of *politics*.

First there is the question of who is "man" and who is (the) "sex." Taking sex seriously would mean that women would cease to be both the second sex and *the* sex. The terms "man" and "humanity" would no longer denote the human species by simultaneously including a connotation of one-dimensional male-identity to this species. Men would (have to) identify themselves, even publicly, as a sex; and, thus, contribute to the realization that sex is never absent from the force of social circumstances whether we call these circumstances personal or public or whatever. This does not mean that sex or gender should always be seen as *the* important feature in understanding or explaining social situations. Nor do I see any contradiction between men identifying themselves publicly as a sex, and acting against sexual harassment and all kinds of male violence against women. On the contrary, the first seems to be a necessary condition for the other to become effective. For instance, if the idea of establishing, somehow, "public zones of erotic peace"[27] is meaningful at all, it seems to presuppose that sex gains some kind of public status as a basis of social interests in a community where women and men can act out gendered conflicts and solve problems by civilized means. Needless to say, men and women would also continue to act politically as individuals or as members of other collectives.

The point is that men, by identifying themselves as the socially significant sex they are, would begin to loose the power they have today of determining *when sex is relevant and how it is relevant as a circumstantial factor* in various social contexts. Considering the unions, for instance, and the parties on the labor market at large, where issues related to sex/gender are usually more inflammable than in many other contexts; taking sex seriously would mean that men would have no legitimate reason for refusing to discuss openly the positions of power they hold and steadily reproduce with respect to women.

To take sex seriously also implies successive insight into the fact that sex actually refers to something as complex as class; it refers to a specific social structure. As in the case of class, sex as a structure can be understood in at least two ways. First, and more immediately visible, sex is women and men as parallellities, as aggregates or groupings of people who can be compared and who constitute and are constituted by a multifaceted pattern of ascribed or achieved attributes. This is the way we understand sex when it is used as a variable to show statistical differences and similarities between women and men, and of course this is useful. Until now, however, in political science, the common assumption has been that this is the only way sex can be taken theoretically seriously as a structure. This is why facts identified through the application of the variable "sex" so often lack a substantial theoretical base.

If sex as a pattern of attributes or variable positions is the only way we think structurally about women and men we cannot say anything about causal or dependency relationships *between* women and men. Being two separate values of the sex variable, women and men exclude each other, so to speak. They change position, or remain unchanged, depending on changes in each group's achievements in *other* circumstances/variables (age, education, wages, occupation, etc.). But there can be no causally operative, inherent relationship between the two values, women and men. Limited in this fashion, sex is thus not thought of as a relationship, a relationship with an inherent connection between the related parties/values, a *social circumstance of its own*. Taking sex seriously in social and political theory means taking into account and developing further the standpoint that sex is *also* a structure in the realist/materialist sense, that is, a structural *relationship* that, in turn, both conditions history and is conditioned by it.

In terms of Alford and Friedland's (1985) three perspectives on politics and the state (pluralist, managerial, and class perspective) sex is empirically relevant on all three levels of analysis, the individual, the organizational, and the societal/class-relational. But, besides that, sex would work to signify its own perspective, having its specific theoretical field parallel to that of class, namely, on the relational level of society.

Traditionally, there are two main ways of defining "politics" and the "political" in terms of what it is and where it takes place. From the liberal viewpoint, politics is generally a conscious, deliberate activity that—in order to be political—must take place in certain specific arenas and not in others. An opposing viewpoint, adhered to traditionally by Marxists and now by feminists as well, sees politics as the "working out of *relationships* within an already given 'power structure' " (Randall, 1987.10). Accordingly, the view of where politics take place is usually less restricted. Yet common to both the liberal and Marxist viewpoints is the assumption that certain activities, spheres, and relationships are somehow naturally (or conventionally) apolitical and should therefore be excluded from that which is actually and potentially viewed as politics. These activities are termed "personal," and sexual matters hold a special position among these supposedly apolitical, personal matters.

The core of feminist thinking is to denaturalize, poblematize, and politicize the exclusiveness of the *personal*, sexuality and love included. This has been said repeatedly and in various ways for almost thirty years. Historically this can be seen as being comparable with, and simultaneously a relative displacement of, the socialist critique of the *private* conditions of economy and work that began in the early nineteenth century. The socialist analysis emerged when the new class relationship was becoming clearly visible; or rather when its consequences were becoming conspicuous. Opposing interests were organized more and more consciously within the socioeconomic system in which people produced the means of life and reproduced the conditions of this particular mode of production.

Comparable developments in the formation of sociosexual interests are visible now. Sex/gender based interest struggles can be discerned throughout society as a whole. As in the case of the class struggle, which encompasses groups of wage laborers with partly different interests, so also the sex struggle includes both latent and manifest conflicts among women.

Toward a "Womanish"-Feminist Continuum

Today, the women's movement is built on both formal organizations and informal activities, both voluntary and state feminist arrangements, and on both separatist organizations and alliances with men who hold feminist sympathies. For me a plurality of this kind is the only way possible. Impetus for the transformation of vital societal power structures come, necessarily, from both inside and outside the structure itself.

This means that neither positive government action for sexual equality nor union or corporate strivings to bring about practical reforms meant to respond to the *collective material needs* of laboring women, do preclude or eliminate the need for women in general to struggle for their individual *rights* in various settings. There is no reason either to believe that ever so "women-friendly" government arrangements will rule out the necessity for women to engage in personal, private, and public matters as a specifically *interested* socio-sexual collective, a collective with both common and conflicting needs and wants.

It is common knowledge by now that women engaged in party politics, for instance, tend to face two kinds of opposition in the political system. Like their male co-partisans women face party opponents and opposition in the traditional sense. But in addition women often have to cope with both overt and covert sexual-political opposition from their party brethren. This illustrates the need for more or less radical separatist activities and institutionalized arrangements, as a partial strategy for building a better society. These kinds of separatist strategies should not be confused with the vision of totalitarian "femalism" that Lynne Segal criticizes in her book *Is the Future Female?* (1987).

As things look now, at a time when "all that is solid" seems to be "melting into air," it is not surprising that some believe that the solution to sex/gender conflicts lies either in the establishment of a "lesbian continuum"[28] or in the cultivation of a play-ground of genderless desires. In reality, however, it seems to be as necessary as ever to establish a more distinct and aware "womanish"-feminist continuum,[29] developed in various ways adequate to each society or section of society. Sisterhood and solidarity between women as well as alliances between feminists (including male sympathizers) may sound ever so out of it or trivial in today's trendy discourses. But practicing these relations in more or less organized ways is simply the only way to move closer to a women-worthy society and, thus, closer to a viable future for all people, men, women, and children.

Neither an invisible hand nor "angels"[30] are likely to tread in to solve the problems of the sex struggle, which ranges from nonconscious discrimination to murders and cruelty of almost unthinkable kinds. There is nobody here but us—women and men—persons[31] to act out, consciously and deliberately and on practically every social arena, the relationships "within [the] already given 'power structure'" that is us: human enminded bodies in need of love.

Notes

Chapter 1

1. The content of this book is exclusively theoretical. I have built my analysis on empirical material from other researchers. In addition, my own as well as many other people's undocumented experiences have on a number of points informed this study and provided it with data.

2. Generally, the limitations of all the prevailing academic views on how the pattern of inequality ought to be described and explained were becoming more and more obvious. Analytical models "sex roles" (developed mostly within structural-functionalist sociology beginning in the 1940s) and "sex differences" (the key concept applied in this field within empiricist psychology), which had dominated academic research on women and men in the 1950s and 1960s, became main targets of early feminist criticism. Within both these fields enormous quantities of data have been produced on the role patterns as well as the attitudinal attributes of women and men. The point of the feminist criticism was that the sex-role system itself as well as the dualist, empiricist sex difference model had to be problematized and explained, in both a historical context and a larger social and political context.

3. The concrete societies in question also comprise relations other than those between the sexes (such as class relations and many others). The formulation in the text above expresses a choice of theoretical perspective. I choose to theorize society primarily from the perspective of *sex/gender relations* and not from any perspective where, for instance, *class relations, individuals,* or *organizations* are the key concepts that determine different levels of theoretical analysis. This means that such other perspectives' theoretical concepts are of empirical rather than theoretical interest to my analysis. See, for example, Alford and Friedland, 1985, for a closer account for the implications of such theoretical perspectivism. See also my discussion of a "relative dual systems theory" in Chapter 2.

4. In her *Sexual Politics* (1970) radical feminist Kate Millett draws on Weber in order to "prove that sex is a status category with political implications"

(p. 32). To my knowledge, only two other explicit feminist attempts have been made to relate to Weber for theorizing about patriarchy. The first is in an article by the socialist feminist Linda Phelps (1981), in which she also presents her arguments for leaving the theoretical guidance of Marxism. The second is in Roberta Hamilton's (1978) book, *The Liberation of Women: A Study of Patriarchy and Capitalism*, in which she combines Weber's view of the historical importance of Protestantism with historical materialism. (Besides this, Randall Collins [1971] explains the persistence of male dominance by combining Weberian ideas on social power with a biologically reductionist view on the role of men's physical strength.)

When one considers that both Marxist and Weberian thinking were tried by radical feminists and socialist feminists alike, it is rather surprising that there was so little attempt by feminists to develop a Marx-Weber synthesis. This is all the more surprising when we think about the 1970s as a decade when much of the revitalized (more Marx-sympathetic than earlier; e.g., Wiley, 1987) Marx-Weber debate dealt with such a synthesis. On the other hand, the Weberian/managerial perspective has been brought to use more concretely (on what Chafetz [1990: 21–22] calls a mezo-structural level) in organization studies, such as Kanter, 1977. Furthermore, the longstanding discussion on gender in stratification research (see Chapter 4, note 11) of course draws on Weber. An interesting feminist reading of Weber's political theory (to my knowledge the first thorough feminist confrontation with this part of his works) is to be found in Brown, 1988.

5. For a critical investigation of the shift in radical feminist analysis during the 1970s, see Eisenstein, 1983. Regarding the "divorce from the left and from Marxism" (Eisenstein, 1983:125), a number of quick-witted formulations exist in radical feminist writings. For instance, Robin Morgan (1977) declared "Goodbye to All That," and Adrienne Rich (1979:193) resolutely spoke of "the dead-endedness—for women—of Marxism in our time." Catharine MacKinnon's "Agenda for Theory" could appear to be a prominent exception from the assumed general break of radical feminism with Marxism. (Presumably because of the time factor, Eisenstein did not deal with MacKinnon in her criticism of radical feminism, although she listed MacKinnon's two articles in *Signs* [1982, 1983] in her bibliography.) MacKinnon, however, broke with Marxism in a more elaborated manner (see her preface in 1989).

6. What I mean by this is: In the later phase of radical feminism, governed by ideals of "women-centeredness" and "unmodified feminism," MacKinnon, for instance, relates to Kate Millett's way of approaching sexuality in terms of politics and dominance. But she does not face the fact that Millett had, by applying these concepts the way she did, started a critical feminist confrontation with one of the most influential paradigms in contemporary social, political, and historical analysis. At the same time MacKinnon's own "dominance approach" (MacKinnon, 1987) goes very much in the same tracks as conventional Weberian informed thinking (otherwise named "elite theory" or "managerial theory"), building on notions of "coercion," "hierarchy," struggles over positions in hierarchies, and the like.

7. Feminists have made various kinds of uses of Marxism by allying more or less closely with the main lines or schools of contemporary Marxist thought. Leaving aside unitary Marxist-feminism (such as the theories of domestic labor), a distinction can be made between four or five such feminist-historical-materialist relationships. First, many feminists have been influenced by the *alienation school*, a line of thinking most notably developed by Georg Lukács (combined with thoughts from Lenin and Antonio Gramsci). The so-called feminist standpoint theory—developed in Canada and the United States by Dorothy Smith, Nancy Hartsock, Sandra Harding, Jane Flax, and others (see also remarks in Chapter 9)—is the result of an attempt to reverse the Lukácsian theory of "privileged" class consciousness and substitute women for class. The program of these feminists was to unite feminist and Marxist analysis "symbiotically," that is, in such a manner that "there will be no recognizable marxism" left (Harding, 1981:139). Zillah Eisenstein (1979) represents a different way of relating to the alienation school. Second, several aspects of *structural Marxism* (originating in Louis Althusser), especially its critique of economist reductionism in much of conventional Marxism, have had a wide range of effects on the development of feminist theory, perhaps most significantly in England and through English feminist writers. The thrust on ideology and consciousness as relatively independent forces in society seemed to open up a "room" for women. The linking of structural Marxist conceptions of ideology to psychoanalytical theory meant much for feminist analysis from Juliet Mitchell on, to say the least. Third, the subsequent (after the "fall" of Althusserianism) development of different *structuration theories* stimulated further feminist thinking (see, e.g., Connell, 1987; Walby, 1986, 1990).

Diametrically opposed to structural Marxism is the *empiricist stance* (within Marxism) developed most strongly by the English historian Edward Thompson (1978). Many feminist historians and sociologists relate explicitly to such a stance (see my discussion in Chapter 9, note 4). Finally, *critical theory*, especially as developed by Jürgen Habermas, is very popular among feminists. Here, also, the critique against classical Marxism for concentrating too much on economy/production and too little on politics, culture, and "communicative action" attracts many feminists. The combination of this displacement of "orthodox Marxism," the longstanding interest in psychoanalytic theory, and Habermas's historico-sociological writings on the public/private split in modernity makes up a pattern of thought that suits feminists in many respects (see, e.g., Benhabib, 1987; Fraser, 1987; Haug, 1980, 1983; Hernes, 1987; Nicholson, 1986, 1987). See also my criticism in Chapter 9, note 3.

It seems that the various schools of thought themselves imply barriers to the development in feminist analysis of an autonomous theory of patriarchy or women's oppression, which was the aim of the feminist-historical-materialist relationship in the first place.

8. See note 14 below.

9. Since about 1985–86 I have found the realist approach to be the branch of historical materialism most in tune with my own understanding of Marxist

method. References to realist pieces of work are dispersed throughout the essays in this volume (see, e.g., Chapter 4, note 22, and the section on "difference" in Chapter 8). Apart from a few points in Chapter 2, however, no substantial treatment of Marxist method in general or the realist view in particular is included. Among the aspects of the realist view that I embrace are, in short, the following: its way of combining a belief in the objective existence of social reality (including human nature) with the belief that it is socially constructed; the way it distinguishes theoretical works from politics (see, e.g., Benton, 1984:1–2, and chap. 10); its concept of "structure" (which differs fundamentally from that of the French linguistic structuralism; see Sayer, 1984:82); and its way of conceiving power and causality (which differ fundamentally from the mechanistic, Humean way; see Chapter 9, note 17.

The realist approach also means that I reject Engels's scienticism and approve of Marx's antipositivist and critical view of how to seek knowledge about society and history. What has meant most to me—besides reading Marx and Engels—is the reading of Terence Ball (1984, 1987), James Farr (1984, 1986), Terrell Carver (1975, 1982, 1984b) and Paul Thomas (1976). In an early phase of my study I benefited from the works of Mats Dahlkvist (1978), Isaac Deutscher (1970), and Gunnar Olofsson (1979), especially concerning the understanding of the different levels of theory in Marx, and how to relate the basic theory of capitalism and empirical studies of concrete societies to one another. For much valuable reading on the never-ending debate about the qualitative-quantitative distinction in the social sciences, see Glassner and Moreno, 1989.

10. See note 6 above.

11. I have dealt briefly with early radical feminism as well as with MacKinnon in Jónasdóttir, 1984.

12. See note 7 above.

13. The most substantial work in this field is Hartsock (1983), "The Feminist Standpoint: Toward a Specifically Feminist Historical Materialism."

14. The aim of my study has been to work out notes toward an analytically isolated theory of contemporary patriarchy, by drawing on what seemed to be usable in historical materialism, and not to fill in the underdeveloped areas of historical materialism. Still, and perhaps because of this, my results seem to imply some unintended consequences for historical materialism. If my theses on love as an human/materialist alienable power and social practice that is basic in the reproduction of patriarchy are valid, it means that labor looses its position as the central analytical concept in the materialist conception of history. Thus, the concepts of "love" and "love power" would be of an immediate interest to this conception's historically dependent transformative potential. "Socially organized love" would be actualized to fill the "potential gap" in the materialist conception of history that, for instance, the prominent British Marxist historian Eric Hobsbawm spoke of in a lecture he gave at the Marx Centenary Conference organized by the Republic of San Marino in 1983 (Hobsbawm, 1984:41). Such a gap opens up if, or when, "comparable analytical discoveries," actualized by the given process of history, can be identified. Such an "other central analytical

concept" would, then, "enable thinkers to reinterpret history" (p. 41). Further-more, given the significance of love as a "practical, human sensuous activity" in the development of contemporary Western society, the concept of "love" seems to displace not only that of "labor" but also the two variants of "rational action" that critical theorists on one hand and analytical Marxists on the other propose as having filled (or made sense of) this gap.

15. Of course this statement does not mean that nothing of value has been done to this program yet. Quite the contrary. It means that the very perspective envisioned here, the one where women and men constitute the producers (and reproducers) of the prevailing patriarchal society *and* the potential augmentors of a better society, demands a rather comprehensive reorganization of intellectual work.

16. Recently, I have met many women—politicians and others—who have begun to formulate, at least metaphorically, what happens in this kind of situation. They use expressions like, "We hit our heads against a wall that seemingly does not exist." The question is, What does the wall consist of?

Chapter 2

1. The terminological and conceptual problems of patriarchy are discussed in more detail in Jónasdóttir, 1984:115–27. The problems include the question whether "patriarchy" can be used as a term for present-day male domination or if it should be confined to father-domination prevailing in the past. Gayle Rubin (1975), for example, prefers the latter as does Elizabeth Fox Genovese (1982). The radical feminists like Kate Millett (1970) launched the expression "patriar-chy" at the end of the 1960s, giving it a new significance, that is, roughly, the social dominance of men over women and in comparison with women. Another problem concerns whether the systematic character and the *relative autonomy* that "patriarchy" confers on male dominance and the oppression of women are theoretically and empirically justifiable. This is a point made by increasing numbers of feminist researchers who accept the concept, while others, e.g., Michèle Barrett (1980), reject the concept of patriarchy on just these grounds. For a further discussion of whether the concept of "patriarchy" is useful, see also Chapter 9.

2. My concepts "sociosexual" and "sociosexual system" should be seen as a way of surpassing Rubin's concepts "sex/gender" and "sex/gender system," and when I use her I use them as synonyms to mine. The concept "sex/gender system" was coined by Rubin in order to distinguish "between the human capacity and necessity to create a sexual world, and the empirically oppressive ways in which sexual worlds have been organized." According to her: "Sex/gender system [in contrast to patriarchy] is a neutral term which refers to the domain [i.e., the "sexual world"] and indicates that oppression is not inevitable in that domain, but is the product of the specific social relations which organize it" (Rubin, 1975:168). This distinction between empirically open concepts and more substantial ones is what unites the rationale of the two sets of terms. What

separates them is that Rubin's sex/gender system actually refers to females (and males) as socialized by the "system," whereas my sociosexual system refers to the set of relations between the sexes as well as among members of each sex, in a society. But I used her terms for my aims until my own came into being.

3. For differences of opinion about the origins of patriarchy, or as I have termed it, the anthropological question, see Jónasdóttir, 1984:129–34.

4. For a closer examination of the historical question concerning patriarchy, see Jónasdóttir, 1984:134–40.

5. The theoretical issue is dealt with in Jónasdóttir, 1984:140–56.

6. Jónasdóttir, 1984:114; see notes 3–5 above.

7. With the question "Why has the sex/gender system become visible only now?" Sandra Harding (1983) underlines the gender system's historical changeability and its uniqueness today and suggests that its specific visibility today is due to the women's movement's "discovery" of a particular feminist perspective.

8. In all academic subjects, criticism has resulted in a number of books and articles. The following are only a few examples from political science and political sociology of authors whose works are either wholly or in part critical of the subject: Boals (1975); Bourque and Grossholtz (1974); Carroll (1979–80); Dahlerup (1974); Elshtain (1974); Evans (1980); Goot and Reid (1975); Halsaa-Albrektsen (1977); Jaquette (1974); Jónasdóttir and Hedlund-Ruth (1981); Lovenduski (1981); Pateman (1988); Shanley and Schuck (1975).

9. Friedan 1963; de Beauvoir (1949) 1972.

10. For more on Parson's work, see especially Parsons, 1954; and Parsons and Bales, 1956. For a feminist critique of Parsons, see, e.g., Mitchell, 1986:104; Berg, 1977; Beechey, 1978.

11. In Jónasdóttir, 1984, there is a lengthy description of the various directions in feminist theory. Jaggar (1983) gives an even more detailed account, and she divides feminist theory into liberal feminism, Marxist feminism, radical feminism, and socialist feminism. Mitchell's term "abstract socialists," quoted in the text above, and Jaggar's "Marxist feminism" connote largely the same line of class reductionist reasoning that I, elsewhere in this book, refer to with the term "unitary theory." Briefly, this line of reasoning argues that in order to understand and investigate the oppression of women, no new feminist theories are needed. What is needed is to apply classical Marxist theory correctly and, if possible, to develop that theory further.

12. Several feminist writers have pointed out that the division of work according to gender or, rather, gender-determined social practice (the concept "division of work according to gender" is usually used in a very wide sense) affects women and men not only in terms of their psychology and attitudes, but also physically—e.g., muscle strength, how we move, even ability to breast feed! For more material on this, see, e.g., Jaggar, 1983:126; Cockburn, 1981:41–58; and Cockburn, 1983.

13. This quotation from Bacon's essay has been taken from the excerpt included in Agonito, 1977:93.

14. Gilligan's book (1982) has received a great deal of attention in the

United States as well as elsewhere. For example, the journal *Social Research* devoted a whole issue (50, no. 3 [1983]) to it. Briefly, Gilligan finds that women tend to develop a different moral philosophy and idea of justice than men do. Women's moral ideas tend to deal with issues of responsibility and caring for others more than with formal principles of justice. A usual way of interpreting observed differences in women's and men's responses to moral issues was to apply a theory of moral development, which placed women at a low stage of development and seldom, if ever, did they reach the highest stage. Among other things Gilligan questions the use of "higher" and "lower" stages in determining moral development.

Carole Pateman shows, in her article " 'The Disorder of Women': Women, Love, and the Sense of Justice" (1980a and 1989) that the idea that women in principle lack a consciousness of justice has existed for a long time in political philosophy. According to Rousseau and Hegel, for instance, this means that women comprise a lethal threat to the state. Hegel claims that women are "the enemy that the state creates for itself within its own walls" (Pateman, 1980a:29). Clearly, the idea of the withering away of the state has more than one meaning!

15. In addition to Mitchell (1974), who makes use of Freud's core theories, I refer here mainly to the feminist "object relation" theorists like Chodorow (1978) and others.

16. See, e.g., Barrett, 1980; Haug, 1983; Kuhn, 1978.

17. Jónasdóttir, 1984: 117n.2, 37.

18. Hartmann, 1976, 1981a, 1981b; Young, 1980, 1981.

19. "Teorin som inte finns" (The theory that does not exist), *Kvinnovetenskaplig tidskrift*, no. 1 (1980).

20. A literary critic and feminist suggested that the following books would be interesting to study from this perspective: Sven Lindqvist's *En gift mans dagbok* (A married man's diary) and *En älskares dagbok* (A lover's diary), and Sun Axelsson's autobiographical books. Other examples could be *Praxis* by Fay Weldon, Inger Alfvén's *Arvedelen* and, especially, *Ur kackerlackors levnad*; and last but not least the clear, powerful depictions in Joyce Carol Oates's *Do with Me What You Will*.

21. For a closer examination of how "appropriation" can be understood, see Chapter 5.

22. See Jónasdóttir, 1984:131.

23. See references in other notes, especially note 8 above. Also among others: Brown, 1988; Eduards, 1986, 1988, 1992; Eduards, Gustafsson, and Jónasdóttir, 1989; Elshtain, 1981; Evans et al., 1986; Hartsock, 1983; Hernes, 1982, 1984, 1987; Jones and Jónasdóttir, 1988; Klein, 1984; Lloyd, 1984; MacKinnon, 1989; Pateman, 1983a, 1983b; Randall, 1987; Sapiro, 1979, 1981, 1983; Siltanen and Stanworth, 1984; Stiehm, 1984.

24. Jónasdóttir, 1980:5, and Jónasdóttir and Hedlund-Ruth, 1981:16–37.

25. Compare Laswell's and Easton's definitions of politics.

26. See, e.g., Eduards and Gunneng, 1983.

27. From Morgan, 1970:633.

Chapter 3

1. In the following I use "basic theory" and "general theory" interchangeably. See note 5.

2. In Anthias and Yuval-Davis, 1983, the notion of "ethnic division" is more comprehensive than "race." They mean that when "race" has been used (within socialist feminism), it has focused on color and has thus singled out the divisions between black and white women. The concept of ethnicity is supposed to grasp "all migrant women."

3. In Chapters 2 and 4 I criticize the different lines of thought in regard to patriarchy and women's oppression, within socialist feminist theory. Among other things I reject what I call the totality view of thinking as it is proposed by, for instance, Iris Young (1980 and 1981), Veronica Beechey (1979), and Zillah Eisenstein (1979). From my point of view we should not conceptualize society as a "single process" (Beechey, 1979:79).

4. I am using "abstract" in the Marxist/realist sense of singling out in thought certain layers and elements of reality in order to understand its composite nature. See, for instance, Sayer, 1984:80.

5. The expression "theories of the middle-range" can be traced to the American sociologist Robert Merton. During the 1940s and 1950s he was involved in a discussion with Talcott Parsons about what kind of social theory—basic theory ("basic theory," "general theory," and "comprehensive theory" were used interchangeably in their discussion) *or* theories of the middle-range—should be the most important to develop at the time. Parsons called for more conscious strivings to elaborate a common general theory while Merton thought that the middle-range level should be given priority. The latter standpoint made a strong impact on mainstream thinking in all the social sciences. There is a shortage of serious discussion about the nature of these different kinds or levels of theorizing as well as about the relationship between them.

In her *Kvinnor och politik*, Maud Eduards (1977:76–77) distinguishes between "comprehensive theories" (*helhetsteorier*) and "partial theories" (*delteorier*) in regard to the various theories that are used to explain the differences in women's and men's behavior in politics and their different positions in the political system.

6. See Haavind, 1980:55. Insofar as Haavind relates her assumptions to a basic theory of patriarchy, she refers primarily to Øystein Holter's (1980) capitallogical explanation of patriarchy. See Haavind, 1985:20.

Juliet Mitchell (1966) divides women's position analytically into what she calls four structures: production, reproduction, socialization, and sexuality. Berit Aas (1975:2–3) presents a model of women's (versus men's) culture including the five dimensions of (1) language and communication, (2) organizations: leadership style, goal, and recruitment patterns, (3) relations to tools (technology) and resources (finances), (4) self-evaluation, and (5) time perspective, availability of own time, future time, and planning possibilities.

7. I use "structure" in the sense of a "necessary relationship," as distin-

guished from "contingent relationships." For further elaboration of these concepts see Sayer, 1984:82.

8. Ulla Wikander (1989) provides an example of the last part of the periodization question. She criticizes Rolf Torstendahl's way of dividing Western industrial capitalism into periods because he ignores the changing character of the gender division of labor in these periods. She also has suggestions about how to surpass his scheme in this respect. (See Torstendahl, "Technology in the Development of Society, 1850–1980: Four Phases of Industrial Capitalism in Western Europe," *History and Technology* 1 [1984]: 157–74.)

Chapter 4

1. See Mitchell, 1966, 1974, 1986; Rubin, 1975; and Hartmann, 1976, 1981a, 1981b. Since the mid-1970s Heidi Hartmann (an American economist and feminist researcher) has attracted a great deal of attention because of these articles, in which she attempts to explain patriarchy through an interweaving of Marxist and feminist analysis.

In Chapter 2 I divide the problem of explaining patriarchy into three questions or subdivisions: the anthropological one (What is the genesis of patriarchy?), the historical one (How has patriarchy changed historically, and how did the particular form of male dominance we live under today arise?), and the theoretical one (How is patriarchy structured and reproduced in our type of society?). Given these divisions, Hartmann, 1976, deals with all three aspects, although the historical aspect is the central one. In this article, her theoretical points of departure are criticisms of the traditional social and economic analysis, neoclassical economics as well as Marxist theory. In Hartmann, 1981a, the anthropological aspect is absent, and her critique is directed toward feminist theoretical discourse. Here her emphasis is on the theoretical question that is a further development from the first article, but the empirical discussion included is primarily historical. The third article (1981b) is mainly empirical, a closer illumination of the class and gender struggle in household work. In this chapter my own critical analysis is primarily based on Hartmann, 1981a, since I am mainly interested in the theoretical question.

For further work on the various socialist feminist orientations, see Chapter 2 in this volume and Jónasdóttir, 1984. For the, perhaps, most comprehensive discussion available of socialist feminism in relation to other orientations in contemporary feminist theory (radical feminism, Marxist analyses of the "woman question," and liberal feminism), see Jaggar, 1983.

2. On the other hand, Linda Phelps (1981), who, like Hartmann, at an early stage used the terms of dual systems (she is said to have coined the expression "dual systems theory"; cf. Jónasdóttir, 1984:115, 164), turned to Weber's ideas on power and authority in order to approach patriarchy theoretically. Otherwise, it is a tricky question (and hardly important to investigate in any sort of detail) who of the pioneer women theoreticians adopted Marxism and who did not. The fact is that a large part of the comprehensive theoretical discussion of

women's oppression and patriarchy has been conducted in one way or another in relation to historical materialism. In addition to this, and often as a complement to historical materialism, there are primarily three (or four, depending on how one counts) programmatic research orientations that feminist theoreticians use: the French structuralism (in the manner of Lévi-Strauss) and, successively, poststructuralism, psychoanalysis, and to a certain degree, Anglo-American structural functionalism. Pure sociobiological approaches also occur, but only exceptionally among feminists themselves.

3. In Chapter 2 I use the term "total theory" to designate the opposite of the dual systems theory. Within the socialist feminist theoretical discussions we can also distinguish as a separate orientation the point of view that declares the sex/gender problematique at bottom theoretically irrelevant. This standpoint is expressed for example through the rejection of the concept of patriarchy because it ascribes too great an independence to sex/gender questions. Michèle Barrett (1980), for instance, takes this point of view. See also my analysis of Barrett in Jónasdóttir, 1984: 146–51.

In *Patriarchy at Work*, Sylvia Walby (1986) details certain interconnected social structures through which men exploit women. One of these structures consists of the domestic or household relation, which, according to Walby, comprises the patriarchal mode of production (p. 50). She also provides empirical evidence for her theories in several chapters. I believe, however, that Walby warrants a similar sort of criticism as Hartmann.

4. Hartmann, 1981a: 3, 10–11, 13–19.

5. Hartmann, 1981a: 11. See also Mitchell, 1971: 81.

6. Hartmann, 1981c: 20–23. In *Capitalism and Women's Work in the Home*, Hartmann (1981c) writes about this family wage system. My intention here is not to test whether her idea of the family wage as an economic fact or social norm (see Hartmann, 1981a:39n.40) holds empirically. My criticism is on another level. I claim that her economic perspective and focus on women and men as working beings leads in the wrong direction—given her expressed aim to explain the foundations of patriarchy—regardless of whether the family wage as such can be empirically confirmed.

7. See the Introduction in Ganetz, Gunnarsson, and Göransson 1986:10.

8. See, for instance, Carlsson et al., 1983. The article contains the results of the authors' joint reading of *Women and Revolution*, in which Hartmann's article "The Unhappy Marriage" was crucial (see Hartmann, 1981a). Here I take up only those points that are interesting in the light of my own argument. For further criticism, see the other articles in *Women and Revolution*. See also Burnham and Louie (1985), who criticize the dual systems approach from the point of view of Leninist rectification.

9. On the different parts of Marxism, see for example, Liedman, 1977: 35, or (somewhat revised) Johansson and Liedman, 1981:129.

10. See, for example, my presentation and critique of Holter, "Det verdifulle patriarkatet" (1982) in Jónasdóttir, 1984:151–56.

11. E.g. Rita Liljeström's (1980:4) critique of Walter Korpi's project, *Arbe-*

tarklassen i välfärdskapitalismen (The working class in welfare capitalism), published in *Jämställdhetsperspektiv i forskningen* (The perspective of gender equality in research), report from a symposium, April 24–25, 1980, Riksbankens jubileumsfond. For an English counterpart, see Michelle Stanworth (1984) and John Goldthorpe's (1984) exchanges in *Sociology.* See also Crompton and Mann, 1986.

In fact, the question whether gender is theoretically relevant or not in the macrosociological field of studies of class formation, class action, and the like has been a standing object of dispute ever since Joan Acker (1973) published her essay, "Women and Social Stratification: A Case of Intellectual Sexism." Class/stratification analysis is one of the few fields of theory and research where defenders of conventional views converse openly and seriously with their feminist opponents. As a first step in a project in which I plan to investigate a certain number of such controversies (in order to see what theoretical significance—if any—the participants in these controversies ascribe to gender) I have written a short paper (Jónasdóttir, 1991) presented at a conference arranged by JÄMFO (the Swedish Commission for Research on Equality between Men and Women), November 24–25, 1990.

12. See, for example, Gunnar Qvist's and Gunhild Kyle's studies of the position of women in the Swedish labor movement; Carlsson, 1986b; *Kvinnorepresentationsutredningen*, 1986–87; Balas et al., 1982. Walby (1986) has written about the sex/gender struggles within the English trade union movement.

13. Cf. particularly the section on Feuerbach in Marx and Engels, 1970. See also the special chapter on the premises of the materialist method and history's fundamental conditions.

14. See Barrett, 1980:93–106, for an account of especially the British discussion of ideology and theory. See also Haug, 1980, 1983.

15. For example, Gordon Allport's classic definition of the concept connects the individual's manner of relating to both the nervous system and to experience. He defines "attitudes" as "A mental and neural state of readiness, organized through experience, exerting a directive or dynamic influence upon the individual's response to all objects or situations with which it is related" (Allport, 1935: 810; quoted from Kelvin, 1969: 41).

16. A study that emphasizes this is Hearn and Parkin, 1987.

17. See, e.g., Ruddick (1980), who argues that mothers have not only hearts but also minds. See also Gilligan, 1982.

18. The terms "involved" and "detached" are taken from Elias, 1956: 226–52; the quotation is from p. 227. Elias is one of the very few social scientists who has for decades (much earlier than Foucault) advocated/defended what I would call a human-materialist or physical/body-materialist view. In addition to his history of civilization, see also his *What Is Sociology?* (1978). Individual studies that contain a serious discussion of the fact that "human beings have bodies and are bodies" (not just ideas) indicate a rising interest in this aspect. See, for example, Turner, 1984.

19. See, for example, Zillah Eisenstein's two chapters in Eisenstein, 1979.

20. In daily discussions the question is sometimes put in terms of guilt and responsibility: whether men alone are responsible for/guilty of oppressing women throughout the ages, or whether women can wholly or in part blame themselves.

21. An expression taken from Rubin, 1975:168.

22. The idea of causality that I indicate here is of the nonmechanical generative type that is found in the work of Roy Bhaskar, Rom Harré, and later, in Andrew Sayer's and Jeffrey Isaac's work. See, for example, Bhaskar, 1978, 1979; Harré and Madden, 1975; Sayer, 1984; and Isaac, 1987.

23. I wish to underline two things: when I refer to women and men as the main parties in the sociosexual process I do not mean that heterosexuality as such necessarily involves relations of oppression. We have to distinguish between "heterosexuality" and "obligatory heterosexuality" (cf. Rubin, 1975:129). Nor do I intend to make lesbian or other homosexual relations invisible. My point is that if we see sexuality—not economy—as the complex foundation on which patriarchy's varied historical forms are based, then women and men, more than women/women or men/men, are the primary parties in this oppressive sex/gender structure. This structure in turn forms the conditions for other sociosexual practices.

24. Increasingly, during the 1980s, another type of a reductionist treatment of sex/gender than the economic one Hartmann presents became popular, that is, one developed under the aegis of French structuralism and poststructuralism. Here gender and sexuality are reduced to differences and dichotomies on symbolic and textual levels. The historical significance of sexual symbols and signs is then that they strengthen *other* power relationships. See, e.g., Scott, 1986.

25. The expression alludes to Beckman, 1981.

26. This means that, among other things, I do not agree with Jaggar when she states that the socialist feminist analysis of patriarchy must be placed *within* the "theoretical domain of political economy" (Jaggar, 1983:134).

27. Marx, 1977b. See, e.g. Liedman, 1965:83–85.

28. Karin Widerberg very likely expresses many women's experiences when she describes her attempt to obtain help from her often more knowledgeable male Marxist comrades. See Widerberg, 1986:172.

Chapter 5

1. See Macpherson's (1973) critique of liberal democracy. A core idea of his is that a "net transfer of powers" from some people to other people occurs in the "market society" (p. 15). Despite a certain economist reductionism in Macpherson, his work encouraged me to continue with the mode of analysis begun here.

2. See Delphy, 1976, 1977; and Lange, 1976. See also the anthology, *Dependence and Exploitation in Work and Marriage* (Barker and Allen, 1976). In these studies exploitation is used exclusively to portray economic exchange or the labor aspect of production. Sylvia Walby (1986, 1990), although widening the range of patriarchal structures, continues to move in the same tracks.

3. Both Jansen-Jurreit (1979) and O'Brien (1981) focus on the procreative feature of the sociosexual relationship. They assume that patriarchy is built on the principle that men appropriate the progeny, and, as a precondition to this, they must have power over women as the means of procreation. In the former the claim is assumed to be founded on economic interest. In the latter it is more a question of existential interests; unlike women, who carry the whole process through, men are alienated from biological procreation. They must prove their potency as fathers and, in virtue of fatherhood, as whole human beings, through a social power system. But women themselves are not assumed to be of any primary interest to men. My point is that neither economic power nor the (existential or other aspects of) power of parenthood is vital in contemporary patriarchy. Today, men must prove themselves above all as *men*, not as fathers. For this women as *women* (not primarily as mothers to men's children) are a necessary source of social existential power.

4. Here I refer to Hartmann's essay, 1981a. The Introduction in this book (Sargent, 1981) deals among other things with the social aspects of the research environment.

5. In the text below, the references to Jon Elster, Marianne Gullestad, and, later, Fredrik Engelstad may be seen as a Norwegian example of this, that is, they reveal the double-faced potential for feminism of many Marxist intellectual milieus.

6. For a discussion of this, see, e.g., Liedman, 1981.

7. Farr Tormey (1976) applies the concept of exploitation to nature as well (see further below). Giddens does this also (1981:59).

8. Gouldner (1960:166) cites a dictionary definition of exploitation: "an unfair or unjust utilization of another." Elster (1981) defines exploitation as "all economic injustice which rests upon economic power, especially ownership of the means of production." For my present purposes the extent to which "exploitation" is or is not a normative concept is in no way a central issue. What is important is that the "technical" element that can be distinguished in the exploitation concept can guarantee among other things its analytical usefulness. See further below. For an example of how Marx's exploitation concept is seen as both technical and normative, see Arneson, 1981. For an example of a study that postulates that it is normative and investigates what and how, see Elster, 1980.

9. The incest taboo is often seen (Freud, Lévi-Strauss) as the norm that marked the origins of civilization—the first rule of law people established over themselves. Gouldner (1960) uses Malinowski (1932) and Westermarck (1908) as his main references in regard to how widespread the norm of reciprocity is. He also refers to Piaget's studies of moral judgment in children (1932).

10. I am aware that during the 1980s Marx's theory of surplus value and with it the concept of exploitation have been at the center of a multifaceted controversy among Marxists, a controversy in which so-called rational choice, or analytical Marxists (one of them being Jon Elster) play the leading role. This is not the place, however, to account for this in any detail. A particular investigation of what eventual significance this internal debate of Marxist theory might

have for the development of historical-materialist feminist theory must await its own work. Anyway, the arguments in this debate have not convinced me to give up, or to change fundamentally my attempt to explain patriarchy along the lines begun here.

A good introduction to the (somewhat varying) approaches to exploitation developed by the so-called analytical Marxists can be found in Roemer, 1988. The bibliographical notes in Roemer's book give an excellent overview of the central themes in this debate and the main works it has generated.

11. It is common to refer to Marx's three main sources as being: English political economy from the eighteenth and early nineteenth centuries, French Utopian socialism, and German philosophy.

12. The disappearance of the term "exploitation" from American sociology soon after it began to be used was due, according to Gouldner, to the struggle of sociology (in the behaviorist era, we might add) to assert itself as a science free of value judgments. As a matter of fact the concept of exploitation was a cornerstone in socialist criticism of modern society.

13. Recently, a political-theoretical approach to exploitation that differs from Macpherson's (see note 1 above) has begun to be developed (or redeveloped). This might be called the domination approach. It stands on a Weberian ground, or, rather, on the ground of the Marx-Weber synthesis that has been growing strong in the West for about twenty years. Anthony Giddens's concept of exploitation, referred to elsewhere in this chapter, represents this domination approach.

14. Farr Tormey discusses two important aspects on which there is no reason to expand in this context. In the first place she isolates the forgoing of one's own things, which is associated with parenthood. In the second she highlights the importance of looking beyond the dichotomy: self-sacrifice/egoism.

15. Farr Tormey argues convincingly that neither exploitation nor oppression requires that the "guilty" party act *with the intention* of exploiting or oppressing. The consequences of the action can be such anyway (1976:209).

Hanne Haavind (1980) has constructed a very usable model for modern gender roles built on symbolical interactionism, in which femininity and masculinity are assumed to aim at the maintenance of a seemingly equal but in reality unequal balance of power. But when she speaks of power and love in marriage (1982) she does so rather like Farr Tormey, about women's specific *burdens* (although she does not employ the concept of exploitation). Generally, her approach is only descriptive; it lacks the level of analysis on which assumptions about *what causes* women's "burdens" can be made.

16. Farr Tormey's concrete examples refer only to the housewife. (The analysis could, however, be extended to embrace working life where the division of work between the sexes displays the same traits as in the home.) I interpret her "menial tasks and unpleasant burdens" as referring primarily to housework. She does not delineate this specifically, but her discussion suggests that my reading is correct.

17. Cynthia Cockburn (1981) has distinguished between the material and

the economic, but her alternative "materiality" refers only to a sort of muscle-power–technical materiality. It deals with "questions of bodily physique and its extension in technology, of buildings and clothes, space and movement" (p. 43). Cockburn does not identify the kind of materiality that I seek to formulate in this chapter.

18. This short phrase by Marx is from the 1844 manuscripts, quoted here according to Giddens (1981:60). In a section entitled "The Problem of Exploitation" Giddens attempts to "widen Marx's standpoint" so that exploitation can be applied not only to human relationships but also to the use of nature by man. But typically enough, Giddens neglects men's specific use of (nature in) women.

19. My assertions here should be treated as philosophical and not empirical; the nature of work as well as love changes historically and cannot therefore in an antihistorical way be generalized empirically.

20. I do not use the term "contract" explicitly elsewhere in this book. It should be clear, however, that the historical type of formally equal patriarchy that I am dealing with here is one that also can be described in terms of contract. Compare, for instance, Carole Pateman, 1988, and Aaström and Hirdman, 1992.

21. Of course it is important not to see these two relationships as identical, that is, they have both similarities and differences.

22. Engelstad suggests that the work process and the process in which men and women interact share the same formal structure, the same pattern of conduct. A model of exploitation can be applied to both that includes three types of relationships: (i) an object relationship (the participants exchange things of the same value; labor for money), (ii) a premise relationship (the participants acknowledge one another as nonequal; power and subordination) and (iii) a mystification relationship (attempts to allow the appearance that the two other conflicting principles are reconciled) (1978:351–53).

23. See Mario Bunge on "emergentist materialism" (1980:2).

24. Raymond Williams postulates this in his discussion of Timparano and materialism (1978:10). His assertion is representative of the conventional Marxist view of what, apart from work, is considered to constitute praxis. (Others would add language to the complex of unique human capacities characteristic of human nature.) Compare also Karel Kosik's discussion of the concept of "praxis" (1978).

25. According to Karel Kosik's critical reading of Heidegger (from a historical materialist point of view), focusing on "care" instead of "labor" leads to a "philosophy founded upon *mystified praxis*" (Kosik, 1978:83). Kosik, however, is writing about "economy and philosophy" (p. 77) and, from this, generalizes to the "*whole* life" (p. 80). In many respects I find the kind of critique that Kosik raises against the phenomenological centering on care, convincing. But my assumption is that the application of the concept of "care" to the human relationships and activities with which I am dealing here needs a particular *feminist* materialist philosophy and feminist critique. A central idea to be developed in such an enterprise would be that *love* as a human sensuous, practical activity takes its place in the concept and the philosophy of praxis.

26. Empirical or phenomenological descriptions of what happens, more concretely, in the love-process (the process through which the "male surplus value" is produced) have to wait. As mentioned in Chapter 2, I think that the best descriptions available as yet are to be found in fiction. But there are also a great number of observations in feminist research literature that would back up my ideas. Dorothy Dinnerstein's book *The Mermaid and the Minotaur* (1976) could be a good example of this. What has not been done is to take men's use of women's love theoretically seriously as the most essential process through which contemporary patriarchy is reproduced.

27. The question of what kind of causality should be assumed here awaits further elaboration. Some maintain that unequal power between women and men must be demonstrated in each individual case. This is hardly reasonable in the light of the massive body of systematic evidence that already exists of inequality and abuse. But the question remains: Which sort of causal mechanisms does the pattern of this evidence assume? The likelihood is that we must think in terms of probabilities and stocastic correlations rather than from the basis of deductive causality.

Chapter 6

1. This paragraph is based on what I think can be regarded as the standard work in the field: Alice Clark, *Working Life of Women in the Seventeenth Century* ([1919] 1968).

2. Filmer (1588–1653) wrote the work for which he is now best known, *Patriarcha; or, The Natural Power of Kings*, partly in the form of pamphlets, around 1640. It was not published in its entirety until after his death, in 1680 (Laslett, 1967:57).

3. Ambjörnsson says that Locke occupies "an interesting intermediate position" between pure individualism and the Aristotelian tradition's view of society (1978:15).

4. Hobbes shifts between *society, commonwealth,* and *body politic,* while Locke speaks foremost of *civil society* and *political society.* Hobbes for the most part refers to the state as *the sovereign state,* but also as *the public state* or simply *the state,* while Locke most often speaks of *government.*

5. Locke puts these drives in the opposite order of strength. See 1978:62.

6. The concept of the state of nature has been the subject of much learned dispute, for instance, with regard to whether it referred to a historical reality or was purely a thought construction. It is only during recent decades that attention has been paid to the individual/family "contradiction" (see also note 15 below). Schochet (1967) indicates (old-)patriarchal pronouncements in Hobbes's writings, and suggests that " 'every man' can certainly be understood as 'every independent father' (or patriarch) without changing Hobbes' basic argument" (p. 441; see also, e.g., p. 431).

7. Strictly speaking it is not right to confront Hobbes with such a question, formulated as it is on the basis of a modern conception of knowledge that clearly

distinguishes between *is* and *ought*, because he did not think in this way. Nevertheless it can still be meaningful to ask this type of question provided one does so on Hobbes's own terms. This means that a merely empirical statement does not have philosophical/scientific status, while "taking a stand"—if based on proper conceptual analysis—corresponds to an affirmed truth. (For Hobbes's position on the theory of knowledge, see, e.g., 1969:16, 21–22, and 1968: 165–83.)

8. Except where stated otherwise, page-references in the section on Locke are to Carpenter's edition of *Two Treatises of Government* (Locke, 1978).

9. Christopher Hill, *Century of Revolution, 1603–1714*, quoted in Zaretsky, 1976:1737.

10. How controversial it was in powerful circles to, for instance, question women's duty to passively suffer the pangs of childbirth is apparent from Adrienne Rich, *Of Woman Born: Motherhood as Experience and Institution* (1976:117): "In 1591 a midwife, Agnes Simpson, was burned at the stake for having attempted to relieve birth pangs with opium or laudanum."

11. See Butler, 1978, and Shanley, 1979. Butler maintains that it is in Locke that the earliest roots of liberal feminism are to be found. According to Shanley, Locke's treatment of marriage as an institution based on contract was the culmination of fifty years of political discussion in which varying images of marriage were interwoven.

12. Milton went furthest in calling for new marriage legislation. According to Shanley, he was anxious to end an unhappy marriage. In 1644, when Parliament was at war with the king, Milton seized the opportunity to publish *Doctrine and Discipline of Divorce*, with a letter "To the Parliament of England with the Assembly" (Shanley, 1979: 84–85).

13. For the sake of amusement we can put side by side Locke's and Filmer's justification of the man's dominion. According to Filmer the man is the nobler, according to Locke the abler and stronger. One can be so bold as to suggest that each justification is related to a specific historical epoch or mode of production: under feudalism it was important to be the nobler, under capitalism the abler.

14. Locke's thoughts on how to bring up children are a subject in themselves, and one that I have not been able to go into here. His utilitarian program was intended for bringing up and educating the sons of the upper class. In response to a mother's direct question, he briefly expressed himself on the upbringing of girls: it should not be essentially different from that of boys. (See further Butler, 1978, and Shanley, 1979). Locke's principles of upbringing and education were "progressive" to the extent that he advocated less flogging and more humane treatment. But the message comes through loud and clear: Children's wills are inexorably to be bent and shaped, and open defiance or refractoriness is to be suppressed with beating if necessary—which is a part of parental love.

15. The understanding of Hobbes and Locke as neopatriarchal thinkers has come chiefly, I think, from two sources: from historians of ideas who have begun treating the family as problematic, and from the research of recent decades into

the position of women from the point of view both of the history of ideas and of ideology. However, in the first of these two sources one cannot take for granted any special awareness of the problems of relations between the sexes, though on the other hand one can rely on there being an awareness of the parents (fathers)/children (sons) relationship. Besides Schochet, 1967 and 1975, see Hinton, 1967 and 1968, and Chapman, 1975.

16. Quoted in Sachs and Wilson, 1978:241. The words are those of Sir William Blackstone (1723–80), the renowned judge and writer on law. It was not until 1972 that the same basic position was officially abandoned in American law (p. 242).

17. Here I think of controversies over the theoretical significance of gender that have been acted out predominantly among British sociologists and Norwegian historians. The expression "conventional views" alludes to the title of John Goldthorpe's article (1983) "Women and Class Analysis: In Defence of the Conventional View." See on this subject Chapter 4, note 14.

18. In a recent work, David Miller (1987) comments on the feminist phrase. For him "the personal is political" hardly makes any sense besides that which has become a truism in political science proper, namely, that "any issue— protection of rare breeds of animals, or the construction of a tunnel under the English Channel—may properly become political" (p. 391). On the other hand, he accepts "the practice of referring to politics within corporations, trade unions, universities and other such sub-state institutions [as being] proper and illuminating" (p. 391). According to the theoretical stance I am arguing in this book it is also, and for similar reasons, "proper and illuminating" to refer to politics within those sub-state institutions by means of which the relations between the sexes and their specific production of people are organized.

Chapter 7

1. I use "scientific studies of politics" and "studies of politics" to include the main ways of approaching politics: political science (which tends to look at politics from a state perspective), political sociology (which more often starts in society), Marxist studies of politics (which takes class-structure as an important point of departure); and feminist studies of politics (whose common denominator is the perspective of sex/gender as a social relationship which organizes society).

2. When I speak about women versus men as being the essential parties in the sexual process, I am not cancelling out lesbian or homosexual relationships. My point is that if we take sexuality (as opposed to economy) to be the complex fundament on which patriarchy, in its various historical forms, is based, the main parties in this *oppressive* sex/gender structure are women versus men (rather than women versus women or men versus men). This oppressive relationship, in turn, forms the conditions on which people practice other social relationships.

Furthermore, my standpoint implies a view opposed to that of, for instance,

Hartmann (1981) as she asserts that the basic relation of patriarchy is a relation between men. Defining it that way she misses the whole point of the new feminist use of the term.

3. This theme has been one of the burning issues within the multi-branched (methodological) debate on power studies. "Interest" and "power," in this debate, used to be defined in terms of each other and are characterized by Lukes (1974) as "essentially contested concepts" (see Lukes, 1974, for references and an introduction to this debate). For an overview of the main contributions to the more limited (analytical) debate on the concept of interests in politics, see the references in Parks, 1982:n.1, and Reeve and Ware, 1983:n.1. Benton (1982) argues that while "power" can be conceived and applied without "moral or political bias," the concept of interests is indispensably both cognitive and evaluative" (p. 8).

4. Sapiro's view is similar to this. She argues that it can be expanded from its present customary use to include sex/gender concerns, such as the production and reproduction of children.

5. One of the greatest weaknesses in modern, mainstream political science is the lack of such historically grounded theorizing about politics. The way in which *interests* is usually handled today is a good example of the "poverty of theory." On one hand, there is a lot of philosophical (logically or morally oriented) conceptual analysis that is almost entirely unrelated to historical or empirical conditions; on the other hand, the term "interests" is much used in empirical studies—but then usually without any clearly stated theoretical frame of references.

6. Ethel Klein (1984) provides certain evidence that is relevant here. According to her, women's support for feminism is part of their personal identity or consciousness (and, thus, as I see it, part of their bodies-and-minds as human-material entities); and "consciousness . . . is derived from personal experiences that prompt people actually to change the political agenda" (p. 104). The significance of men's support for feminism differs from women's. "For men, feminism is an abstract issue of rights and obligations," a cause that they can sympathize with (if they want to) on ideological grounds. "Men's concern for feminism is similar to the concern that whites express about race discrimination" (p. 104). It should be added here that the survey questions that these results are based on are mainly about feminism in the meaning of efforts to end sex-discrimination and sexism in general. To what extent nurturing (or "mothering") fathers, for instance, come to such issues as child-care facilities "from the path of personal experience," instead of that of ideology, is thus another question.

7. "Interest" in the sense of financial interest rates or gains has its roots in the Middle Ages. Money lending was carried on for centuries before openly taking out interest on borrowed money was allowed. The prohibition on interest was circumvented by allowing compensation for those damages a borrower might cause a creditor's property. This compensation subsequently was called interest (s.v. "Interest" in *International Encyclopedia of the Social Sciences*). My references regarding the history of the concept include, further, works such as Gunn, 1969; *Philosophisches Wörterbuch*, 1975b; and Hirschman, 1977.

8. Allusion to Birnbaum, 1976.

9. My arguments in this essay imply a use of "form" and "formal" that transcends their common meaning of juridico-legal formalism, that is, legal rules for what individual citizens have to do, or are allowed to do, as members of the state/political community. In short I use "form" and "formal" as meaning: the power of forming or shaping societal processes. So the fact that women are fighting for an openly acknowledged presence as *women* in those processes, and the idea, derived from this fact, that women and men as gendered persons are interested parties in the political processes, challenges the reified genderlessness of the existing forms. Women are demanding gender-based social "intervention" into the seemingly gender-neutral institutionalized arrangements (forms) that shape, or direct, the substantial/material processes (the work-process, the process of producing and reproducing people, etc.) of society.

10. This line of reasoning as well as the whole discussion here of women and interest theory leads into the question of the status of women as women (and of men as men) in relation to the state; or the question of sex/gender as a component capacity in citizenship. In the last few years a feminist theory of the state has begun to emerge. For further references, see Chapter 8, notes 1 and 2, and note 9 above.

11. A review of the literature shows that there are at least three different ways of linking interests to some source or base: (1) Interests *are* the preferences of context-free subjects; (2) Interests are related to some externally determined principles or standards, which in turn can be of two kinds: (a) some ethical principles or ideals, or (b) some objectively stated standards for human need fulfillment; and (3) Interests emerge from people's social experiences, from the social arrangements in which people practice their lives. My own standpoint is of the third kind.

12. Even if there are other "memberships," such as class and race, they do not *cancel out* gender ones. In fact, they are always mediated by it. Of course, the particular intersections of race, class, and sex/gender and the ways these vary in different historical and cultural contexts need to be articulated carefully in theory and studied empirically.

13. The behavioral revolution in Anglo-American political science brought with it, among other things, much ado about how to define the concept of "group" in general and "interest group" in particular. This depended on methodological individualism's being one of the main points of the behavioralist credo. A central issue in the definition discussions was whether to define "interest group" by considering some objectively confirmable characteristics of individuals (such as class position, sex, age, etc.) or if shared attitudes, or consciousness of some common concerns, between individuals was needed for "interest group" to be a meaningful concept. Against this background Klein (1984), for example, distinguishes between women as an interest category or a status in the objective sense, and women as an interest group in the sense of a class of people who, through a social and political movement, have become aware of some common concerns. In traditional political theory similar distinctions have been made be-

tween grouping and group (Easton) and potential interest group and interest group (Truman).

14. Siedentop (1983), for instance, criticizes existing political theory for taking the concept of "individual" as a neutral or descriptive term synonymous to "the social agent" in general, while it is, in fact, historically specific and related to another problematic concept—"the state." "*De facto* development of the 'state' [as one species of government] is a necessary condition for the emergence of the individual as a social role," according to Siedentop (1983:61).

15. This is an allusion to the book with that title (1973) by Hanne Haavind et al. in which the authors criticize several dubious scientific results and interpretations of the mother/child relationship.

16. There are at least two different discourses on need-based political theory. On one hand what might be called a reformist theory of social justice and on the other a radical, or Marxist, theory of social community. Representative authors of the first discourse are Bay (1965, 1968, 1980), Etzioni (1968), and Miller (1976).

A radical theory of needs and community, built on Marx, has been developed by such authors as Herbert Marcuse and Agnes Heller. For further studies on this subject see, for example, Jones, 1978.

My critical comments in the text refer mainly to the first mentioned discourse (the justice theory of needs) as being the more relevant one for looking at existing welfare societies (and in fact Diamond/Hartsock link together the two by quoting Bay). On the other hand, it seems to me that the Marxists hitherto, when they claim that people's concrete needs should be the raison de societé, also take things for granted that must be discussed. The whole dimension of agency and organization: the formulating of wants, potential conflicts, decision-making, implementation, and so on, is hardly problematized at all. Of course we are here touching on the question of the underdevelopment of *political* theory in Marxist thought, and there is no space here to go further into that question.

17. This way of defining "interests" as control over the conditions of choice is both like and unlike the way Brian Barry (in his *Political Argument*, 1965) conceives interests: as generalized means (or actions) to ends (or results), and not the ends or results themselves (pp. 176, 183). The similarity is in drawing such a boundary and the focus on action rather than the content; the dissimilarity is that Barry treats the two aspects as two separate or isolated things while my understanding here (and my reading of Parks) aims at treating the two aspects of interests (the form and the content) as dialectically related. Another dissimilarity is that Barry's concept "generalized means" refers exclusively to money, while my action component in the concept of interest refers to a power of agency as a specific political "means."

18. Dahlerup refers to Matthew A. Crenson: *The Un-Politics of Air Pollution: A Study of Non-Decisionmaking in the Cities* (1971). This is one of the few empirical studies carried out with the help of the controversial non-decision theory. The conundrum concerns how one can, and from a scientific point of view should, investigate power in society. "Objective" or "real interest" is included as one of the controversial concepts. See also note 4 above.

19. The expression is Tocqueville's "l'ancien régime." He wrote about the "great transformation," that is, the transition from the Middle Ages to the new age in western Europe. "L'ancien régime" refers more specifically to the royal autocracy: the middle phase between the medieval decentralized social organization and the political/civil, gradually democratic modern societies.

20. The historical line of reasoning I am aiming at should not be confused with the type of argument that says, for example, that women have the right of participation because they comprise half the population. To speak about objective interests in terms such as these would be to derive women's interests from some principle of quantitative justice. That is not analytically fruitful, even if it sometimes is ideologically forceful. In short we can say that the notion of "objective" or "real" interests, actualized in Crenson's (1971) study, refer to biological criteria; the justice argument, as usually formulated, refers to an ahistorical general principle; while my notion of "objective" interest refers to subjects or agents motivated by experienced historically specific forces.

21. See Balas et al. 1982:103–6. Several sections of this book support my arguments here.

22. In his book *Democracy: The Threshold of Freedom* ([1948] 1977: 61–63), Harold F. Gosnell relates how the principle of equal distribution of sexes among the delegates to a party convention was practiced during the second and third decades of this century in a state in the United States, and how it was a disappointment for the women because the men, who were already in power, could see to it that "difficult" women disappeared and that accommodating women were chosen for the places designated for women.

Lenin's berating of Clara Zetkin for allowing working-class women to discuss marriage problems at their meetings is well known. Less well known is how she was actually treated in the party at home in Germany, how, for example, in 1908 (when German women obtained the right to organize politically), at the designation of a women's place in the party executive, she had to step back in favor of Luise Zietz, a woman who increasingly identified herself with the party executive and not with women (cf. Honeycutt, 1976:139).

Anita Dahlberg (1984:138) takes up for instance how the unions (read union's dominating men) see a threat in women's "internal solidarity." Similarly, recent reports from the Swedish JÄMO (the ombudsman for the equality between the sexes) show that some of the women who have contacted JÄMO because of discrimination on the job have afterward been harassed by their bosses and by their union officials as well.

23. In real life, not even these dialectics exhaust the multifold of reality. Presumably, surrender sometimes *is* "control," as for example in sado-masochistic relationships.

Chapter 8

1. About women and men having different relations to the state, especially the welfare state, see Hernes, 1984, 1987. About women and various state inter-

ests, see Randall, 1987, chap. 4, esp. pp. 195–204. The earliest writings on women and the welfare state underlined the oppressive and controlling state function, see, e.g., Wilson, 1977. Later works tend toward a more nuanced view; besides Hernes, 1984, 1987, see, e.g., Siim, 1988. About inherent contradictions in the Swedish equality policy, see Eduards, 1986.

2. Besides Pateman's work in this field, see Lange, 1976; Gould, 1983; Gutmann, 1988.

3. This paragraph is a summing up of a discussion in the ECPR workshop, *Political Theories of Gender and Power*, 1986, in Gothenburg, where I was asked: "What, exactly, do you mean by 'women as women'?"

4. Robbins (1955), for instance, discusses these two strands of thought (under the heading " 'Natural rights' and Utility") in connection with his presentation of the classical English liberal view of individual freedom versus state authority. Kraditor (1971) also writes about a similar shift in arguments in American history and within the suffragist movement. My point is that we should look closer at these two lines of thought when analyzing "women's freedom versus male authority."

5. Compared with Susan Moller Okin (1979), who argues that from Plato on a functionalist view of women has prevailed in Western political thought, I want to stress the point of being observant to historical shifts in types of arguments related to other societal changes.

6. See, e.g., Thomas (1958) on women's emancipatory efforts within the Civil War sects in the seventeenth century in England.

7. About the ideological shift from Divinity to Humanity, see Vernon, 1986:pts. I–II.

8. My reasoning here on the aristocratic *chain* image being substituted by a modern masculine one was inspired by Vernon, 1986; his own analysis, though, reflects a seemingly sexless world.

9. About the idea, "deeply rooted in England for many centuries," of the importance of men having property in women, see Thomas, 1959. See also Hirschon, 1984.

10. See Dolan, 1988.

11. See, e.g., Crompton and Mann, 1986.

12. Interestingly, Stoper (1988) argues that a gender gap has in fact existed for many decades in American politics within several issue areas but has been concealed because of "certain peculiarities of the American political system."

13. Here I have in mind especially the Women's List in Iceland, which now holds 8 percent of the seats in the Icelandic parliament.

14. See, e.g., Hedlund, 1986.

15. See, e.g., Haavind, 1984.

Chapter 9

1. A "distinctive theoretical project" is taken from Alison Jaggar (1983:118). The term "research tradition" belongs to a particular standpoint in

the perpetual methodological discussion of how to deal with questions of rationality and progress in scientific inquiry. If Thomas Kuhn's "paradigm" and "paradigm shifts" is taken as a relatively fixed starting point in this discussion, and Imre Lakatos's "progressive" (i.e., content-increasing) versus "degenerative" "research programs" provide a strong alternative in the second phase of this discussion, then Larry Laudan's "more or less fruitful" "research traditions" is central among a third generation's attempts to modify Lakatos's rather strict, although liberalized, Popperianism concerning shifts in scientific discourse, without falling into the irrationalism of (at least the early) Kuhn.

Of course, from a pure linguistic point of view, it seems strange to introduce or propose a tradition. But apart from that, Laudan's ideas on research traditions seem to be well to square with the history of what actually has been happening between Marxism and feminism (also, for that matter, between feminism and, as it seems, every other established methodological program) since the late 1960s, and also with the continuing development within the various feminist idioms of inquiry.

My account here of Laudan's work (1977) relies partly on Ball, 1987.

2. It should be noticed that the five-to-ten-year period when most of the leading works of current socialist feminist theory were written (starting at about 1975) was also a period during which discussions about sexuality, especially "normal" heterosexuality, became almost nonexistent among socialist feminists, and even among heterosexual feminists at large. Because of the—often very traumatic—political conflicts within the women's movement between separatist and nonseparatist feminists, even theoretical analyses of patriarchal heterosexuality, which did not rest on separatist ideology, became almost impossible. These conflicts exploded in many countries in the late 1970s. Experiences of male opposition, ranging from sexist comments or other male authoritarian expressions at seminars to direct hostility and violence, presumably also contributed to silence nonseparatist women on this matter (see, e.g., Sargent, 1981; Segal, 1983). Recently, socialist feminists in England and the United States have begun to discuss sexuality, even heterosexuality, again, and especially the reasons for their own years of silence (see, e.g., Campbell, 1987; English, Hollibaugh, and Rubin, 1987; Segal, 1987. Yet these reflections do not seem to have made much of an impact on the more comprehensive theory-building within socialist feminism.

3. In the editorial introduction to *Feminism as Critique* (1987) Seyla Benhabib and Drucilla Cornell claim that "the confrontation between twentieth-century Marxism and feminist thought requires nothing less than a paradigm shift of the former" (p. 1). Furthermore, they describe this shift as the "displacement of the paradigm of production" (p. 1). However, neither these authors nor Linda Nicholson, whose chapter "Feminism and Marx: Integrating Kinship with the Economic," according to the editors, provides a programmatic statement for the volume as a whole (p. 4), actually carry through any such shift. In all their statements of the alternative conceptualization needed to displace the monopoly position of (economic) "production" they still cling to what I would call a *work paradigm*. A closer examination of what feminist critical theorists argue on this point is in progress.

4. This is presumably a point around which a great deal of misunderstanding of what I am actually saying may arise. I want to underline that, for me, to insist on the importance of isolating in theory the structural basis of contemporary patriarchy does not go against, for instance, those feminist historical or sociological approaches that (often explicitly following the British Marxist historian Edward P. Thompson) emphasize "experience" as mediating between "social being" and "social consciousness" (or between "basis" and "superstructure," a metaphor that Thompson explicitly rejects as being more harmful than useful).

As Ellen Kay Trimberger (1984) shows in her examination of Thompson's approach, his way of filling the "silences" "as to cultural and moral mediations" he finds within the historical materialist research tradition does not render superfluous the Marxist theory of structured and determined social being. On the contrary, "Thompson's concept of social being also allows for those structured relationships that, despite their origins in intended actions, come to confront actors as limiting structures outside themselves" (Trimberger, 1984:220). For Thompson, certain basic elements of Marx's structural theory of capitalist social being (the base) are given and accepted; that is, the basic theory is accepted as long as it does not follow that the theory of the logic of capital could substitute concrete studies of how this logic—the functioning of the capitalist work-process and structural relationship—is experienced and handled in various cultural contexts.

What I am arguing is that the theoretical project of feminist historical materialism has not hitherto had any such given, or relatively stabilized, theory of contemporary "social being" *as structured by sociosexual relations in carrying on human-material processes specific for these relations.* My notes toward a theory of men's exploitation of women's love power in the name of free and equal exchange of sociosexual goods is an attempt to fill this particular "silence."

A similar mix of approval and critique could be formulated about the feminist-standpoint theorists, who, at present, tend to concentrate on experiental *differences* among women in such a way as to run the risk of cancelling out conceptions of the structural commonalities of women's conditions (see, e.g., Harding, 1988).

5. Deploring the lack of adequate theory reflects not only feelings of academic dissatisfaction. The need for a more complete conception of social existence is experienced repeatedly in the practical political struggles against the many barriers to sociosexual equality. In her *The Past Is Before Us: Feminism in Action Since the 1960s* (1989), Sheila Rowbotham claims that "lurking behind the practical and strategic problems is the lack of a theory" (p. 179). Rowbotham is one of the feminist historians who acknowledges her debt to E. P. Thompson's approach (see note 4 above) and who seems to conclude from the emphasis on experience (which always, necessarily, is complex and composit, emerging from class, sex/gender, race, and other sources) that feminist analysis can do without a distinct basic theory of patriarchy. Thus, she thinks that the kind of theory that is missing should be one that can "take on the whole range of human activity" (p. 179). According to my view, a theory cannot (or, rather, should

not) provide direct *solutions* to practical political problems arising in concrete situations, especially not solutions that "take on the whole range of human activity." In order to interpret and make practical decisions about particular situations we should not simply try to *apply* a Marxist or feminist or any other grand, or less grand, theory as such. Basic, substantial theoretical ideas should be used in a cautious "dialogue with the evidence," to borrow a phrase from Trimberger (1984:227). (For further arguments about the usefulness and limits of the kind of theorizing I am working on, see the last section of Chapter 4.)

6. This is a quotation from Jane Jaquette's "Review Essay," on political science in *Signs* (1976:163). She brings the "arena of personal interactions," or, "the politics of everyday life," as a research focus, into her argument for how feminist political scientists should revise the discipline. Very little has been done yet in this direction.

7. Robert Connell (1987:41) uses the conceptual pair intrinsic–extrinsic to distinguish between the kind of theories where gender inequality is produced internally, that is, within the very gender system itself, and theories in which determinants of gender inequality are looked for elsewhere (externally), for instance, in the class relations of the capitalist ideology.

8. The materialist (in a bodily sense of that word) phenomenology of Maurice Merleau-Ponty (1962) seems to be in harmony with my way of theorizing about sexuality and love as a specific and structured current in human existence.

9. I have always seen Firestone's technological solution to the "tyranny of nature" over women's bodies more as an expression of irony than as a serious vision. Besides that, reproductive technologies are being developed in male-dominated science independent of this or that feminist vision. Anyway, her "solution" does not necessarily follow from her basic propositions, namely, to take sexuality and love seriously as core entities and processes in a new division, or epoch, of the historical materialist research tradition. Nor does it follow from her fundamentally optimistic view on the future of love. For an essay on the different views on love in radical feminism and a comparison with Rousseau, see Rapaport, 1976.

10. For a discussion about problems of materialism, the risk of degeneration into closed systems and "frozen world-views," see, e.g., Williams, 1978.

11. See, e.g., the critique of Joan Scott in Jones and Jónasdóttir, 1988:6–7.

12. I do not yet have a permanent set of terms to use in these discussions. In my previous essays I mostly used the production/reproduction vocabulary from the key formulation of the materialistic conception of history in Engels, (1884) 1972 (see quotation in Chapter 2). However, I also use the concepts creation/re-creation as synonyms to production/reproduction when I refer to the field of sexuality (or the production of human beings themselves). Procreation, then, as it is commonly used, refers literally to the creation of new people, that is, giving birth to children.

13. The expression "enminded bodies" is mine. It plays with the more common "embodied minds."

14. This is the line of argument pursued by those feminist anthropologists

who emphasize cultural meaning as the crucial thing for understanding gender asymmetry. In an influential essay from 1980 Michelle Zimbalist Rosaldo writes: "It now appears to me that women's place in human social life is not in any direct sense a product of the things she does (or even less a function of what, biologically, she is) but of the meaning her activities acquire through concrete social interactions" (p. 400). But as soon as questions are asked about sources or causes of gender asymmetry, this line of argument seems to come very close to the biologism it set out to reject in the first place. It is difficult to find determinants, other than ones of biological or physiological necessity, when the establishment and change of the cultural configuration of meaning is not seen as related to any specific material practice, or transformative, social activity (what people *do*).

15. The quotations in the text are from Kate Soper's critical account of a dispute between Lucien Sève and Louis Althusser on the reading of the sixth thesis in Marx's *Theses on Feuerbach* ("The human essence is no abstraction inherent in each single individual. In its reality it is the ensemble of social relations").

16. The term "economy" as it is used here embraces the entire work process in a society, including unpaid housework.

17. For a clarifying account of the difference between the realist concept of power and the mechanistic one, see, e.g., Farr, 1986:210–11. See also Isaac, 1987, and Sayer, 1984.

18. In addition, many would see the power embedded in human language as the most vital power in history, a stance I find disputable. This is not the place, however, to dwell on a dispute on that matter.

19. For a fruitful view on how functionalist approaches as well as political (or agency) ones should be seen as two related aspects of a theoretical perspective, and not necessarily as two approaches that cancel out each other, see Alford and Friedland, 1985.

20. For a discussion of the challenges to existing theories and power structures, which rest in feminist notions of women's collective agency, see, e.g., Eduards, forthcoming.

21. This is made most strongly by Foucault, see, e.g., *Power/Knowledge* (1980:59).

22. To be sure, the argument of women's inferior nature survived alongside the utilitarian view, especially in continental philosophy. But even there the usefulness-of-women view has, if not precedence, a prominent position. Of course, it is possible to perceive these two different modes of oppressive ideology as two different sides of one composite line of argument. I think, however, that utilitarianism (which allows some groups of people to exploit others in the name of a common interest) can be seen as an epoch-specific form of power to control women, which the inferior-nature argument alone could not provide. This is the hegemonic power to define what is useful in women as well as when, where, and how it might be so, independently of how women's nature is defined. Moreover, the strength of this male hegemony is increased by the fact that women

themselves are very much forced to argue in these same terms. Women often find it unnatural, but necessary, to argue for their own wants in terms of their complementary usefulness, since it is the only way for them to be acknowledged.

The somewhat lengthy remarks made here on this issue can be seen as an indirect response to some of Carole Pateman's comments on my article (Chapter 8) in Pateman, 1990.

23. For a closer account of the feminist-standpoint theory, see Jaggar (1983, pp. 370ff., 392). This direction of thought was developed by Dorothy Smith (1974, 1979), Nancy Hartsock (1983), Jane Flax (1983), and others.

24. A "device for backing values with power" is Arthur Stinchcombe's definition of a "social institution" (1968:182).

25. The kind of authority I envision on behalf of women is neither a superior position relative to men in a social hierarchy (a female *Herrschaft* position in the Weberian sense) nor entitlement to the kind of restricted virtue of cognitive rationality that Hannah Arendt (1961) idealizes. It seems to me that the kind of authority women in the West today actually tend to demand, is more of a position of strength that enables them (and men) to act politically to augment new "virtues"—in public, in private, as well as personally. They demand that a space be allowed, openly for emotive and compassionate judgments so that the cognitive-rational choices will be kept within reason—and vice versa. See also Jones, 1987, 1990.

26. See, e.g., Rustin, 1989; Harvey, 1989.

27. This idea was included in a program on sexual policy presented by The National Federation of Social Democratic Women in Sweden in 1984.

28. The expression "lesbian continuum" is used by Adrienne Rich to designate what she thinks is the appropriate way to embrace the whole range of social and political bonding among women, not only lesbian connections in the more usual and narrower sense (Rich, 1980:648–49).

29. Beatrice Halsaa (1988) distinguishes between "womanism" and "feminism"; "womanism" refers to ideas seen as a precondition for feminism, which in turn is seen as a more full-fledged "ideology in itself" (p. 325).

30. This alludes to the impressive gesture in the well-known chapter on behavioralist democratic theory in *Voting*, by Berelson, Lazarsfeld, and McPhee (1954). They ascribe to elitist politics a similar self-regulating, mystical force as "the invisible hand" is thought to bring about in the market economy, where private vices are thought to become public benefits: "Where the rational citizen seems to abdicate, nevertheless angels seem to tread" (p. 311).

31. This can be taken as a correction of the idea expressed in the title of Robert Paul Wolff's essay "There's Nobody Here but Us Persons" (1976).

References

Aas, Berit. 1975. "On Female Culture: An Attempt to Formulate a Theory of Women's Solidarity and Action." *Acta Sociologica* 18(2–3): 142–61.

Aaström, Gertrud, and Yvonne Hirdman, eds. 1992. *Kontrakt i kris: Om kvinnors plats i välfärdsstaten.* Stockholm: Carlssons Förlag.

Acker, Joan. 1973. "Women and Social Stratification: A Case of Intellectual Sexism." *American Journal of Sociology* 78 (4): 936–45.

Agonito, Rosemary. 1977. *History of Ideas on Woman: A Source Book.* New York: G. P. Putnam's Sons.

Alford, Robert R., and Roger Friedland. 1985. *Powers of Theory: Capitalism, the State, and Democracy.* Cambridge: Cambridge University Press.

Allport, Gordon W. 1935. "Attitudes." In C. Murchison, ed., *Handbook of Social Psychology.* Worcester, Mass.: Clark University Press.

Ambjörnsson, Ronny. 1978. *Familjeporträtt: Essäer om familjen, kvinnan, barnet och kärleken i historien.* Stockholm: Gidlunds.

Anthias, Floya, and Nira Yuval-Davis. 1983. "Contextualizing Feminism: Gender, Ethnic and Class Divisions." *Feminist Review*, no. 15:62–75.

Arendt, Hannah. 1961. "What Is Authority?" In *Between Past and Future.* New York: Viking Press.

Arneson, Richard J. 1981. "What's Wrong with Exploitation?" *Ethics* 91 (January): 202–27.

Avineri, Shlomo. 1968. *The Social and Political Thought of Karl Marx.* Cambridge: Cambridge University Press.

Balas, Gro, et al., eds. 1982. *Faglig kvinnepolitikk: Hvor gaar LO?* (Union politics concerning women: where is the [TUG] going?) Oslo: Pax Förlag.

Balbus, Isaac D. 1971. "The Concept of Interest in Pluralist and Marxism Analysis." *Politics and Society* 1:151–77.

Ball, Terence. 1984. "Marxian Science and Positivist Politics." In Terence Ball and James Farr, eds., *After Marx.* Cambridge: Cambridge University Press.

———. 1987. "Is There Progress in Political Science?" In Ball, ed., *Idioms of Inquiry: Critique and Renewal in Political Science.* Albany: State University of New York Press.

269

Barker, Diana Leonard, and Sheila Allen, eds. 1976. *Dependence and Exploitation in Work and Marriage.* London: Longman.

Barrett, Michèle. 1980. *Women's Oppression Today: Problems in Marxist Feminism Analysis.* London: Verso and NLB.

————. 1987. "The Concept of 'Difference.' " *Feminist Review,* no. 26:29–41.

Barry, Brian. 1965. *Political Argument.* London: Routledge and Kegan Paul.

Bay, Christian. 1965. "Politics and Pseudo-Politics: A Critical Evaluation of Some Behavioral Literature." *American Political Science Review* 59:39–51.

————. 1968. "Needs, Wants, and Political Legitimacy." *Canadian Journal of Political Science* 1(33): 241–60.

————. 1980. "Peace and Critical Political Knowledge as Human Rights." *Political Theory* 8(3): 293–318, 331–34.

de Beauvoir, Simone. (1949) 1972. *The Second Sex.* Harmondsworth: Penguin Books.

Beckman, Svante. 1981. *Kärlek paa tjänstetid: Om amatörer och professionella inom vaarden* (Love in working hours: on amateurs and professionals within the caring professions). Stockholm: Arbetslivscentrum.

Beechey, Veronica. 1978. "Women and Production: A Critical Analysis of Some Sociological Theories of Women's Work." In Annette Kuhn and A. M. Wolpe, eds., *Feminism and Materialism: Women and Modes of Production.* London: Routledge and Kegan Paul.

————. 1979. "On Patriarchy." *Feminist Review,* no. 3:66–82.

————. 1987. *Unequal Work.* London: Verso.

Benhabib, Seyla. 1986. "The Generalized and the Concrete Other: The Kohlberg-Gilligan Controversy and Feminist Theory." *Praxis International* 5(4): 402–24.

————. 1987. "The Generalized and the Concrete Other: The Kohlberg-Gilligan Controversy and Feminist Theory." In Seyla Benhabib and Drucilla Cornell, eds., *Feminism as Critique: Essays on the Politics of Gender in Late-Capitalist Societies.* Cambridge: Polity Press.

Benhabib, Seyla, and Drucilla Cornell. 1987. "Beyond the Politics of Gender." In Benhabib and Cornell, eds., *Feminism as Critique: Essays on the Politics of Gender in Late-Capitalist Societies.* Cambridge: Polity Press.

Benston, Margaret. 1969. "The Political Economy of Women's Liberation." *Monthly Review* 21(4): 13–27.

Benton, Ted. 1982. "Realism, Power and Objective Interests." In Keith Graham, ed., *Contemporary Political Philosophy.* Cambridge: Cambridge University Press.

————. 1984. *The Rise and Fall of Structural Marxism: Althusser and His Influence.* London: Macmillan.

Berelson, Bernard R., Paul E. Lazarsfeld, and William N. McPhee. 1954. *Voting: A Study of Opinion Formation in a Presidential Campaign.* Chicago and London: University of Chicago Press, Phoenix Books.

Berg, Anne Marie. 1977. "Kvinneforskning og konjunkturer." In Anne Marie Berg, Aase Berge, Annemor Kalleberg, and Arnlang Leira, eds., *I kvinners bilde: Bidrag til en kvinnesosiologi.* Oslo: Pax Förlag.

Berman, Harold J. 1983. *Law and Revolution: The Formation of the Western Legal Tradition.* Cambridge, Mass., and London: Harvard University Press.

Bernard, Jessie. 1971. *Women and the Public Interest: An Essay on Policy and Protest.* Chicago: Aldine/Athertone.

Bhaskar, Roy. 1978. *A Realist Theory of Science.* Brighton: Harvester Press.

————. 1979. *The Possibility of Naturalism.* Brighton: Harvester Press.

Birnbaum, Pierre. 1976. "Power Divorced from Its Sources: A Critique of the Exchange Theory of Power." In Brian Barry, ed., *Power and Political Theory.* London: John Wiley.

Boals, Kay. 1975. "Review Essay: Political Science." *Signs* 1(1): 161–74.

Bourque, Susan C., and Jean Grossholtz. 1974. "Politics as Unnatural Practice: Political Science Looks at Female Participation." *Politics and Society* 4(2): 225–66.

Brecht, Arnold. 1959. *Political Theory: The Foundations of Twentieth-Century Political Thought.* Princeton: Princeton University Press.

Brekke, Live, and Haukaa, Runa. 1980. "Teorin som inte finns." *Kvinnovetenskaplig tidskrift* 1(1): 30–44. (Summary in English, p. 44.)

Brennan, Teresa, and Carole Pateman. 1979. "Mere Auxiliaries to the Commonwealth: Women and the Origins of Liberalism." *Political Studies* 27(2): 183–200.

Bridenthal, Renate, and Claudia Koonz, eds. 1977. *Becoming Visible: Women in European History.* Boston: Houghton Mifflin.

Brown, Wendy. 1988. *Manhood and Politics: A Feminist Reading in Political Theory.* Totowa, N.J.: Rowman & Littlefield.

Bunge, Mario. 1980. *The Mind-Body Problem: A Psychobiological Approach.* Oxford: Pergamon Press.

Burnham, Linda, and Miriam Louie. 1985. *The Impossible Marriage: A Marxist Critique of Socialist Feminism.* Special issue of *Line of March: A Marxist-Leninist Journal of Rectification* 17 (Spring).

Butler, Melissa A. 1978. "Early Liberal Roots of Feminism: John Locke and the Attack on Patriarchy." *American Political Science Review* 72(1): 135–50.

Campbell, Angus, Philip E. Converse, Warren E. Miller, and Donald E. Stokes. 1960. *The American Voter.* New York: Wiley.

Campbell, Beatrix. 1987. "A Feminist Sexual Politics: Now You See It, Now You Don't." In Feminist Review, ed., *Sexuality: A Reader.* London: Virago Press.

Carlsson, Christina. 1986a. "Kön och klass ur ett historiskt perspektive." In *Feminism och marxism: En föräslkelse med förhinder.* See Ganetz, Gunnarsson, and Göansson, 1986.

————. 1986b. *Kvinnosyn och kvinnopolitik: En studie av svensk socialdemokrati, 1880–1910.* Lund: Arkiv.

Carlsson, Christina, et al. 1983. "Om patriarkatet: En kritisk granskning." *Kvinnovetenskaplig tidskrift* 4 (1): 55–69. (Summary in English, p. 68.)

Carroll, Berenice. 1979–80. "Review Essay: Political Science." Part I, "American Politics and Political Behavior." *Signs* 5(2): 289–306. Part II, "International Politics, Comparative Politics, and Feminist Radicals." *Signs* 5(3): 449–58.

Carver, Terrell. 1982. *Marx's Social Theory.* Oxford: Oxford University Press.
————. 1984a. "Marx, Engels and Scholarship." *Political Studies* 32, no. 2:249–56.
————. 1984b. "Marxism as Method." In Terence Ball and James Farr, eds., *After Marx.* Cambridge: Cambridge University Press.
————. 1987. *A Marx Dictionary.* Cambridge: Polity Press.
————, trans. and ed. 1975. *Karl Marx: Texts on Method.* Oxford: Basil Blackwell.
Chafetz, Janet Saltzman. 1990. *Gender Equity: An Integrated Theory of Stability and Change.* Newbury Park, Calif.: Sage.
Chapman, Richard Allen. 1975. "*Leviathan* Writ Small: Thomas Hobbes on the Family." *American Political Science Review* 69(1): 76–90.
Chodorow, Nancy. 1978. *The Reproduction of Mothering: Psychoanalysis and the Sociology of Gender.* Berkeley: University of California Press.
Clark, Alice. (1919) 1968. *Working Life of Women in the Seventeenth Century.* London: Frank Cass & Co.
Clark, Lorenne M. G., and Lynda Lange, eds. 1979. *The Sexism of Social and Political Theory: Women and Reproduction from Plato to Nietzsche.* Toronto, Buffalo, and London: University of Toronto Press.
Cockburn, Cynthia. 1981. "The Material of Male Power." *Feminist Review,* no. 9:41–58.
————. 1983. *Brothers: Male Dominance and Technological Change.* London: Pluto Press.
Collins, Randall. 1971. "A Conflict Theory of Sexual Stratification." *Social Problems* 19(1): 3–21.
Connell, Robert W. 1987. *Gender and Power: Society, the Person and Sexual Politics.* Cambridge: Polity Press.
Connolly, William E. 1983. *The Terms of Political Discource.* 2d ed. Oxford: Martin Robertson.
Crenson, Matthew A. 1971. *The Un-Politics of Air Pollution: A Study of Non-Decisionmaking in the Cities.* Baltimore and London: Johns Hopkins University Press.
Crompton, Rosemary, and Michael Mann, eds. 1986. *Gender and Stratification.* Cambridge: Polity Press.
Dahlberg, Anita. 1984. *Jämt eller ibland: Om jämställdhet* (Always or sometimes: on equal rights). Forskningsrapport 43 i AJDA-projektet. Stockholm: Arbetslivscentrum.
Dahlerup, Drude. 1974. "Betragtninger over de nye kvindestudiers baggrund, indehold og perspektiv." *Politica* 2–53.
————. 1980. "Approaches to the Study of Public Policy Towards Women." Paper prepared for Department of Political Science, Aarhus University, Aarhus, Denmark.
————. 1984. "Overcoming the Barriers: An Approach to the Study of How Women's Issues are Kept from the Political Agenda." In *Women's Views of the Political World of Men. See* Stiehm, 1984.

Dahlkvist, Mats. 1978. *Att Studera Kapitalet: Första boken.* Lund: Cavefors.

Delphy, Christine. 1976. "Continuities and Discontinuities in Marriage and Divorce." In Diana Leonard Barker and Sheila Allen, eds., *Sexual Division and Society: Process and Change.* London: Tavistock.

———. 1977. *The Main Enemy: A Materialist Analysis of Women's Oppression.* Exploration in Feminism, no. 3. London: Women's Research and Resources Centre Publications. Originally published in French in 1970.

———. 1984. *Close to Home: A Materialist Analysis of Women's Oppression.* Translated and edited by Diana Leonard. Amherst: University of Massachusetts Press.

Deutscher, Isaac. 1970. "Att upptäcka 'Kapitalet.'" In *Den socialistiska människan och andra essäer.* Stockholm: Pan/Norstedts. Originally published in *Monthly Review,* December 1967.

Diamond, Irene, and Nancy Hartsock. 1981. "Beyond Interests in Politics: A Comment on Virginia Sapiro's 'When Are Interests Interesting? The Problem of Political Representation of Women.'" *American Political Science Review* 75(3): 717–23.

Dinnerstein, Dorothy. 1976. *The Mermaid and the Minotaur: Sexual Arrangements and Human Malaise.* New York: Harper & Row.

Dolan, Frederich M. 1988. "Postwar Political Science and the History of Metaphysics: The Rhetoric of Rationality in David Easton's Behavioralism." Paper presented at the Western Political Science Association Annual Meeting, San Francisco, March 10–12.

Donovan, Josephine. 1985. *Feminist Theory: The Intellectual Traditions of American Feminism.* New York: Frederick Ungar.

Edsall, Thomas B. 1984. *The New Politics of Inequality.* New York; London: W. W. Norton.

Eduards, Maud. 1977. *Kvinnor och politik: Fakta och förklaringar.* Stockholm: Liber Förlag.

———. 1986. "Kön, stat och jämställdshetspolitik." *Kvinnovetenskaplig tidskrift* 7(3): 4–15. (Summary in English, pp. 14–15.)

———. 1988. "Att studera politik ur ett könsperspektiv." *Statsvetenskaplig tidskrift* 91(3): 207–21.

———. 1992. "Against the Rules of the Game: On the Importance of Women's Collective Actions." In *Rethinking Change: Current Swedish Feminist Research.* Stockholm: HSFR.

———. Forthcoming. "Human Agency and Sex/Gender: The Feminist Tradition and Beyond." In Björn Wittrock, ed., *Social Theory and Human Agency.* London: Sage.

———, ed. 1983. *Kön, makt, medborgarskap: Kvinnan i politiskt tänkande fraan Platon till Engels.* Stockholm: Liber Förlag.

Eduards, Maud, and Hedda Gunneng. 1983. "Medborgaren och hans hustru: Om Aristoteles' syn på kvinnan." In *Kön, makt, medborgarskap. See* Eduards, 1983.

Eduards, Maud Landby, Gunnel Gustafsson, and Anna G. Jónasdóttir. 1989.

"Könsmakt och maktlöshet i nationalstaten." In *Kvinnors makt och inflytande: Forskningsöversikt och forskningsbehov*. Report no. 15. Stockholm: JÄMFO.

Ehrmann, Henry W. 1968. *International Encyclopedia of the Social Sciences*. S.v. "Interest Groups."

Eichler, Margrit. 1980. *The Double Standard: A Feminist Critique of Feminist Social Science*. London: Croom Helm.

Eisenstein, Hester. 1983. *Contemporary Feminist Thought*. Boston: G. K. Hall & Co.

Eisenstein, Zillah R. 1979. "Developing a Theory of Capitalist Patriarchy and Socialist Feminism." In Z. R. Eisenstein, ed., *Capitalist Patriarchy and the Case for Socialist Feminism*. New York: Monthly Review Press.

———. 1981. *The Radical Future of Liberal Feminism*. New York and London: Longman.

Elias, Norbert. 1956. "Problems of Involvement and Detachment." *British Journal of Sociology* 7(3): 226–52.

———. 1978. *What is Sociology?* New York: Columbia University Press.

Elshtain, Jean Bethke. 1974. "Moral Woman and Immoral Man: A Consideration of the Public/Private Split and Its Political Ramification." *Politics and Society* 4(4): 453–73.

———. 1981. *Public Man, Private Woman: Women in Social and Political Thought*. Princeton, N.J.: Princeton University Press.

Elster, Jon. 1980. "Exploitation and the Theory of Justice." Paper presented at the 2d CIA Colloquium on Exploitation, London, September 12–14.

———. 1981. *Pax Leksikon*. S.v. "Utbytting" (Exploitation).

———. 1982. "Roemer versus Roemer: A Comment on 'New Directions in the Marxian Theory of Exploitation and Class.'" *Politics and Society* 11(3): 363–73.

Engels, Friedrich. (1884) 1972. *The Origin of the Family, Private Property, and the State*. Introduction and notes by Eleanor Burke Leacock. London: Lawrence & Wishart.

Engelstad, Fredrik. 1978. "Kjaerlighet og utbytting." In Laris Hem and Harriet Holter, eds., *Sosialpsykologi: Familie, ungdom og kjønnsroller*. Oslo: Universitetsforlaget.

English, Deirdre, Amber Hollibaugh, and Gayle Rubin. 1987. "Talking Sex: A Conversation on Sexuality and Feminism." In Feminist Review, ed., *Sexuality: A Reader*. London: Virago Press.

Etzioni, Amitai. 1968. "Basic Human Needs, Alienation, and Inauthenticity." *American Sociological Review* 33(6): 870–84.

Evans, Judith. 1980. "Women in Politics: A Reappraisal." *Political Studies* 28(2): 210–21.

Evans, Judith, et al. 1986. *Feminism and Political Theory*. London: Sage.

Farr, James. 1984. "Marx and Positivism." In Terence Ball and James Farr, eds., *After Marx*. Cambridge: Cambridge University Press.

———. 1986. "Marx's Laws." *Political Studies* 34, no. 2:202–22.

Farr Tormey, Judith. 1976. "Exploitation, Oppression, and Self-Sacrifice." In

Carol Gould and Marx W. Wartofsky, eds. *Women and Philosophy: Toward a Theory of Liberation*. New York: Capricorn Books.

Ferguson, Ann. 1979. "Women as a New Revolutionary Class in the United States." In Pat Walker, ed. *Between Labor and Capital*. Boston: South End Press.

Firestone, Shulamith. 1971. *The Dialectic of Sex: The Case for Feminist Revolution*. New York: Bantam Books.

Flax, Jane. 1983. "Political Philosophy and the Patriarchal Unconscious: A Psychoanalytic Perspective on Epistemology and Metaphysics." In Sandra Harding and Merrill Hintikka, eds., *Discovering Reality: Feminist Perspectives on Epistemology, Metaphysics, and Philosophy of Science*. Dordrecht, Boston, and London: D. Reidel.

Foucault, Michel. 1980. *Power/Knowledge: Selected Interviews and Other Writings, 1972–1977*. Edited by Colin Gordon. Brighton: Harvester Press.

Fraser, Nancy. 1986. "Toward a Discourse Ethic of Solidarity." *Praxis International* 5(4): 425–29.

———. 1987. "What is Critical about Critical Theory? The Case of Habermas and Gender." In Seyla Benhabib and Drucilla Cornell, eds., *Feminism as Critique: Essays on the Politics of Gender in Late-Capitalist Societies*. Cambridge: Polity Press.

Friedan, Betty. 1963. *The Feminine Mystique*. Harmondsworth: Penguin Books.

Fuchs Epstein, Cynthia, and Rose Laub-Coser, eds., 1981. *Access to Power: Cross-National Studies of Women and Elites*. London: Allen and Unwin.

Fukuyama, Francis. 1992. *The End of History and the Last Man*. New York: Free Press.

Ganetz, Hillevi, Evy Gunnarsson, and Anita Göransson, eds. 1986. *Feminism och marxism: En förälskelse med förhinder*. Stockholm: Arbetarkultur.

Gardiner, J. K. 1983. "Power, Desire, and Difference: Comment on Essays from the *Signs* Special Issues on Feminist Theory." *Signs* 8(4): 733–37.

Gatens, Moira. 1987. "Feminism, Philosophy and Riddles Without Answers." In Carole Pateman and Elizabeth Gross, eds., *Feminist Challenges: Social and Political Theory*. Boston: Northeastern University Press.

Genovese, Elizabeth Fox. 1982. "Placing Women's History in History." *New Left Review*, no. 133 (May–June): 5–29.

Giddens, Anthony. 1981. *A Contemporary Critique of Historical Materialism*. London: Macmillan.

Gilliam, Mikael, and Lennart Nilsson. 1985. "Svenska folkets aasikter om den offentliga sektorn." *Statvetenskaplig tidskrift* 88(2):123–39.

Gilligan, Carol. 1982. *In a Different Voice: Psychological Theory and Women's Development*. Cambridge, Mass.: Harvard University Press.

Glassner, Barry, and Jonathan D. Moreno, eds. 1989. *The Qualitative-Quantitative Distinction in the Social Sciences*. Dordrecht: Kluwer Academic Publishers.

Goldthorpe, John. 1983. "Women and Class Analysis: In Defence of the Conventional View." *Sociology* 17(4): 465–88.

———. 1984. "Women and Class Analysis: A Reply to the Replies." *Sociology* 18(4): 491–99.

Goode, William. J. 1959. "The Theoretical Importance of Love." *American Sociological Review* 24(1): 38–47.

Goot, Murray, and Elizabeth Reid. 1975. *Women and Voting Studies: Mindless Matrons or Sexist Scientism?* London: Sage.

Göransson, Anita. 1987. "Innovation och institution: Om receptionen av kvinnohistoria och kön som analytisk kategori." In Birgit Sawyer and Anita Göransson, eds., *Manliga strukturer och kvinnliga strategier: En bok till Gunhild Kyle.* Göteborg: Historiska institutionen, Göteborgs universitet.

Gosnell, Harold F. (1948) 1977. *Democracy: The Threshold of Freedom.* Westport, Conn.: Greenwood Press.

Gould, Carol C. 1983. "Private Rights and Public Virtues: Women, the Family, and Democracy." In *Beyond Domination: New Perspectives on Women and Philosophy.* Totowa, N.J.: Rowman & Allanheld.

Gouldner, Alvin W. 1960. "The Norm of Reciprocity: A Preliminary Statement." *American Sociological Review* 25(2): 161–78.

Gullestad, Marianne. 1981. *Pax Leksikon.* S.v. "Undertrykking."

Gunn, J.A.W. 1969. *Politics and the Public Interest in the Seventeenth Century.* London: Routledge and Kegan Paul.

Gutmann, Amy, ed. 1988. *Democracy and the Welfare State.* Princeton, N.J.: Princeton University Press.

Haavind, Hanne. 1980. "Kvinnelighet og frigøring." In *Teori och metode i kvinneforskningen: Rapport fra en konferense.* Oslo: NAVFs sekretariat for kvinneforskning.

———. 1982. "Premisser for personlige forhold mellom kvinner." In Harriet Holter, ed., *Kvinner i felleskap.* Oslo: Universitetsforlaget.

———. 1984. "Love and Power in Marriage." In Harriet Holter, ed., *Patriarchy in a Welfare Society.* Oslo: Universitetsforlaget.

———. 1985. "Förändringar i förhaallandet mellan kvinnor och män." *Kvinnovetenskaplig tidskrift* 3:17–27. (Summary in English, p. 27.)

Haavind, Hanne, et al. 1973. *Myten om den gode mor.* Oslo: Pax.

Halsaa, Beatrice. 1988. "A Feminist Utopia." *Scandinavian Political Studies* 11(4): 323–36.

Halsaa-Albrektsen, Beatrice. 1977. *Kvinner og politisk deltakelse.* Oslo: Pax Forlag.

Hamilton, Roberta. 1978. *The Liberation of Women: A Study of Patriarchy and Capitalism.* London: Allen and Unwin.

Harding, Sandra. 1981. "What Is the Real Material Base of Patriarchy and Capital?" In Lydia Sargent, ed., *Women and Revolution: The Unhappy Marriage of Marxism and Feminism: A Debate of Class and Patriarchy.* London: Pluto Press.

———. 1983. "Why Has the Sex/Gender System Become Visible Only Now?" In Sandra Harding and Merrill Hintikka, eds., *Discovering Reality: Feminist Perspectives on Epistemology, Metaphysics, and Philosophy of Science.* Dordrecht, Boston, and London: D. Reidel.

———. 1988. "Feminisms Federated Against Patriarchy?" Paper presented at the 14th World Congress of the International Political Science Association (IPSA), Washington, D.C., August 28–September 1.

Harré, Rom, and E. H. Madden. 1975. *Causal Powers*. Oxford: Blackwell.

Harrison, Brian. 1978. *Separate Spheres: The Opposition to Women's Suffrage in Britain*. New York: Holmes and Meier.

Hartmann, Heidi. 1976. "Capitalism, Patriarchy, and Job Segregation by Sex." Originally published as a supplement to *Signs* 1(3), pt. 2.

————. 1981a. "The Unhappy Marriage of Marxism and Feminism: Towards a More Progressive Union." In Lydia Sargent, ed., *Women and Revolution: The Unhappy Marriage of Marxism and Feminism: A Debate on Class and Patriarchy*. London: Pluto Press.

————. 1981b. "The Family as the Locus of Gender, Class, and Political Struggle: The Example of Housework." *Signs* 6(3): 366–94.

————. 1981c. *Capitalism and Women's Work in the Home*. Philadelphia: Temple University Press.

Hartsock, Nancy. 1983. *Money, Sex and Power: Toward a Feminist Historical Materialism*. Boston: Northeastern University Press.

Harvey, David. 1989. *The Condition of Postmodernity: An Enquiry into the Origins of Cultural Change*. Oxford: Basil Blackwell.

Haug, Frigga, ed. 1980. *Frauenformen 1: Alltagsgeschichten und Entwurf einer Theorie weiblicher Sozialisation*. Berlin: Argument-Sonderband (AS 45).

————, ed. 1983. *Frauenformen 2: Sexualisierung der Körper*. Berlin: Argument-Sonderband (AS 90).

Hearn, Jeff, and Wendy Parkin. 1987. *"Sex" at "Work": The Power and Paradox of Organisation Sexuality*. Brighton: Wheatsheaf Books.

Hedlund, Gun. 1986. "Varför ska just gruppen kvinnor öka sin representation i beslutande organ?" In *Hit—men inte längre? Rapport fraan seminariet "Kvinnor och politisk makt."* Delrapport fraan utredningen om kvinnorepresentation. Government report, Ds A, no. 5. Stockholm.

Held, David. 1987. *Models of Democracy*. Stanford, Calif.: Stanford University Press.

Held, Virginia. 1976. "Marx, Sex, and the Transformation of Society." In Carol Gould and Marx W. Wartofsky, eds., *Women and Philosophy: Toward a Theory of Liberation*. New York: Capricorn Books.

Heller, Agnes. 1976. *The Theory of Need in Marx*. New York: St. Martin's Press.

Hermodsson, Elisabet. 1980. *Gör dig synlig*. Stockholm: Rabén & Sjögren.

Hernes, Helga Maria. 1980. "Predicting Support for the Women's Movement: A Diffusion Model." *Scandinavian Political Studies* 3(3): 265–73.

————. 1982. *Staten—Kvinner ingen adgang?* Oslo: Universitetsforlaget.

————. 1984. "Women and the Welfare State: The Transition from Private to Public Dependence." In Harriet Holter, ed., *Patriarchy in a Welfare Society*. Oslo: Universitetsforlaget.

————. 1987. *Welfare State and Woman Power: Essays in State Feminism*. Oslo: Norwegian University Press.

Herring, Pendleton. 1968. *International Encyclopedia of the Social Sciences*. S.v. "Public Interest."

Hill, Christopher. 1969. "Reformation to Industrial Revolution." *The Pelican Economic History of Britain*. Vol. 2. Harmondsworth: Penguin Books.

Hinton, R. W. K. 1968. "Husbands, Fathers and Conquerors I." *Political Studies* 15(3): 291–300.

———. 1969. "Husbands, Fathers and Conquerors II." *Political Studies* 16(1): 55–67.

Hirschman, Albert Q. 1977. *The Passions and the Interests: Political Arguments for Capitalism Before Its Triumph*. Princeton, N.J.: Princeton University Press.

Hirschon, Renée, ed. 1984. *Women and Property: Women as Property*. London: Croom Helm.

Hobbes, Thomas. 1968. *Leviathan; or, The Matter, Forme & Power of a Common-Wealth Ecclesiasticall and Civill*. Edited and with an introduction by C. B. Macpherson. Har-Middlesex: Penguin Books.

———. 1969. *The Elements of Law*. Edited and with a preface and critical notes by Ferdinand Tönnies. 2d ed. with a new introduction by M. M. Goldsmith. London: Frank Cass & Co.

———. 1972. *Man and Citizen*. Edited and with an introduction by Bernard Gert. London: Harvester Press.

Hobsbawm, Eric. 1984. "Marx and History." *New Left Review*, no. 143 (January–February): 39–50.

Hole, Judith, and Ellen Levine. 1974. *Rebirth of Feminism*. New York: Quadrangle.

Holmberg, Sören, and Kent Asp. 1984. *Kampen om kärnkraften: En bok om väljare, massmedier och folkomröstningen 1980*. Stockholm: Liber.

Holter, Øystein Gullvaag. 1980. *Sjekking: Kaerlighet og konnsmarked*. Oslo: Pax.

———. 1982. "Det verdifulle patriarkatet." In Runa Haukaa, Marit Hoel, and Hanne Haavind, eds., *Kvinneforskning: Bidrag til Samfunnsteori*. Festskrift til Harriet Holter. Oslo: Universitetsforlaget.

———. 1984. "Gender as Forms of Value." In Harriet Holter, ed., *Patriarchy in a Welfare Society*. Oslo: Universitetsforlaget.

Honeycutt, Karen. 1976. "Clara Zetkin: A Socialist Approach to the Problem of Woman's Oppression." *Feminism Studies* 2(3–4): 131–44.

Isaac, Jeffrey C. 1987. *Power and Marxist Theory: A Realist View*. Ithaca and London: Cornell University Press.

Jaggar, Alison M. 1983. *Feminist Politics and Human Nature*. Totowa, N.J.: Rowman & Allanheld.

Jansen-Jurreit, Marielouise. 1979. *Sexism*. In Swedish. Stockholm: Norstedts.

Jaquette, Jane. 1976. "Review Essay: Political Science." *Signs* 2(1): 147–64.

———. 1984. "Power as Ideology: A Feminist Analysis." In J. S. Stiehm, ed., *Women's Views of the Political World of Men*. Dobbs Ferry, N.Y.: Transnational Publishers.

———, ed. 1974. *Women in Politics*. New York: John Wiley & Sons.

Johansson, Ingvar, and Sven-Eric Liedman. 1981. *Positivism och marxism*. Stockholm: Norstedts.

Jónasdóttir, Anna G. 1980. "Women and politics." Paper presented at the annual meeting of the Swedish Political Scientist Association, Baastad, June.

———. 1984. *Kvinnoteori. Naagra perspektiv och problem inom kvinnoforskningens teoribildning*. Research Reports ser. 32. Högskolan i Örebro.

————. 1985. "Kvinnors intressen och andra värden." *Kvinnovetenskaplig tidskrift* 6(2): 17–33. (Summary in English, pp. 32–33.)
————. 1991. "Könsbegreppet i samhällsvetenskapen: Tre kontroverser." In *Könsrelationernas betydelse som vetenskaplig kategori.* Stockholm: JÄMFO.
Jónasdóttir, Anna G., and Gun Hedlund-Ruth. 1981. "Manspräglad valforskning: En kritisk analys av dess tolkningar och förklaringsmodeller." Paper presented at the annual meeting of the Swedish Sociologist Association, Uppsala, January.
Jonasson, Birgit, 1985. "Aasikter i tre jämställdshetsfrågor." *Kvinnovetenskaplig Tidskrift* 6(2):54–62. (Summary in English, p. 62.)
Jones, Kathleen B. 1978. "The Marxian Concept of Community." Ph.D. diss., City University of New York, New York.
————. 1987. "On Authority; or, Why Women Are Not Entitled to Speak." *Nomos* 29.
————. 1990. "Citizenship in a Woman-Friendly Polity." *Signs* 15(4): 781–812.
Jones, Kathleen B., and Anna G. Jónasdóttir, eds. 1988. *The Political Interests of Gender: Developing Theory and Research with a Feminist Face.* London: Sage.
Kanter, Rosabeth Moss. 1977. *Men and Women of the Corporation.* New York: Basic Books.
Kelly, Joan. 1984. *Women, History and Theory: The Essays of Joan Kelly.* Chicago and London: University of Chicago Press.
Kelly-Gadol, Joan. 1984. "The Social Relation of the Sexes: Methodological Implications of Women's History." In *Women, History, and Theory. See* Kelly 1984.
Kelvin, Peter. 1969. *The Bases of Social Behavior.* London: Holt, Rinehart and Winston.
Klein, Ethel. 1984. *Gender Politics: From Consciousness to Mass Politics.* Cambridge, Mass., and London: Harvard University Press.
Kosik, Karel. 1976. *Dialectics of the Concrete.* Translated by Karel Kovanda and James Schmidt. Boston Studies in the Philosophy of Science, vol. 52.
————. 1978. *Det Konkretas dialektik.* In Swedish. Göteborg: Röda bokförlaget AB.
Kraditor, A. S. 1971. *The Ideas of the Woman Suffrage Movement, 1890–1920.* New York: Anchor Books.
Kuhn, Annette. 1978. "Structures of Patriarchy and Capital in the Family." In Annette Kuhn and A. M. Wolpe, eds. *Feminism and Materialism: Women and Modes of Production.* London: Routledge and Kegan Paul.
Kvinnorepresentationsutredningen (Investigation of the representation of women). 1986–87. Government reports, Ds A (1986), no. 4; Sou (1987), no. 19. Stockholm.
Lafferty, William M. 1980. "Sex and Political Participation: An Exploratory Analysis of the 'Female Culture.' " *European Journal of Political Research* 8:323–47.
Laird, John. 1934. *Hobbes.* London: Oxford University Press.
Lange, Lynda. 1976. "Reproduction in Democratic Theory." In John King-Far-

low and William R. Shea, eds., *Contemporary Issues in Political Philosophy*. Canadian Contemporary Philosophy Series. New York: Science History Publications.

Laslett, Peter. 1967. Introduction to John Locke, *Two Treatises of Government*, a critical edition with an introduction and apparatus criticus. London: Cambridge University Press.

Laudan, Larry. 1977. *Progress and Its Problems: Towards a Theory of Scientific Growth*. Berkeley: University of California Press.

Liedman, Sven-Eric. 1965. *Människans frigörelse: Ett urval ur Karl Marx Skrifter* (Human liberation: a selection of Karl Marx's writings). Stockholm: Aldus/ Bonniers.

———. 1977. *Motsatsernas spel, Del I*. Lund: Cavefors.

———. 1981. "Marxism." In *Positivism och marxism*. See Johansson and Liedman, 1981.

Liljeström, Rita. 1980. "Jämställdhet, arbetarklass och välfärdskapitalismen." In *Jämställdhetsperspektiv i forskningen* (Perspectives of gender equality in research). Report from a seminar, April 24–25. Stockholm: Riksbankens jubileumsfond 4.

Lipset, Seymour Martin. 1960. *Political Man*. Garden City, N.Y.: Doubleday.

Lloyd, Genevieve. 1984. *The Man of Reason: "Male" and "Female" in Western Philosophy*. London: Methuen.

Locke, John. 1916. *Tankar om uppfostran (Some Thoughts Concerning Education)*. Translated by J. Reinius. Uppsala.

———. 1978. *Two Treatises of Government*. Edited and with an introduction by W. S. Carpenter. London: Dent; New York: Dutton.

Lovenduski, Joni. 1981. "Toward the Emasculation of Political Science." In Dale Spender, ed., *Men's Studies Modified*. London: Pergamon Press.

Lukes, Steven. 1974. *Power: A Radical View*. London: Macmillan.

MacKinnon, Catharine A. 1982. "Feminism, Marxism, Method, and the State: An Agenda for Theory." *Signs* 7(3): 515–44.

———. 1983. "Feminism, Marxism, Method, and the State: Toward Feminist Jurisprudence." *Signs* 8(4): 635–58.

———. 1987. *Feminism Unmodified: Discourses on Life and Law*. Cambridge, Mass., and London: Harvard University Press.

———. 1989. *Toward a Feminist Theory of the State*. Cambridge, Mass.: Cambridge University Press.

Macpherson, Crawford B. 1962. *The Political Theory of Possessive Individualism: Hobbes to Locke*. London and New York: Oxford University Press.

———. 1973. *Democratic Theory: Essays in Retrieval*. Oxford: Oxford University Press.

Mainardi, Pat. 1970. "The Politics of Housework." In *Sisterhood Is Powerful*. See Morgan, 1970.

Malinowski, Bronislaw. 1932. *Crime and Custom in Savage Society*. London: Paul, Trench, Trubner.

Marx, Karl. (1859) 1977a. "Preface to 'A Critique of Political Economy.' " In

David McLellan, ed., *Karl Marx: Selected Writings*. New York: Oxford University Press.
————. 1977b. *Economic and Philosophic Manuscripts of 1844*. Moscow: Progress Publishers.
Marx, Karl, and Friedrich Engels. 1970. *The German Ideology*. Edited by C. J. Arthur. London: Lawrence & Wishart.
Merleau-Ponty, Maurice. 1962. *Phenomenology of Perception*. Translated by Colin Smith. London: Routledge and Kegan Paul.
Milbrath, L. W., and M. L. Goel. 1977. *Political Participation*. 2d rev. ed. Chicago: Rand McNally.
Miller, Arthur H., Anne Hildreth, and Grace L. Simmons. 1988. "The Mobilization of Gender Group Consciousness." In *The Political Interests of Gender*. See Jones and Jónasdóttir, 1988.
Miller, David. 1976. *Social Justice*. Oxford: Clarendon Press.
————. 1987. "Politics." In *The Blackwell Encyclopedia of Political Thought*. Oxford: Blackwell.
Miller, Jean Baker. 1978. *Toward a New Psychology of Women*. Harmondsworth: Penguin Books.
Millett, Kate. 1970. *Sexual Politics*. New York: Doubleday.
Mitchell, Juliet. 1966. "Women: The Longest Revolution." *New Left Review* 40 (November–December): 11–37.
————. 1974. *Psychoanalysis and Feminism*. New York: Pantheon Books.
————. 1986. *Women's Estate*. Harmondsworth: Penguin Books. Originally published in 1971.
Morgan, Robin. 1977. *Going Too Far: The Personal Chronicle of a Feminist*. New York: Random House.
————, ed. 1970. *Sisterhood Is Powerful: An Anthology of Writings from the Women's Liberation Movement*. New York: Vintage Books.
Nicholson, Linda. 1986. *Gender and History: The Limits of Social Theory in the Age of the Family*. New York: Columbia University Press.
————. 1987. "Feminism and Marx: Integrating Kinship with the Economic." In Seyla Benhabib and Drucilla Cornell, eds., *Feminism as Critique: Essays on the Politics of Gender in Late-Capitalist Societies*. Cambridge: Polity Press.
O'Brien, Mary. 1981. *The Politics of Reproduction*. London: Routledge and Kegan Paul.
Okin, Susan Moller. 1979. *Women in Western Political Thought*. Princeton, N.J.: Princeton University Press.
Olofsson, Gunnar. 1979. *Mellan klass och stat: Om arbetarrörelse, reformism och socialdemokrati*. Lund: Arkiv.
Østerberg, Dag. 1978. *Sociologins nyckelbegrepp och deras ursprung*. Göteborg: Bokförlaget Korpen.
Parks, Robert Q. 1982. "Interests and the Politics of Choice." *Political Theory* 10(4): 547–65.
Parsons, Talcott. 1954. *Essays in Sociological Theory*. New York: Free Press.
Parsons, Talcott, and R. F. Bales. 1956. *Family: Socialization and Interaction Process*. London: Routledge and Kegan Paul.

Pateman, Carole. 1980a. " 'The Disorder of Women': Women, Love, and the Sense of Justice." *Ethics* 91:20–34.
————. 1980b. "Women and Consent." *Political Theory* 8(2):149–68.
————. 1983a. "Feminist Critique of the Public/Private Dichotomy." In S. I. Benn and G. F. Gaus, eds., *Public and Private in Social Life.* London: Croom Helm.
————. 1983b. "Feminism and Democracy." In Graeme Duncan, ed., *Democratic Theory and Practice.* Cambridge: Cambridge University Press.
————. 1985a. *The Problem of Political Obligation: A Critique of Liberal Theory.* Cambridge: Polity Press.
————. 1985b. "Women and Democratic Citizenship." The Jefferson Memorial Lectures. Delivered at the University of California, Berkeley, February.
————. 1988. *The Sexual Contract.* Cambridge: Polity Press.
————. 1989. *The Disorder of Women: Democracy, Feminism and Political Theory.* Cambridge: Polity Press.
————. 1990. " 'Does Sex Matter to Democracy?': A Comment." *Scandinavian Political Studies* 13(1): 57–63.
Patinkin, Don. 1968. *International Encyclopedia of the Social Sciences.* S.v. "Interest."
Petchesky, Rosalind Pollack. 1980. "Reproductive Freedom: Beyond a Woman's Right to Choose." *Signs* 5(4): 661–85.
————. 1983. *Abortion and Women's Choice.* New York: Longman.
Peterson, Abby. 1981. "Kvinnofrågor, kvinnomedvetande och klass." *Zenit* 70:5–21.
Phelps, Linda. 1981. "Patriarchy and Capitalism." In *Building Feminist Theory: Essays from "Quest."* New York: Longman. Originally published in *Quest: A Feminist Quarterly* 2 (2) (1975).
Philosophisches Wörterbuch. 1975a. S.v. "Form." Leipzig: VEB Bibliographisches Institut.
————. 1975b. S.v. "Interessen." Leipzig: VEB Bibliographisches Institut.
Piaget, Jean. 1932. *The Moral Judgment of the Child.* New York: Harcourt, Brace.
Pitkin, Hanna Fenichel. 1972. *The Concept of Representation.* Berkeley: University of California Press.
Putnam, Robert D. 1976. *The Comparative Study of Political Elites.* Englewood Cliffs, N.J.: Prentice-Hall.
Qvist, Gunnar. 1980. "Om periodindelning i kvinnohistorien." *Kvinnovetenskaplig tidskrift* 1(1): 45–52. (Summary in English, pp. 51–52.)
Randall, Vicky. 1987. *Women and Politics: An International Perspective.* 2d rev. ed. London: Macmillan.
Rapaport, Elizabeth 1976. "On the Future of Love: Rousseau and the Radical Feminists." In C. Gould and M. Wartofsky, eds, *Women and Philosophy: Toward a Theory of Liberation.* New York: Capricorn Books.
Reeve, Andrew, and Alan Ware. 1983. "Interests in Political Theory." *British Journal of Political Science* 13(4): 379–400.
Rich, Adrienne. 1976. *Of Woman Born: Motherhood as Experience and Institution.* New York: Bantam Books.

————. 1979. *On Lies, Secrets, and Silence: Selected Prose, 1966–1978.* New York: W. W. Norton.

————. 1980. "Compulsory Heterosexuality and Lesbian Existence." *Signs* 5(4): 631–60.

Riley, Denise. 1988. *"Am I That Name?" Feminism and the Category of "Women" in History.* Minneapolis: University of Minnesota Press.

Robbins, Lionel. 1955. *The Theory of Economic Policy in English Classical Political Economy.* In Swedish. Stockholm: Natur och kultur.

Roemer, John E. 1988. *Free to Lose: An Introduction to Marxist Economic Philosophy.* Cambridge, Mass.: Harvard University Press.

Rosaldo, Michelle Zimbalist. 1980. "The Use and Abuse of Anthropology: Reflections on Feminism and Cross-cultural Understanding." *Signs* 5(3): 389–417.

Rowbotham, Sheila. 1974. *Women's Consciousness, Man's World.* Harmondsworth: Penguin Books.

————. 1989. *The Past Is Before Us: Feminism in Action Since the 1960s.* London: Pandora Press.

Rubin, Gayle. 1975. "The Traffic in Women: Notes on the 'Political Economy' of Sex." In Rayna R. Reiter, ed., *Toward an Anthropology of Women.* New York and London: Monthly Review Press.

Ruddick, Sara. 1980. "Maternal Thinking." *Feminist Studies* 6(2): 342–67.

Rustin, Michael. 1989. "The Politics of Post-Fordism; or, The Trouble with 'New Times.' " *New Left Review,* no. 175:54–77.

Sachs, Albie, and Joan Hoff Wilson. 1978. *Sexism and the Law: A Study of Male Beliefs and Legal Bias in Britain and the United States.* Oxford: Martin Robertsson.

Sapiro, Virginia. 1979. "Sex and Games: On Oppression and Rationality." *British Journal of Political Science* 9:385–408.

————. 1981. "Research Frontier Essay: When Are Interests Interesting? The Problem of Political Representation of Women." *The American Political Science Review* 75(3):701–16.

————. 1983. *The Political Integration of Women: Roles, Socialization, and Politics.* Urbana: University of Illinois Press.

Sargent, Lydia. 1981. "New Left Women and Men: The Honeymoon Is Over." In Sargent, ed., *Women and Revolution: The Unhappy Marriage of Marxism and Feminism: A Debate of Class and Patriarchy.* London: Pluto Press.

Sayer, Andrew. 1984. *Method in Social Science: A Realist Approach.* London: Hutchinson.

Schochet, Gordon J. 1967. "Thomas Hobbes on the Family and the State of Nature." *Political Science Quarterly* 82(3): 427–45.

————. 1975. *Patriarchalism in Political Thought.* Oxford: Blackwell.

Schumpeter, Joseph A. (1942) 1976. *Capitalism, Socialism, and Democracy.* London and Boston: Allen and Unwin.

Scott, Joan W. 1986. "Gender: A Useful Category of Historical Analysis." *American Historical Review* 91(5): 1053–75.

284 *References*

Segal, Lynne. 1983. "Sensual Uncertainty; or, Why the Clitoris Is Not Enough." In Sue Cartledge and Joanna Ryan, eds., *Sex and Love: New Thoughts on Old Contradictions*. London: The Women's Press.

———. 1987. *Is the Future Female? Troubled Thoughts on Contemporary Feminism*. London: Virago Press.

Shanley, Mary L. 1979. "Marriage Contract and Social Contract in Seventeenth Century English Political Thought." *Western Political Quarterly* 32(1): 79–91.

Shanley, Mary L., and Victoria Schuck. 1975. "In Search of Political Woman." *Social Science Quarterly* 55: 632–44.

Sichtermann, Barbara. 1986. *Femininity: The Politics of the Personal*. Cambridge: Polity Press.

Siedentop, Larry. 1983. "Political Theory and Ideology: The Case of the State." In David Miller and Larry Siedentop, eds., *The Nature of Political Theory*. Oxford: Clarendon Press.

Siim, Birte. 1988. "Towards a Feminist Rethinking of the Welfare State." In *The Political Interests of Gender*. See Jones and Jónasdóttir, 1988.

Siltanen, Janet, and Michelle Stanworth. 1984. "The Politics of Private Women and Public Men." *Theory and Society* 13: 69–90.

———, eds. 1984. *Women and the Public Sphere: A Critique of Sociology and Politics*. London: Hutchinson.

Smith, Dorothy. 1974. "Women's Perspective as a Radical Critique of Sociology." *Sociological Inquiry* 44.

———. 1979. "A Sociology for Women." In *The Prism of Sex: Essays in the Sociology of Knowledge*. Madison: University of Wisconsin Press.

Soper, Kate. 1979. "Marxism, Materialism and Biology." In John Mepham and D-H. Ruben, eds., *Issues in Marxist Philosophy*. Vol. 2, *Materialism*. Brighton: Harvester.

Stanworth, Michelle. 1984. "Women and Class Analysis: A Reply to John Goldthorpe." *Sociology* 18(2): 159–70.

Stiehm, Judith H., ed. 1984. *Women's Views of the Political World of Men*. Dobbs Ferry, N.Y.: Transnational Publishers.

Stinchcombe, Arthur L. 1968. *Constructing Social Theories*. New York: Harcourt, Brace & World.

Stoper, Emily. 1988. "The Gender Gap Concealed and Revealed: 1936–1984." Paper presented at the Western Political Science Association Annual Meeting, San Francisco, March 10–12.

Thomas, Keith. 1958. "Women and the Civil War Sects." *Past and Present* 13: 42–62.

———. 1959. "The Double Standard." *Journal of the History of Ideas* 20:195–216.

Thomas, Paul. 1976. "Marx and Science." *Political Studies* 24(1): 1–23.

Thompson, Edward P. 1978. *The Poverty of Theory and Other Essays*. London: Merlin Press.

Togeby, Lise. 1984. *Politik: Ogsaa en kvindesag*. Aarhus: Politica.

Trimberger, Ellen Kay. 1984. E. P. Thompson: Understanding the Process of History." In Theda Skocpol, ed., *Vision and Method in Historical Sociology*. Cambridge: Cambridge University Press.

Turner, Bryan S. 1984. *The Body and Society: Explorations in Social Theory*. Oxford: Blackwell.

Ve, Hildur. 1982. "Kvinnefelleskap og relasjonslogikk: Om altruisme som samhandlingspremiss." In Harriet Holter, ed., *Kvinner i felleskap*. Oslo: Universitetsforlaget.

———. 1984. "Women's Mutual Alliances: Altruism as a Premise for Interaction." In Harriet Holter, ed., *Patriarchy in a Welfare Society*. Oslo: Universitetsforlaget.

Vernon, Richard. 1986. *Citizenship and Order: Studies in French Political Thought*. Toronto: University of Toronto Press.

Walby, Sylvia. 1986. *Patriarchy at Work*. Cambridge: Polity Press.

———. 1990. *Theorizing Patriarchy*. Oxford: Basil Blackwell.

Walker, Nancy J. 1986. "Are Women More Peaceminded than Men?" Paper presented at the ECPR Joint Session of Workshops, Gothenburg, April 2–7.

Westermarck, Edward. 1908. *The Origin and Development of the Moral Ideas*. London: Macmillan.

Widerberg, Karin. 1986. "Fraan marxism till feminism, till könskamp till . . . —ett könskampsperspektiv paa arbetsdelningen och rätten." In *Feminism och marxism*. See Ganetz, Gunnarsson, and Göransson, 1986.

Wikander, Ulla. 1989. "Periodisering av kapitalismen: Med kvinnor." *Arbetarhistoria* 13(3): 7–11.

Wiley, Norbert. 1987. "Introduction." In Wiley, ed., *The Marx-Weber Debate*. Newbury Park, Calif.: Sage.

Williams, Raymond. 1978. "Problems of Materialism." *New Left Review*, no. 109 (May–June): 3–17.

Wilson, Elisabeth. 1977. *Women and the Welfare State*. London: Tavistock.

Wolff, Robert Paul. 1976. "There's Nobody Here But Us Persons." In Carol Gould and Marx W. Wartofsky, eds., *Women and Philosophy: Toward a Theory of Liberation*. New York: Capricorn Books.

Young, Iris. 1980. "Socialist Feminism and the Limits of Dual Systems Theory." *Socialist Review*, nos. 50–51:169–88.

———. 1981. "Beyond the Unhappy Marriage: A Critique of the Dual Systems Theory." In Lydia Sargent, ed., *Women and Revolution: The Unhappy Marriage of Marxism and Feminism: A Debate of Class and Patriarchy*. London: Pluto Press.

Zagorin, Perez. 1968. *International Encyclopedia of the Social Sciences*. S.v. "Thomas Hobbes."

Zaretsky, Eli. 1976. *Capitalism, the Family and Personal Life*. New York: Harper & Row.

Index

Carlsson, Christina, 50, 250n.8
causality, typology of injustice and,
  106–8, 256n.27
choice: contemporary citizenship
  theories and women in, 191–92;
  feminist interest theory and,
  233–35; interest theory and,
  164–70, 261n.17
citizenship: contemporary inferiority
  of, 188–92; role of, in interest
  theory, 155, 260n.10; sexual
  differentiation and, 178; women's
  individuality and, 182–84
civil society, Locke's view of, 139–43
Clark, Alice, 142
class structure: commonalities of sex/
  gender and, 34, 41–42; differences
  in love relations and, 61–64; dual
  systems theory and, 76–77; "empty
  places" theory in Marxism and,
  53–54, 251n.11; feminism in
  relation to, 14–15; gender
  dominance and, 66–69;
  Hartmann's dual systems theory
  and, 73–74; historical aspects of
  partriarchy and, 59–60; impact of
  historical change on, 44–45;
  interest theory and, 150–52,
  152–53, 162–64, 260n.12;
  Lukácsian theory of, 243n.7;
  Marxist concept of exploitation
  and, 90–91; oppression and
  exploitation and, 82–85; race/
  ethnicity issues, 39–40; sex/gender
  issues in relation to, 26–27, 39–40;
  societal theory and, 241n.3; theory
  of sexuality and, 236–38
Cockburn, Cynthia, 254n.17
cognitive rationality, 268n.25
collectivity, vs. individualism,
  199–201
"common" issues in sex/gender
  relations, 40–46
commonwealth: Hobbes's philosophy
  concerning, 118–19; woman-man
  relationship in, 129–30

competence, role of, in contemporary
  theory, 191–92
"conditional liberation," 171–72,
  373n.33
consciousness theory, patriarchy and,
  230–31
"contested concepts," 146
"Contextualizing Feminism: Gender,
  Ethnic and Class Divisions," 41
contract relationships, exploitation
  and oppression in terms of, 98,
  255n.20
Cornell, Drucilla, 264n.3
creation/recreation terminology,
  219–21, 266n.12
Crenson, Matthew, 168–70, 261n.18
critical theory, popularity of, among
  feminists, 243n.7

Dahlberg, Anita, 262n.22
Dahlerup, Drude, 147, 158, 168–70
de Beauvoir, Simone, 15
Democracy: The Threshold of Freedom,
  190
democratic theory: contemporary
  theorists overlooking of, 189–92;
  sex/gender system and, 177–203
dialectics: dual systems theory and,
  60–64; total theory and, 35
Diamond, Irene, 146–49, 159–64
difference: feminist state theory and,
  181–82, 184; importance and
  limits of, 197–99; individuality
  and, 196–97; interest theory and,
  233–35
Dinnerstein, Dorothy, 256n.26
distribution of goods, typology of
  injustice and, 104–8
dominance: in dual systems theory,
  58–59; exploitation and oppression
  in terms of, 97–98; Hobbes's state
  of nature and, 122–29; patriarchy
  theory and, 3–5, 231–32, 242n.6;
  socialist feminist theory and, 213;

oppression (*cont.*)
  252n.23; Marxist theory and,
  82–85, 96–103; motherhood and,
  138, 257n.10; race, sex, and class
  issues regarding, 39–40;
  reproduction as, 216–17, 266n.9;
  theoretical status of men and, 209
organization studies: interest theory
  and, 169–73; societal theory and,
  241n.3, 242n.4
original sin, Hobbes's state of nature
  and, 125–29
*Origin of the Family, Private Property,
  and the State, The*, 19
Østerberg, Dag, 90–91

"paradigm of production," 208,
  264n.3
parenthood: doctrine of self-sacrifice
  and, 254n.14; exploitation and,
  253n.3; interest theory and,
  163–64, 174; Locke on wife's role
  in, 140–43, 257n.14; woman-man-
  child in state of nature and, 123–29
Parks, Robert Q., 165–68, 170
Parsons, Talcott, 15–16, 37, 248n.5
partial theory of patriarchy, 37–38,
  248n.5
party politics, women's experiences
  in, 171, 262n.22
*Past Is Before Us: Feminism in Action
  Since the 1960s, The*, 265n.5
Pateman, Carole, 247n.14; on
  democracy and feminism, 178–95;
  patriarchy theory and, 231–32,
  268n.22
*Patriarcha; or, The Natural Power of
  Kings*, 110, 256n.2
patriarchy: anthropological, historical,
  and theoretical aspects of, 249n.1;
  basic mechanisms of, 13–14;
  capital-logical explanation of,
  248n.6; class-related aspects of,
  26–27; commonality and specificity
  of issues concerning, 34; conditions

of sexual love and, 4; dialectic
  approach to, 61–64; dual systems
  theory and, 47–52; Hartmann's
  concept of, 64–69; historical
  background on theories of, 109–15;
  historical materialism and,
  244n.14; Hobbes's woman-man
  relationship in commonwealth and,
  129–30; labor-capital aspects of,
  45–46; limits to theory of, 231–32;
  marriage society and, 229–33;
  materialist analysis of, xiii; partial
  theories of, 37–38; political theory
  and, 1–9, 27–29; power
  relationships and, 12, 179, 218–21,
  245n.1; procreative aspects of,
  253n.3; radical feminism and,
  59–60; rejection of concept of, by
  some theorists, 250n.3;
  reorientated feminist materialism
  and, 214–17; research tradition of,
  205, 264n.1; royal autocracy as
  form of, 115–18; sex, class, and
  race issues and, 39–40; similarity
  of, to capitalism, 229; socialist
  feminism and, 6–9, 245n.15;
  terminological and conceptual
  problems of, 12, 245n.1; total
  ambition and, 211–12, 264n.4;
  woman-man-child in state of nature
  and, 123–29; work theory and,
  23–25
Patriarchy at Work, 250n.3
periodization, sex/gender system and,
  42–46
Petchesky, Rosalind Pollack, 147,
  161, 164
Peterson, Abby, 147, 156–57
Phelps, Linda, 242n.4, 249n.2
pluralistic interests, 149–52
political economy, feminist theory
  and, 228–29
political participation, gender
  differences in, 30
political sexuality, 227–29
political theory: gender-related

surplus value, theory of, exploitation and, 253n.10, 256n.26

theoretical project, socialist feminism as, 207, 264n.2
theoretical separatism, regarding patriarchy, 7
Thompson, Edward, 243n.7, 265n.5
Togeby, Lise, 157
Torstendahl, Rolf, 249n.8
total ambition theory, 211–12, 265n.4
total theory: definition and concepts of, 34–37, 248n.3; vs. dual systems theory, 250n.3. *See also* partial theory of patriarchy
Treatise on Human Nature, A, 183
Trimberger, Ellen Kay, 265n.4
Two Treatises of Government, 113
typology of interests, interest theory and, 151

"unitary theory," 246n.11
Un-Politics of Air Pollution: A Study of Non-Decisionmaking in the Cities, The, 261n.18
utilitarianism: antifeminism and, 184–88, 263nn.4–5; Locke's concept of, 141–43; power of love and, 226–27, 267n.22

"values backed with power," 232, 267n.24
Veblen, Thorstein, 86
violence, role of, in sociosexual relations, xiii
von Wiese, L., 86
Voting, 268n.30

Walby, Sylvia, 250n.3
Weber, Max: dual systems theory influenced by, 249n.2; political feminist theory and, 3, 241n.4
welfare state, women and, 177–78, 262n.1

"When Are Interests Interesting? The Problem of Political Representation of Women," 146
wholes, concept of, basic patriarchal theory and, 35–37
Widerberg, Karin, 252n.28
Wikander, Ulla, 249n.8
will, freedom and, 139–40
Williams, Raymond, 102, 255n.24
Wollstonecraft, Mary, 185–86
"womanish"-feminist continuum, 238–40
"womanism," 268n.29
Women and the Public Interest: An Essay on Policy and Protest, 147
Women and Revolution, 250n.8
"Women and Social Stratification: A Case of Intellectual Sexism," 251n.11
woman-man-child-property concept, 133–39
women's issues: definition of, 156–57; historical aspects of oppression, 114–18; interest theory and, 146–49
women-worthy society, sexual equality and, 201–3
work, theories of: dual systems theory and, 75–77; essential relationships and, 221, 267n.16; exploitation and oppression in terms of, 97–100; Hartmann's concept of, 69–74; in historical materialism, transcendence of, 6–9; limitations of, 23–25; paradigm, 264n.3; socialist feminism and, 207–8. *See also* gender-based division of labor

Young, Iris, 23–26, 50–51
Yuval-Davis, Nira, 41

Zetkin, Clara, 262n.22
Zietz, Luise, 262n.22